WHO IS MY ENEMY?

WHO IS MY ENEMY?

RICH NATHAN

welcoming

people

the church

rejects

ZONDERVAN™

GRAND RAPIDS, MICHIGAN 49530

We want to hear from you. Please send your comments about this book to us in care of the address below. Thank you.

ZONDERVAN™

GRAND RAPIDS, MICHIGAN 49530

WWW.ZONDERVAN.COM

ZONDERVAN™

Who Is My Enemy?
Copyright © 2002 by Rich Nathan

Requests for information should be addressed to:

Zondervan, *Grand Rapids, Michigan 49530*

Library of Congress Cataloging-in-Publication Data

Nathan, Rich, 1955-.
    Who is my enemy? : welcoming people the church rejects / Rich Nathan.
       p. cm.
    Includes bibliographical references and index.
    ISBN 0-310-23882-X
    1. Church and the world. I. Title.
    BR115.W6 N26 2002
    261—dc21

                                     2001005382

Interior design by Susan Ambs

Printed in the United States of America

02 03 04 05 06 07 08 /❖ DC/ 10 9 8 7 6 5 4 3 2 1

To Marlene, my wife and best friend,
From you I first heard the message
that Jesus' love is free.
Through you I daily feel
that Jesus still loves me.
With you I want the world to know
that Jesus' love is true.
To you I pray my life to show
that Jesus is in love with you.

Contents

Preface

On September 11, 2001, terrorists hijacked four jumbo jets filled with businesspersons, students, wives, husbands, Christians, non-Christians, children, people living wisely, people living unwisely—and everyone in between. Two of the hijacked jets smashed into the twin towers of the World Trade Center in New York City, causing the towers' collapse and the presumed deaths of approximately 5000 people. Another jet was flown into the side of the Pentagon in Washington, D.C. A fourth jet crashed in a rural county southeast of Pittsburgh, Pennsylvania—the reported result of a heroic attempt by some of the passengers to retake the plane. In all, nearly 6000 people from 80 countries died (although the precise numbers are difficult to determine with certainty at this point).

In the wake of this terrorist attack, a nationally known Christian leader made these comments: "The ACLU's got to take a lot of blame for this.... I really believe that the pagans, and the abortionists, and the feminists, and the gays and the lesbians who are actively trying to make that an alternative lifestyle, the ACLU, People for the American Way—all of them who have tried to secularize America—I point the finger in their face and say, 'You helped this happen.'"

This Christian leader later apologized for his intemperate remarks. His comments, however, created a firestorm of negative reaction. Numerous editorials blasted this Christian leader. Some, unfairly I believe, compared him to the terrorists who had carried out the attacks.

My own heart was broken by the profound lack of Christian welcome implicit in these comments and the barrier that was erected that will undoubtedly keep some from considering the claims of the gospel. The manuscript for this book was completed well before the attacks on the World Trade Center and the Pentagon, and well before this Christian leader's remarks gained such notoriety. But in some sense, the book you now hold is my response to the viewpoint announced not only by that Christian leader but sincerely held by some of my good and decent Christian brothers and sisters. I would like this book to be an extended challenge to the perspective shared in that unfortunate television interview. I hope that after reading this book, many of my Christian brothers and sisters will gain new perspectives on the question "Who is my enemy?" and will join me in saying, "We must stop shutting the door of the kingdom in the faces of those whom God is inviting in. We will reserve our harshest judgments for ourselves. As we carry out our ministry of welcome, we will season our moral stances with profound mercy and compassion for a hurting world."

Acknowledgments

To James Mumford, who believes that I assisted him in the writing of this book. Thank you for your immense help in researching and critiquing.

To Jeff Cannell, who has become a new parlor game, replacing Kevin Bacon. You are the world's master networker and my Web guru.

To Eric and Julia Pickerill, thank you, in particular, for standing your ground on my chapters on feminism. You helped me think more clearly.

To Jay Pathak and Joshua Weir, thank you for your research help in the early stages of this book.

To Shelley McWherter, you are more than my assistant—you are my friend and trusted confidante.

To my wife, Marlene, who edited and commented on every page of this book. You are my daily reminder of how much Christ loves me.

1

Who Is My Enemy?

My son is an excellent baseball player. Throughout his childhood and teenage years he played on all-star teams formed from several communities around our city. As you may know, sports activities for children have become far more than a casual recreational pursuit. For good athletes and their parents, participation in youth sports requires a level of devotion reminiscent of the Nuremberg rallies of 1936. One particular year, my son played eighty baseball games in three different states over a four-month period of time. As good parents, we dutifully went to most of his games.

Despite this busy schedule, I relished the opportunity as a pastor to spend that much time with fifteen other families, most of whom were unchurched. Watching my son play baseball got my wife and me outside of our church walls and deeply involved in the lives of other couples.

One day, as I was getting out of my car to watch yet another game, one of the fathers called to me in a loud whisper, "Rich, come over here. I want to show you something." He and several other dads were standing at the back of a car, snickering like junior high boys.

"What's up?" I asked.

He opened the trunk of his car to reveal a cooler full of beer. Excitedly, he said to me, "Hey, Rich, you want some?"

I responded with a real note of appreciation in my voice, "Hey, thanks for the offer, but no, I think I'll just go over and watch the game." I walked toward the field, laughing and thinking to myself, *Guys never outgrow adolescence, do they?* But that wasn't the end of the story.

A Christian couple whose son was on the team, and who regularly sat about fifteen feet away from all of the other parents, got wind of the fact that beer had been brought to the parking lot at one of the games. (Apparently there was a Little League rule that no alcohol could be served within several hundred feet of a game in progress.) This couple petitioned the league to make a ruling on the "beer incident." The league came down against it. They also demanded that the coach speak to all of the parents and ask them to sign a pledge that they would no longer bring beer anywhere near a game in the future.

To this day I believe that this Christian couple was sincere in their religious convictions. They believed that what they were doing was ultimately serving the cause of Christ. The effect of their stand for righteousness, however, was devastating to our witness with the other parents. The unchurched parents were completely turned off to Christianity. For the remaining few weeks of the baseball season, my wife and I had to listen to them angrily denounce Christians. All of our work evaporated, because, in my opinion, a couple of Christians drew their boundary lines in the wrong place.

THE GOOD SAMARITAN REVISITED

On one occasion Jesus told this story:

A man was going down from Jerusalem to Jericho, when he fell into the hands of robbers. They stripped him of his clothes, beat him and went away, leaving him half dead. A priest happened to be going down the same road, and when he saw the man, he passed by on the other side. So too, a Levite, when he came to the place and saw him, passed by on the other side. But a Samaritan, as he traveled, came where the man was; and when he saw him, he took pity on him. He went to him and bandaged his wounds, pouring on oil and wine. Then he put the man on his own donkey, took him to an inn and took care of him. The next day he took out two silver coins and gave them to the innkeeper. "Look after him," he said, "and when I return, I will reimburse you for any extra expense you may have."

Which of these three do you think was a neighbor to the man who fell into the hands of robbers? The expert in the law replied, "The one who had mercy on him." Jesus told him, "Go and do likewise."

—Luke 10:30–37

In the story that has become known as the Parable of the Good Samaritan, Jesus helped his audience see that the category of *neighbor*, those whom they were called to love, was much wider than most of them would allow. Neighbors included those outside the covenant community and beyond the borders of the chosen people. To love God, according to Jesus, meant to love people with the wideness of the heart of God. In other words, loving God, at least in part, means redefining whom we include in our category of neighbor.

The challenge facing the church in the twenty-first century is more basic than the question, "Who is my neighbor?" I believe the first question the church must answer correctly is, "Who is my *enemy*?" Many people believe that the world is our enemy.

PRACTICING THE WELCOME OF THE KINGDOM

Have you ever been in a situation where you knew you were not welcome? I was raised in a conservative Jewish family in New York City. My sister once invited her new Italian Catholic boyfriend, Dominic, over to our house early in their dating relationship. Throughout dinner my sister kept calling her boyfriend "Dom." "Dom, could you pass the butter?" "Dom, what movie do you want to see tonight?" "Dom, could you get me a drink from the refrigerator?"

My very traditional Jewish grandmother kept hearing my sister refer to her boyfriend as Dom. She innocently asked, "Don? Is that short for Donald?"

My sister responded, "It's not *Don*, his name is *Dom*. Dom is short for Dominic."

The blood drained from my grandmother's face as she repeatedly asked in a high-pitched voice, *"Dominic? Dominic? Dominic?"* as she came to the stunning realization that her granddaughter was dating outside of the faith. "Dominic" is obviously not a Jewish name. For the rest of the evening, my grandmother refused to speak. It was obvious that, at least according to my grandmother, Dominic was an unwelcome guest.

How would a feminist or politically liberal person feel in many conservative churches? I don't know, but I fear they would be made to feel like Dominic at my family's dinner table.

Michael Cromartie wrote about a conversation he once had with a very conservative Christian journalist. The journalist insisted that Jimmy Carter could not be a Christian because "no one could be a Christian and have his kind of foreign policy."[1]

I have been told by several people that they keep their political views hidden around their conservative Christian coworkers because they do not want their coworkers to know that they occasionally vote Democrat. They fear a reaction akin to my grandmother's "Dominic? Dominic?" "How could you possibly vote for a Democrat and call yourself a Christian?"

KINDNESS WITH DISCERNMENT

Church members and pastors deeply desire to practice the welcome of the kingdom and to be kind. The English pastor G. A. Studdert-Kennedy reminds us that even kindness has a limit: "Christians in trying to be kinder than Christ cease to be kind at all."[2] Christ was very clear that "the world," in at least one of its biblical senses, is hostile to God and everything God stands for.

What does the Bible mean by "the world?" The term *world* is used in three different senses in the New Testament. First of all, it refers to the earth, or the created order. God, we are told, "made *the world* and everything in it."[3] It is this sense that the apostle John wrote, saying, *"The world* was made through him."[4]

Second, when the Bible speaks of the *world*, it sometimes means simply the world of people—people of various races and ethnicities—

the world of men and women. It is likely in this second sense that the apostle John writes, "For God so loved *the world* that he gave his one and only Son...."[5] It is an unfortunate fact that the majority of men and women have not loved God or served him. Rather, in the case of Jesus Christ, God's Son, they were antagonistic to him, rejected him, and ultimately nailed him to a wooden cross.

So it is not surprising, then, that the Bible uses the term *world* in a third sense to refer to the human race in its opposition to God and in its refusal to receive the truth, to worship God, to believe in Christ, or to follow God's commandments. *The world* in this last sense is the mind-set of unredeemed humanity. Or as David Wells puts it, "The 'world' is the way in which our collective life in society and the culture that goes with it is organized around the self and substitution for God. It is life characterized by self-righteousness, self-centeredness, self-satisfaction, self-aggrandizement and self-promotion, with a corresponding distaste for the self-denial proper to union with Christ."[6] It is the world in this third sense—a way of life hostile to God—that the apostle John was referring to in 1 John 2:15–17 when he wrote these words:

> Do not love the world or anything in the world. If anyone loves the world, the love of the Father is not in him. For everything in the world—the cravings of sinful man, the lust of his eyes and the boasting of what he has and does—comes not from the Father but from the world. The world and its desires pass away.

The world in its hostility murdered Jesus, and the world in its hostility continues to murder Jesus' followers to this very day. It was the world in the form of the Chinese Boxers who slaughtered hundreds of foreign missionaries and tens of thousands of indigenous Christians at the beginning of the twentieth century. E. J. Cooper, a Protestant missionary, wrote to his mother about that world:

> The Lord has honored us by giving us fellowship in his sufferings. Three times stoned, robbed of everything, even

clothes, we know what hunger, thirst, nakedness, weariness are as never before, but also the sustaining grace and strength of God and his peace in a new and deeper sense than before.... Billow after billow has gone over me. Home gone, not one memento of dear Maggie [his wife] even, penniless, wife and child gone to glory, Edith [his other child] lying very sick with diarrhea, and your son weak and exhausted to a degree, though otherwise well.[7]

The world attacked two families and six young children in the Chinese town of Luchen, chasing them from one village to another, hurling sticks and stones and shouting, "Death to the foreign devils." One seven-year-old named Jessie Saunders understood the character of the world when, after being stoned, she said to her mother: "If they loved Jesus, they would not do this."[8]

The world still practices crucifixion at the beginning of the twenty-first century in the Sudan, the largest country in Africa. After enduring more than forty years of civil war, the predominantly Christian population in the southern Sudan is subject to torture, rape, and starvation for their refusal to convert to Islam. Christian children are routinely sold into slavery. Muslims in the north who dare to convert to Christianity are faced with the death penalty. In the decades of the 1980s and 1990s, Sudan's estimated death toll of more than 1.9 million is far greater than the much better publicized slaughter in Rwanda (800,000), Bosnia (300,000), and Kosovo (several thousand as of the beginning of 1999) *combined*.[9]

The world in the form of the modern Chinese government acknowledged "the church played an important role in the change in Eastern Europe" and then it ominously added, "If China does not want such a scene to be repeated in its land, it must strangle the baby while it is still in the cradle."[10]

The world is also found in the "Christian" West. For Western Christians to have the proper perspective on this, they must listen to people who come to the West from other cultures. Eugene Peterson makes this astute observation:

If you listen to a Solzhenitsyn or Bishop Tutu, or university students from Africa or South America, they don't see a Christian land. They see almost the reverse of a Christian land. They see a lot of greed and arrogance. And they see a Christian community that has almost none of the virtues of the biblical community, which has to do with a sacrificial life.... The attractive thing about America to outsiders is the materialism, not the spirituality.... What they want are cars and televisions. They're not [attracted to] our gospel.[11]

IRRELEVANT OR IRRATIONAL?

One way the world's hostility toward Christ is apparent, at least in its Western expression, is in its view that Christianity is either *irrelevant* or *irrational*. At the end of 1997, A. M. Rosenthal, former executive editor of *The New York Times*, candidly confessed that he had helped promote Christianity's irrelevance: "I realized that in decades of reporting, writing, or assigning stories on human rights, I rarely touched on one of the most important [rights]. Political human rights, legal, civil, and press rights, emphatically; but the right to worship where and how God or our conscience leads, almost never."[12]

Religious freedom and the role of the church worldwide simply never show up on the radar screen of the cultural elite in America. Economics are endlessly discussed, as are political considerations, social differentiations, and racial and gender divides. But the cultural elite in America are generally unable to see, much less understand, the role of faith (Christian or otherwise) on the decisions of ordinary people.

Patrick Glynn reflects on his undergraduate days at Harvard in the late 1960s:

When I left my Jesuit High School to attend Harvard in 1969, I plunged into an environment where the death or the disappearance of God was simply taken for granted....

It was not so much that the professors who taught me were anti-religious—the English Department (apart from a couple of practicing Catholics and a few other churchgoers) was marked by a kind of sad yearning for lost Christianity. It was simply assumed that religious belief had become impossible for rational human beings in the modern era, a fact that one accepted with a certain melancholy and nostalgia for previous ages when it was still possible for "men" to believe.[13]

When religion does appear on the radar screen, it almost always does so in its most irrational form, such as the latest battle between science and religion, or the latest witchcraft scare in a local public school, or the most recent completely harmless book being selected for censorship by "fundamentalist" parents. Of course, the term *fundamentalist* is never used in its appropriate historic context (one who subscribes to the fundamentals of the faith) or, even more narrowly (one who takes a position of opposition to modernist tendencies). In the media, *fundamentalist* is almost always used as a shorthand for "religious fanatic." It is often preceded by adjectives (whether appropriate or not) such as right-wing or ultraconservative, or it is followed by "follower of" as in the expression, "right-wing fundamentalist follower of Jerry Falwell" or "ultraconservative fundamentalist follower of Pat Robertson." The portrait is one of blind, unthinking, often intolerant and bigoted commitment to some religion or religious sect. This stereotypical description allows the elites to dismiss Christians without ever taking seriously what a particular Christian may be saying or without ever asking the question whether a Christian's viewpoint may, in fact, be a true one.

Thus, despite all the talk about multiculturalism, contemporary culture regularly balks at including Christianity in its "gorgeous mosaic." This resistance to Christ and Christianity has sometimes been dubbed the "ABC Rule," meaning "anything but Christianity."

DISCERNING WHAT FORM
OUR REAL ENEMY IS TAKING

Throughout this book, I will attempt to clearly identify the world in this third sense. My goal is to discern the form our real enemy is taking in the twenty-first century. We must not shrink from this task—as though Christian love means the absence of moral discernment or any critique whatsoever. We must never find ourselves trying to be kinder than Christ! According to the Swiss theologian Karl Barth, "We are unfeeling, not when we probe deeply into the wound they carry when they come to us for healing, but rather when we pass over it as if we did not know why they had come."[14] Barth was echoing sentiments expressed by the prophet Jeremiah more than six hundred years before the time of Christ: "They [the prophets and priests] dress the wound of my people as though it were not serious. 'Peace, peace,' they say, when there is no peace."[15]

It is relatively easy to practice the welcome of the kingdom yet fail to practice moral discernment at the same time. For example, many churches have adopted the gay-rights perspective, which blurs the distinction between compassion for individual homosexuals and the political and social agenda of gay activists. These churches claim that compassion for individual homosexuals must translate into complete tolerance of homosexuality in all spheres of life. Anything less than viewing homosexuality as a completely equal and valid alternative to heterosexuality (including the blessing of same-sex marriages) is seen as evidence of homophobia.

It is also relatively easy to identify sin in others and fail to practice the welcome of the kingdom. Using my prior example of homosexuality, many churches announce a moral position against homosexuality but fail to emphasize the hope of redemption for homosexual sinners to the same degree as they do for every other kind of sinner.

Again, it is easy to announce a moral position. It is far more challenging to create ministries that offer healing and hope to broken people. To me, the most exciting (and biblical) kind of church to be involved in is a church that maintains clear moral standards but also communicates maximum compassion and mercy through ministries of welcome. Such ministries of welcome may include ministries to drug and alcohol abusers. Or perhaps a ministry to AIDS sufferers or those who are trapped in New Age mysticism. Ministries of welcome might include a "Coffee and Conversation" evening, where folks are invited to listen to someone speak about a controversial subject. They then have the opportunity to discuss (and agree or disagree with) the speaker's viewpoint as they have coffee afterwards with a church member.

People need and deserve straight talk from Christians. If sex outside of God's prescribed boundaries kills us spiritually (and sometimes physically), let's say so without mincing words. But first let's make sure that in our communication we're targeting our greatest firepower toward those who are presently *inside the church*, while showing maximum patience and grace toward those *outside the church*. And let's not merely announce a moral position. (We don't need Jesus to do that; the Pharisees were great at merely announcing moral positions.) Let's couple a "ministry of welcome" with every moral stance taken.

M   D

Before I becam   at a major state university for sev   , the oval on our campus was frequ   d to speak in the name of Jesus Cl   preacher wore a shirt emblazoned   The "G" in "Got," the "A" in "AIDS,   t red and lined up vertically in a co   Y." The preacher employed the mo   or gay people, for those who were   n for women who wore jeans or shorts. He thought he was serving Jesus by attacking those he judged to be *the world*.

Now admittedly, the behaviors of the Christian parents at my son's baseball game and this preacher are not representative of the Christian community in tone and style. Few Christians I know would go to war about beer brought to a baseball game or would use harsh, vulgar language aimed at homosexuals or women.

But I believe the larger Christian community, particularly in the United States, does share the flawed assumptions that undergirded these believers' behaviors. Many Christians err when we try to identify *the world* as "those people out there"—nonchurchgoers such as New Agers, postmodernists, feminists, advocates of diversity, liberals, and homosexuals. What if we discover that *the world* we Christians are to avoid is not "out there," but is *in the church*?

THE WELCOME OF THE KINGDOM AND SET THEORY

What Are Bounded Sets?

Paul Hiebert, a professor at Fuller Theological Seminary's School of World Missions, points out that people around the world categorize things in very different ways.[16] In the West, we tend to look at life in terms of *bounded sets*. An apple is always an apple. Apples may be MacIntosh, Jonathan, Winesap, or Delicious. They may be green, yellow, red, or some combination of these. But everyone knows that an apple is an apple. An apple is never a potato.

In the West, whenever we look at life, we Westerners tend to see clear boundaries. An object is either *in* or *out* of a particular category. Of course, the Bible uses bounded-set language on many occasions. Paul speaks about people being *in Christ* and *outside of Christ*.[17] The apostle John makes it clear that there are boundaries to the Christian life: "We know that we have passed from death to life, because we love our brothers. Anyone who does not love remains in death."[18]

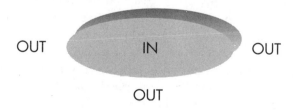

OUT   IN   OUT

OUT

What Are Centered Sets?

Hiebert points out another way of defining things. Rather than drawing a boundary between one category and another, one could define things in terms of *centered-set* theory. In a centered set, the issue is not being in or out of a category (as though everything were static and unchanging). Rather, in a centered set we define things by movement—a person or object is either moving *toward* or moving *away from* the center. In a centered set one recognizes not only movement, but the possibility of a change in direction.

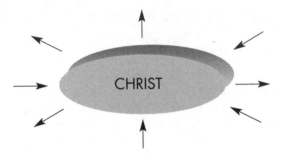

So rather than asking "Are you healthy today?" as though health were an unchanging static category, centered sets help us to understand that a person is either moving toward or away from health. We further recognize that a person who is moving away from health by smoking or eating fatty foods can turn around. In Christianity, the critical question in terms of a centered set is not whether you have *crossed the line* and are *in* or *out*, but rather where are you right now in relationship to the center, namely, Christ? Are you facing Christ, or is your back turned to Christ? Are you moving away from Christ or toward Christ? Rather than merely asking ourselves, "Did I pray the sinner's prayer twenty years ago?" most Christians would be far better off asking, "Who is my Lord today? Today am I moving away from Christ or toward Christ?"

In the past, Christians understood centered-set thinking through their familiarity with John Bunyan's classic *The Pilgrim's Progress*. In Bunyan's story the Christian life is seen as a journey toward (or away from) the Celestial City (heaven). Many Christian leaders have commented that it would be an enormous boon to Christian discipleship if the church could regain "journey" language in addition to "step over the line" language. Classes and book clubs that rediscover *The Pilgrim's Progress*, as well as leadership training on centered sets, move us in the right direction.

Jesus often used centered-set language. He saw that the Pharisees, although they were near to God, had the wrong direction in their lives and were moving away from God. On the other hand, tax collectors and prostitutes, who were far away from God, were moving toward him.

Over the years, I have watched many longtime Christians who have attended church for twenty or thirty years smugly judge and condemn those who have not stepped over the boundary line by praying the sinner's prayer. The question needs to be asked, How do you know that the person *outside* is not moving toward Christ? How do you know that *you* haven't spent the last decade moving away from him?

Centered-set thinking has been an enormous encouragement to evangelism and ministry for the church I pastor. Recently, a young woman came to our church from a background of deep involvement in Wicca and the New Age. She was dressed entirely in black and had no ability to make eye contact with anyone in the church. One of our staff interns talked with her and later confessed, "My first reaction was that this woman was so far-out, she could never be reached. But then I remembered that the issue is not how far or near someone is, but what direction they are headed. At least she was here at church making contact with another Christian. It is obvious that God is at work in her life, drawing her toward Christ. My interaction with her became a lot more fun as I discovered new ways that the Holy Spirit was drawing this former practitioner of Wicca toward Christ."

Centered-set thinking also recently helped a widow in the church. She told me about an encounter she had had with two Mormons who knocked at her door. She welcomed them in and offered them something to eat. As they sat around her kitchen table, she talked with them about a relationship with Christ.

"What church do you go to?" they asked her.

"I attend the Vineyard on the northeast side of town," she replied.

The two young Mormon men looked at each other and laughed. "We thought so. The Christians in your church are the only Christians in town who don't slam the door in our faces and who show us any kindness at all."

As you can imagine, I couldn't have felt more proud of the people in my church than I did when I heard her story!

Throughout this book, centered-set language will show up again and again as a key toward creating ministries of welcome that continue to hold moral standards.

What Are Fuzzy Sets?

Paul Hiebert mentions a third way of forming categories. Some people, especially in Oriental societies, have talked about *fuzzy sets.* Rather than seeing something as being either A *or* B, people in the East will often ask why not both A *and* B? For example, using fuzzy boundaries, they might ask the question, "Where does a mountain begin?" Sometimes things blend into each other.

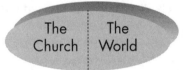

In a culture of increasing diversity, many people have great difficulty filling out the census form with regard to their race. When is someone Hispanic? Must all of their ancestors be Hispanic? What if one of their four grandparents was black? What if two were black? What if one was Northern European? When is a Hispanic Hispanic?

Applying fuzzy-set theory to the Bible, we might ask, When did Peter become a disciple? When Jesus first called him? When he first confessed that Jesus was the Christ? When he got out of the boat and began to walk on the water? When he repented of his sin of disowning Christ? And when was Peter a non-disciple? When he was born? When he told Jesus to depart from him because Peter was a sinful man? When he rebuked Jesus for suggesting that Messiah must suffer and die? When he took his eyes off the Lord as he walked on the water? When he denied three times that he knew Jesus?

In the West, with our bounded sets, someone is either in or out. But with fuzzy sets, one thing may run into the other. Contrary to most Christians' assumptions, fuzzy sets help us understand that the church and the world often blend together.

FOUR IMPORTANT QUESTIONS

I am indebted to one of the world's foremost Jesus scholars, N. T. Wright, and his book *Jesus and the Victory of God,* for offering a practical and biblical way for us to sort through the issues raised by set theory. Specifically, Wright asks us to consider four important questions:

- Who are we?
- Who is our enemy?
- What is our calling?
- What are our methods?[19]

Who Are We?

Jews in Jesus' day defined themselves by certain boundary markers: the temple, the Torah, the keeping of the Sabbath, and the observance of certain dietary restrictions. Boundary markers are those things that tell us who is in and who is out, who is one of us and who isn't. A Pharisee in Jesus' day believed that he could easily discern who was one of God's covenant people by simply examining how that person observed the Sabbath day.[20]

Christians today also have a set of boundary markers, defining who is in and who is out of the community of believers. Read the newsletters from Christian parachurch organizations. Listen to Christian radio. Liberals are out; conservatives are in. Homosexuals are out; heterosexuals are in. Those who are pro-choice on the issue of abortion are definitely out; those who are pro-life are definitely in. Much of conservative Christian thinking is limited by its exclusive use of bounded-set categories.

While I am *strongly* pro-life and have actively worked for twenty years in various pro-life activities, in this book I would like to challenge the use of outward "badges" to identify and define God's people. One way to challenge our thinking is to ask ourselves who drew lines and used identifying badges in the New Testament—the Pharisees, or Jesus? Who said that prostitutes and tax collectors would get into the kingdom before many of those who were supposedly in? Jesus had boundary markers too, but they were quite different from those of the Pharisees and contemporary Christians. Jesus' identifying badges included such things as love ("By this all men will know that you are my disciples, if you love one another") and faith ("For my Father's will is that everyone who looks to the Son and believes in him shall have eternal life").[21] He also used the badges of mercy and compassion for the broken and the outcast,[22] self-denial, cross bearing, and not being ashamed of him or his words.[23] Are these the badges you and I use to determine who is in and who is out?

Who Is Our Enemy?

The Pharisees were quite clear about who were the enemies of God. According to them, God's enemies were obviously the Romans, as well as anyone who deliberately flouted the Torah—people such as prostitutes, tax collectors, and "sinners." Jesus redefined the concept of enemy in a way that caused deep offense to the Pharisees. According to Jesus, the so-called "people of God" were to be God's enemies. He called that generation of Jewish people "wicked and adulterous."[24] He said they were idolatrous and in bondage to the love of money.[25] He told them they might actually be weeds and not wheat, or bad fish and not good fish.[26] In other words, *the world is often found in the church.* (Fuzzy sets!)

Our inquiry concerning what is wrong with the world should always begin with the answer—we are! This echoes G. K. Chesterton's famous two-word answer to an essay contest. In response to "What is wrong with the world?" Chesterton telegraphed, "'I am!' G. K. Chesterton." What is wrong with the world, therefore, is not that there are too many liberals or New Agers or feminists or postmodernists in our schools or in our government. What is most wrong with the world is that *the people of God fail to act and live like the people of God.* Or to put it another way, what is wrong with the world is that there is too much of "the world" in the church. Jesus' strictest scrutiny is always reserved for those who supposedly are in a covenant relationship with God, not for those outside of a covenant relationship with God.

The apostle Paul said much the same thing when he wrote to the Corinthian believers about church discipline: "What business is it of mine to judge those outside the church. Are you not to judge those inside? God will judge those outside."[27]

What Is Our Calling?

Many Pharisees in Jesus' day believed they were called to be victorious over the Gentile world by engaging in revolutionary activity against the Roman government. Jesus challenged Israel to fulfill its calling by choosing an entirely different path—the path of being the salt of the earth and the light of the world.[28] As Wright so aptly puts it, "He . . . [criticized] his contemporaries for being more concerned for victory over the Gentile world than for bringing YHWH's healing and salvation to it."[29]

Could not the same thing be said of the contemporary Christian understanding of calling? Our rhetoric often betrays us. We use holy-war rhetoric and the language of crusades, suggesting that our primary calling is to crush those who oppose us, not to bring healing and salvation to them.

What Are Our Methods?

The method of many of the Jewish people in Jesus' day was to support nationalistic, sometimes violent revolutionary activity against Rome. Jesus rejected the entire way that the people thought the battle would be won. In fact, in the words of Wright, "Jesus was to fight the battle against those who wish to fight the battle."[30] Jesus wept over Jerusalem, saying, "If you, even you, had only known on this day *what would bring you peace*—but now it is hidden from your eyes."[31]

What are the things that "would bring you peace" to which Jesus was referring? What were Jesus' methods for dealing with people who were far from God? First, he challenged Israel to act like Israel. Jesus called God's people to radical repentance and to be the salt of the earth and the light of the world! Salt that has lost its saltiness won't save anyone. Second, he welcomed sinners, ate with them, and offered them the gift of forgiveness and salvation. Third, he brought those outside of the covenant community into God's family. Jesus preached the good news, healed the sick, and delivered those who were oppressed by the devil. Finally, he went the way of the cross. The way of the cross, in part, involves overcoming opposition to God through voluntary suffering rather than retaliation in kind. ("Well, the gays are marching; we Christians need to organize a counter-demonstration!")

Here are some of the things that "would bring you peace" we'll reflect on in this book:

- the continual need on the part of Christians to revisit our categories—specifically, who we are, who our enemy is, what our calling is, and what our methods are
- the need to learn the language of our culture
- the need to listen rather than to speak
- the need to follow the way of the cross and be willing to suffer for Jesus' sake

LEARNING THE LANGUAGE OF THE CULTURE

On the day of Pentecost, Jews from all over the known world gathered in Jerusalem to celebrate one of the three annual Jewish pilgrimage feasts. For some, their trip to Jerusalem was a once-in-a-lifetime pilgrimage. The book of Acts records a miracle that took place on one particular Pentecost:

> Now there were staying in Jerusalem God-fearing Jews from every nation under heaven. When they heard this sound, a crowd came together in bewilderment, because each one heard them speaking in his own language. Utterly

amazed, they asked: "Are not all these men who are speaking Galileans? Then how is it that each of us hears them in his own native language? Parthians, Medes and Elamites; residents of Mesopotamia, Judea and Cappadocia, Pontus and Asia, Phrygia and Pamphylia, Egypt and parts of Libya near Cyrene; visitors from Rome (both Jews and converts to Judaism); Cretans and Arabs—we hear them declaring the wonders of God in our own tongues!"[32]

What was the miracle that took place on that Pentecost day? It wasn't only that a sound like the blowing of a violent wind came from heaven, or even that the disciples saw what seemed to be tongues of fire separating and coming to rest on each of them. The miracle of Pentecost was that people from all over the known world heard God speaking in their own language. "A crowd came together in bewilderment, because each one heard them speaking in his own language." And again, "How is it that each of us hears them in his own native language?" And again, "We hear them declaring the wonders of God in our own tongues!"

Luke, the author of Acts, wants us to understand the shattering impact of God speaking to a person in his or her own language. There is a world of difference between believing that God sent his Son to die for the sins of the world and experiencing the reality that *my* God sent his Son to die for *my* sins. Very often the change from the impersonal, "Christ died for the sins of the world" to the first person, "Christ died for *my* sins," occurs when persons hear God speaking in their own native language.

That is precisely what happened to me. I first heard about Christ through a woman named Marlene, who later became my wife. Through Marlene I first began to understand the basic outline of the gospel. She spoke to me about Christ fulfilling the Old Testament promises. She told me the story of God coming to earth and taking on human flesh. She shared with me Christ's teachings and miracles, his death on a cross for sin, and his resurrection from the dead. But as a person raised in a conservative Jewish family in New York City, there still was a huge cultural distance between the story of Christ and my own life—that is, until I heard God speaking to me in my language. At Marlene's church, a Jewish believer in Christ explained the gospel narrative in terms of the Passover Seder dinner, which we were celebrating together one evening. I finally heard God speaking to me in a language I could understand (the Jewish Passover Seder), and I was able to embrace Christ's death as a death for *my* sins.

The notion that God saves people by allowing them to hear the gospel message in their own language has fueled the modern Bible translation movement. In past centuries, great missionaries such as William Carey, Hudson Taylor, Henry Martyn, and Adoniram Judson were all Bible translators. One of the greatest missionaries in history, a man named Cameron Townsend, felt a calling to missionary service and went to Guatemala as a young adult in 1917. While there, he tried to sell Spanish Bibles to the native Cakchiquel Indians who lived in a remote rural area of Guatemala. Only a few Cakchiquel Indians could read or speak Spanish. One day Cameron Townsend was confronted by an Indian man. "If your God is so smart," he asked, "then why hasn't he learned the Cakchiquel language yet?" Cameron Townsend was so convicted by that question that he spent the next thirteen years of his life translating the Bible into the Cakchiquel language. Based on this experience, Townsend started an organization in 1942 called Wycliffe Bible Translators. Their mission is to provide the Scriptures in every known language on earth so that people can hear God speaking in their own language.[33]

I believe we would do wrong to confine our thinking about God, who speaks many languages, to just Bible translation. I believe we should include, for instance, the experience of an unchurched person who walks into a church and, for the first time in her life, can relate and connect with God. One of the greatest compliments I hear about our church from guests is, "Today when I came to your church, I felt like I had come home!" What they mean is, they didn't have to jump through seventy-two cultural hoops to hear God speaking. It wasn't as though they had been transported back in time seventy-five years and felt completely out of place. The message, the music, the dress, and the issues addressed all served to connect them to Christ.

This is the ongoing task of a church—to recreate in twenty-first-century people the miracle of Pentecost—hearing God's voice in their native language. This includes communicating the gospel in the increasingly diverse dress of America and other Western nations' newest immigrants. This means planting thousands of ethnic churches and creating many multicultural churches. It also includes recognizing that the language of seniors and baby boomers is not the language of young adults. Nor is the language of moderns the language of postmoderns. It includes the recognition that the language of married couples is not necessarily the language of singles, or that the language of men is not the language of women. We must ask ourselves as Christians, "Do we love people enough to try to speak to them about God in their own language?" Not everyone is a churched person. Not everyone speaks "Christian-ese." Do you love people enough to enter their world and really comprehend the way they think and the way they speak? Do you love teenagers enough to speak to them in such a way that God is not simply the "God of their fathers." Do you have enough love for people who have AIDS or who are HIV-positive to communicate the gospel in their language? Do you love feminists and postmodernists enough to even learn their language?

I believe the question posed to Cameron Townsend nearly a century ago is the question being asked of Christians today: "If your God is so smart, then how come he doesn't speak my language?"

LEARNING TO LISTEN

We live in an increasingly diverse culture, and Western Christians can no longer claim the privileged position of guardians of the culture's morals, values, or truth claims. In fact, the Christian's position today more closely resembles the position of Christians in the New Testament world than the position of Christians in the church-dominated world following the Edict of Milan in A.D. 313.[34] Today

Christians are a minority, and so we find ourselves increasingly marginalized by our culture's elite institutions.

Christians must be willing to listen as much as they speak if they ever hope to be heard and taken seriously. Listening communicates more respect than speaking (a very hard task when you are confident you possess the truth). Listening suggests we may actually have something to learn. Since we claim omniscience belongs to God alone and not ourselves, this shouldn't be a novel concept for Christians. Yet it is the rare book on evangelism that advises Christians to actually listen to their non-Christian friends as much as speak. By listening we not only show respect, we also affirm truth in a friend's position, at which point we can point him or her to a greater, more comprehensive, more satisfying truth.

Most of all, the style we adopt should be that of our great example, Jesus, who, when he saw the crowds, "had compassion on them, because they were harassed and helpless, like sheep without a shepherd."[35] Compare Jesus' tone and style to that of the Pharisees, who, when they saw the crowds, disdainfully said, "This mob that knows nothing of the law—there is a curse on them."[36] Which tone and style do you think most Christians use, especially those engaged in today's culture wars? More important, which tone and style do we use as we relate to those outside the church with whom we may strongly disagree? Are we more likely to sound like our overall goal is to crush opposition to God, or to bring healing and salvation to those who oppose the truth?

THE WILLINGNESS TO SUFFER

When I was a business law professor at a midwestern state university, I once hosted a luncheon with other professors, with a time set aside for questions and answers. One young professor, without any sense of incongruity, asked me, "How can I live as a Christian in my university department without having it affect my prospects for tenure and promotion?"

I responded, "Whatever made you think you could live as a Christian and not have it affect your tenure? Didn't the apostle Paul say somewhere that it is appointed to you to not only believe in him, but also *to suffer* for his sake?" When I saw that I wasn't scratching his itch, I talked to him about my own experience, the constitutional protection given to state university professors, and the long-standing tradition of academic freedom that includes the opportunity for Christian professors to be public about their faith.

But that professor's question left me unsettled and shaken, because it sums up why, despite so much religious activity in America, there is so little impact on the public square. Millions of American Christians are asking that professor's question. "How can I serve Christ without paying a price?" The simple biblical answer is, *You can't!* Whatever made you think you could?

The price we pay as Christians is not only the suffering we experience at the hands of the world (as defined by those outside the church). We may also find ourselves in direct opposition to the worldliness found today in the church. Like Jesus, you may find yourself subjected to the cross not only at the hands of the Romans, but also at the hands of God's people. There is a price to pay when one begins to redefine the answer to the question, "Who is my enemy?"

Questions for Reflection and Discussion

?

1. Recall the story of the "beer incident" at the beginning of this chapter. Have you ever been in a situation where you felt torn between taking a moral stand and showing the grace and love of Jesus? What did you do, and what was the outcome?

2. Consider the term *world* in its third sense—hostile opposition to God. What experience can you point to in which you experienced the world this way?

3.   Explain the difference between a bounded set, a centered set, and a fuzzy set. How do you most often categorize people spiritually—by using bounded-set language, centered-set language, or fuzzy-set language?

4.   How might expanding the categories you normally employ assist you in being a follower of Christ? In your witness?

5.   What would you say is the "language" most people speak today at your job, in your neighborhood, in your family, and so forth. Is it the language of young adults? Traditional Christian? Postmoderns? Some other? How well do you as a Christian communicate God in the language that is most prevalent around you?

RECOMMENDED READING

Bunyan, John. *The Pilgrim's Progress*. New York: Penguin Books, 1965.

Wells, David F. *God in the Wasteland*. Grand Rapids: Eerdmans, 1994.

_____. *No Place for Truth*. Grand Rapids: Eerdmans, 1993.

Wright, N. T. *Jesus and the Victory of God*. Minneapolis: Fortress, 1996.

Part 1

Is the Postmodernist My Enemy?

2

The Hodgepodge on the Highway

"I'm an Episcopalian, and I think of myself as a practicing non-Jew," says Katherine Powell Cohen, a 36-year-old English teacher in San Francisco. "I'm a Mennonite hyphen Unitarian Universalist who practices Zen meditation," says Ralph Imhoff, 57, a retired educator from Chandler, Arizona. "I call myself a Christian-Buddhist, but sort of tongue-in-cheek," says Maitreya Badami, 30, who works in the Contra Costa, California, public defender's office.[1]

The *Wall Street Journal* recently wrote about this hodgepodge of beliefs:

> If America has always been a melting pot, these days its religious practices have become a spiritual hash. Blending or braiding the beliefs of different spiritual traditions has become so rampant in America that the Dalai Lama has called the country "the spiritual supermarket." Jews flirt with Hinduism, Catholics study Taoism, and Methodists discuss whether to make the Passover Seder an official part of worship. Rabbi Zalman Schachter-Shalomi, a prominent Jewish scholar, is also a Sufi sheik, and James Ishmael Ford, a Unitarian minister in Arizona, is a Zen sensei, or master. The melding of Judaism with Buddhism has become so commonplace that marketers who sell spiritual books, videotapes, and lecture series have a name for it: "JewBu."[2]

The *Journal* goes on to report that even Christian clergy are caught up in this smorgasbord of beliefs. For example, at St. Gregory of Nyssa, an Episcopal church in San Francisco, two senior ministers have created a service that includes "the worship of Jesus Christ, dancing and the ringing of Buddhist cymbals." The ministers, both of whom have impeccable Episcopalian credentials (with graduate degrees from Cambridge and Princeton universities respectively), had the church built four years ago to their specifications. St. Gregory's has an interior decorated with Eastern Orthodox icons, a Shinto shrine, and a Chinese gong. The ministers wear tie-dyed African vestments. Unlike traditional Episcopal services, their service always includes the Shema (an ancient Jewish prayer), as well as quiet moments of reflection with the ringing of cymbals. People dance forward to join in the Eucharist, and everyone is invited to partake, not just Christians.

HODGEPODGE ON THE HIGHWAY

Richard Mouw, president of Fuller Theological Seminary, wrote an amusing article about how Americans can hold in their minds entirely contradictory ideas without sweating it. He reported that one day on a Chicago expressway he was following a car that had a Playboy bunny decal affixed to its rear window. Curious to see what sort of person would drive a car with a Playboy bunny decal so prominently displayed, Mouw pulled up alongside the car, only to notice a plastic statue of the Virgin Mary on the car's dashboard.

"Was there some intra-family compromise at work," wondered Mouw, "between, say, a would-be Hugh Hefner and [the driver's] pious wife?" Upon further reflection, Mouw recognized that this incident was symptomatic of the entire lack of coherence in people's worldviews.

Mouw went on to tell another story about a time when he was a guest on a call-in radio show. His fellow guest was a liberal church leader who was skeptical about the reliability of the New Testament and the resurrection of Jesus. Mouw, however, defended the reliability of the New Testament text and the historicity of Christ's resurrection. One of the callers was a young woman who identified herself as "Heather from Glendale."

"'I'm not what you would call, like, a Christian,' Heather began. 'Actually, right now I am sort of into—you know, witchcraft and stuff like that. But I agree with the guy from Fuller Seminary. I'm just shocked that someone would, like, say that Jesus wasn't really raised from the dead!'"[3]

Is there a philosophy or worldview that can account for Heather from Glendale (the dabbler in witchcraft who believes in the resurrection), the fellow whose car bore a statue of the Virgin Mary and a Playboy bunny sticker, and St. Gregory's Episcopal Church (which has Christian symbols alongside a Shinto shrine and Chinese gongs)? Yes, the worldview that can account for the melding of seemingly incompatible philosophies into one gigantic collage is called "postmodernism." To make sense of the Western world in the twenty-first century, one must strive to understand the postmodernist worldview.

WHAT IS POSTMODERNISM?

One author said that trying to get a handle on postmodernism is "like trying to nail Jell-O to the wall." Some contend that post-modernism is simply a collection of different forms of antimodernism. Others see it as a rather benign or neutral movement that takes shape within different areas of the arts, physical sciences, and the metaphysical disciplines. Still others view it as a self-contradictory attack on the very concept of truth itself, which would jettison all attempts at a singular worldview.[4]

Some authors, such as theologian Thomas Oden, believe that postmodernism is a misnomer altogether and that we ought to substitute the word "ultramodern" for "postmodern." Oden writes, "What is named 'post' is actually a desperate extension of despairing modernity, which imagines by calling itself another name (post-modern), it can extend the ideology of modernity into the period following modernity."[5]

Because there are so many different perspectives on post-modernism, any attempted definition will be criticized by one camp or another. Instead of trying to define postmodernism, I will describe some of its main features. But first . . .

WHEN DID POSTMODERNISM BEGIN?

The word *post* means "after." Postmodernism, therefore, simply means "after modernism." But just as there is no agreement regarding the definition of postmodernism, there is also no consensus about the exact dating of modernism. Theologian Stanley Grenz would place the birth of the modern era at about 1648, associating it with the beginning of the Enlightenment and the Peace of Westphalia following the Thirty Years War.[6] Thomas Oden marks the modern period by the fall of two great walls: the wall in front of the Bastille Prison in 1789 and the wall in Berlin in 1989.[7] Thus, modernity would cover an exact two hundred-year period marked by the collapse of these two famous walls.

However one dates the birth of the modern period, whether as early as 1648 or as late as 1789, it is clear to most observers that the twenty-first-century Western world is witnessing the end of an era. The philosophical perspective known as modernism is either dying or is already dead.

WHAT ARE THE FEATURES OF MODERNISM?

Although many features of modernism could be cited, some of the more prominent ones include the following:

- a belief in the inevitable progress of humanity
- an extreme confidence in human reason
- an acceptance of autonomy and rejection of authority
- a belief that nature is all that exists
- a quest for unity, with a tendency toward uniformity

A Belief in the Inevitable Progress of Humanity

Modernists are the ultimate optimists. To them, everything is getting bigger and better every day and in every way. Modernists' political slogans speak of New Frontiers, New Deals, and a New Day Dawning. The eighteenth-century French philosopher Condorcet spoke of the gradual perfection and improvement of humanity over time with these enthusiastic words: "The human race, emancipated from its shackles, released from the empire of fate and from that of the enemies of its progress, is advancing with a firm and sure step along the path of truth, virtue, and happiness."[8] John Dewey, whose philosophy of education has permeated the public school system in North America, captured modernism's optimistic belief in inevitable progress this way: "The future rather than the past dominates the imagination. The Golden Age lies ahead of us, not behind us."[9]

But it is by no means self-evident or obvious that we moderns are happier, more moral, more compassionate, more tolerant, or less warlike than our premodern ancestors. The twentieth century provided an abundance of evidence that we are not. While it is certainly the case that we have progressed technologically and scientifically, this past century has witnessed trainloads of Jews delivered to German gas chambers; Soviet gulags; Chinese brainwashing; ethnic cleansing in Rwanda and Bosnia; genocide in Uganda and Cambodia; atomic bombings of Hiroshima and Nagasaki; massacre at Mylai—to name just a few witnesses against the idea of moral progress.

The myth of progress exists not only in the realm of humanity's moral improvement, but also in the modern belief of our intellectual advancement over premoderns. C. S. Lewis coined the phrase "chronological snobbery" to describe the uncritical assumption that what has gone out of date is on that account discredited (in other words, if an idea is no longer fashionable, it must not be true). Lewis wrote the following:

> You must find out why [an idea] went out of date. Was it ever refuted (and if so, by whom, where, and how conclusively), or did it merely die away as fashions do? If the latter, this tells us nothing about its truth or falsehood. From seeing this, one passes to the realization that our own age is also a "period," and certainly has, like all periods, its own characteristic illusions.[10]

An Extreme Confidence in Human Reason

Before the modern age, human reason was employed to understand truth given through biblical revelation. Anselm, the medieval theologian, said, "The believer does not seek to understand, that he may believe, but he believes that he may understand."[11] The theologians of the church in the premodern period used their reason to demonstrate the truth of revelation and to reconcile the human experience of life with the teaching found in the Bible. Beginning with the philosopher René Descartes, however, human reason was uncoupled from revelation and was allowed to wander autonomously toward whatever discoveries could be made through the human senses. According to Stanley Grenz, modernism's confidence in human reason was based on three major assumptions:

- Knowledge is certain. As long as we come up with the right method of investigation, humanity can make absolutely correct statements about all aspects of reality.
- Knowledge is objective. The ideal intellectual is a dispassionate knower who stands apart from what he or she is observing. In other words, the scientist can somehow gain a God's-eye-view of the universe and be an entirely neutral observer of the object of his or her study.
- Knowledge is inherently good. This is taken to be a given. No justification is needed for any scientific enterprise, since all knowledge is inherently good and ignorance is always unquestionably evil.[12]

But are these modernist assumptions valid?

Is knowledge certain? Complete certainty is an impossibility, since every one of our observations and experiences takes place in some context and is, to some degree, a function of interpretation. In other words, everything we know is limited by who we are.

Recently I was asked to speak at a Unitarian-Universalist church. I have made it a practice to accept invitations to speak almost anywhere, as long as there are no constraints put on what I am allowed to say. After my talk (and an hour of questions and answers), a young man came up to me and said, "Rich, I don't think I can believe in Jesus as you've been encouraging us to do this evening. I still have some doubts, and there are still questions that for me remain unanswered."

I said, "Listen, if you're waiting to arrive at a place of total certainty before you trust in Christ, that will never happen. I live life with a constant sense of my three fundamental limits. First of all, I am a creature, not the Creator. I am by design very small and can't possibly comprehend all of the working of my Creator. Second, I am a sinner. Even those things that I could comprehend get twisted in my mind to serve my own self-interest. I recognize that there is a high degree of distortion based on the fallenness of my reason. Third, I am from New York City. That fact inclines me towards a whole set of cultural assumptions and approaches. Therefore, I know that I could never arrive at absolute certainty about anything."

On the other hand, the fact that we can't have absolute certainty does not immediately throw us into a state of total relativity in which one opinion is as good as another. Neither must we stop drawing any lines or making judgments because we know philosophically that what we are saying may only be a very good approximation of reality.[13]

I witnessed the results of extreme uncertainty at a recent conference in which I participated. One of the other speakers, also a pastor, kept asserting that "everything was just a matter of perspective." A friend of mine asked him afterward, "How far would you go with this idea that 'everything is just a matter of perspective'?"

The presenter responded, "In the last several years I've lost my certainty about everything!"

My friend, still wanting to know where the pastor would draw the line, said, "I understand that, but let's say a Jehovah's Witness came into your church and wanted to lead one of your small groups. Would you allow him to lead?"

The presenter said, "As a matter of fact, he would be able to lead in my church."

My friend said, "You mean someone who denies the deity of Christ and the reality of the Trinity would still be able to have a leadership role in your church? Don't you have a Statement of Faith?"

He said, "No. Our only Statement of Faith is 'Follow Jesus, whatever that means to you.'"

The pristine certainty of modernism, which could not be subjected to any corrections, has been appropriately critiqued by twentieth-century philosophers. We shouldn't, however, toss the baby out with the bathwater. Our basic confidence is that God can and does speak in ways appropriate to our limitations, so that we have more than enough knowledge on which to be saved and to live life well.

Is knowledge objective? Knowledge can hardly be said to be objective, since no human being can separate himself or herself from the flow of history and gain a God's-eye-view of the universe. It is not wrong to struggle for objectivity or neutrality, but what we know must be viewed with a high degree of modesty. As scientists have long held, the very presence of an observer alters the results of the experiment.

What's so great about objectivity anyway? In the area of interpersonal relationships, subjectivity may yield more reliable knowledge than objectivity. The existentialists used to talk about the importance of moving from an "I/it" relationship with other personal beings (making other people or God into objects to be analyzed) toward an "I/thou" relationship (making other people or God into subjects to be loved).

Who knows a person better—someone who views them dispassionately and indifferently, like a scientist, or someone who loves them, like a wife or a husband? As Christians, we believe that truth is not merely an abstract proposition, but it is contained in a person, Jesus Christ, who said, "I am the way and the truth and the life."[14]

The addition of the subjective to the objective is not meant to pit words (objective revelation) against experience (subjective revelation). Objective words do not exhaust God's revelation, but then neither does a "mystical experience." We need both to arrive at what is true.

Consider this helpful illustration:

> If you have any doubt that cognitive, propositional communication is at the very heart of relationship, let me ask this to those of you who have dogs at home: Would you say you had a good relationship with them? Probably most of you dog-owning readers of this chapter would say that, yes, you do have a good relationship with your dog. Yet even so, I predict the quality, indeed the very nature of that relationship would change if you were to go home this evening and be greeted verbally by your dog. If your dog introduced speech into the relationship, it would change the nature of that relationship. That dog could both fully know you and be more fully known by you.
>
> Our God is not a mute God. Not only is he active in history [and also in our experience], but he has spoken. And so we must care about cognitive truth. God has revealed himself as a personal God, and part of that personhood is his communication to us of truth [through words].[15]

Is all knowledge inherently good? The Bible would not agree with the modernists. Some knowledge, specifically the knowledge gained through disobedience ("the knowledge of good and evil") is inherently bad. Other kinds of knowledge, such as uncovering the secret of human cloning, may well turn out to be bad. Not only should we as Christians challenge the inherent goodness of knowledge, but we should also reject the idea that human reason is the sole means of gaining and judging knowledge. The Bible speaks of truth coming to human beings through prophecy, revelation, and such nonrational (or suprarational) means as dreams, visions, and angelic visitations. Emotions and intuition, therefore, should be added to human reason as legitimate biblical ways to discover truths.

An Acceptance of Autonomy and Rejection of Authority

The famous mathematician and atheist philosopher Bertrand Russell spoke for many modernists and illustrated another feature of modernism:

In this world we can now begin a little to understand things, and a little to master them by the help of science, which has forced its way step by step against the Christian religion, against the churches, and against the opposition of all the old precepts. Science can help us to get over this craven fear in which mankind has lived for so many generations. Science can teach us, and I think our own hearts can teach us, no longer to look around for imaginary supports, no longer to invent allies in the sky, but rather to look to our own efforts here below to make this world a fit place to live in, instead of the sort of place that the churches in all these centuries have made it. . . . We can conquer the world by intelligence and not merely by being slavishly subdued by the terror that comes from it. The whole conception of God is a conception derived from the ancient Oriental despotisms. It is a conception quite unworthy of free men.[16]

Have you heard John Lennon's song, "Imagine"? It reflects the same mind-set of autonomy. In it, Lennon imagined the utopia that would result from a world where there was "no countries . . . and no religion too."[17]

Russell and Lennon voiced the modernist dream: freedom from the authority of the church, freedom from the authority of Scripture, freedom from the authority of governments, and freedom from the authority of God.

The antiauthoritarianism of modernist philosophy, however, didn't stop with the church, the Bible, or even God. Modernist parents find that their authority has been severely undermined at home. For many of our contemporaries, the family is no longer a refuge from the stresses of life, but rather a battlefield for a war of the wills between parents and children. The authority of teachers has been so undermined that all too many schools are no longer places for learning and the impartation of knowledge. Drug-sniffing dogs patrol the halls, accompanied by uniformed police officers who carry clubs and handcuffs. Students in some school districts have to pass through metal detectors and are no longer allowed to carry backpacks, since these can be used to conceal weapons.

The breakdown of respect for government's authority has resulted in the need to allocate billions of dollars for the construction of new prisons. In some neighborhoods in America, more young men are incarcerated than attend college. The modernist dream of freedom from external authority has turned out to be a nightmare. It has resulted in millions of men and women being locked up in penitentiaries, and many million more being "imprisoned" behind triple-locked apartment doors and in gated communities with twenty-four-hour security checkpoints.

A Belief That Nature Is All That Exists

Modernism is thoroughly naturalistic in its belief that the world is a closed system without any intrusion from the supernatural, whether divine or angelic or demonic. Naturalists attempt to explain everything by means of natural causes. Therefore, the modernist would view as absurd the claim that someone has been healed as a result of praying to God. Perhaps prayer had a calming effect on the endocrine system of the sick person, which then released beneficial hormones in the person's body, causing the person to be healed. But the notion that something from outside the closed system (namely, God) intruded into our world in response to prayer and healed a sick person is viewed as absurd. The universe is closed, and all that exists is nature.

Carl Sagan, the well-known popularizer of astronomy, put it plainly when he said, "The Cosmos is all that is or ever was or ever will be."[18] Therefore, the universe itself cannot be attributed to an eternal Creator God, since it is simply the result of the cosmos itself. To the consistent naturalist, the universe has no beginning point; it has always existed. There are no such things as "answers to prayer" or miracles. There is no ultimate purpose in life beyond doing the best you can while you are here. And there is nothing beyond the grave. The modernist is left with no reason for living and no hope when dying. All the modernist has is the supposedly unalterable "laws of nature."

C. S. Lewis once critiqued naturalism in a beautiful little essay titled "Religion and Science." He lets us listen in to a dialogue between himself and a naturalist:

> *Naturalist*: "I think the laws of nature are really like two and two making four. The idea of their being altered is as absurd as the idea of altering the laws of arithmetic."
>
> *Lewis*: "Half a moment," said I. "Suppose you put six pence into a drawer today, and six pence into the same drawer tomorrow. Do the laws of arithmetic make it certain you will find a shilling's worth there the day after?"
>
> *Naturalist*: "Of course," said he, "provided no one's been tampering with your drawer."
>
> *Lewis*: "Ah, but that's the whole point," said I. "The laws of arithmetic can tell you what you will find, with absolute certainty, *provided that* there is no interference. If a thief has been at the drawer, of course, you will get a different result. But the thief won't have broken the laws of arithmetic— only the laws of England. Now aren't the laws of nature much in the same boat? Don't they all tell you what will happen *provided* there is no interference?"[19]

Lewis argued that the laws of science can merely predict what will happen provided there is no interference from an outside source, such as God. But God does not break the laws of science any more than a thief who steals something out of your drawer breaks the laws of mathematics.

A Quest for Unity, with a Tendency Toward Uniformity

The modernist quest for unity can be seen in institutions such as the United Nations, the International Monetary Fund, and the World Bank. It can be seen in the image of the United States as a "melting pot" in which historic ethnic differences are melted away and a person comes out of the pot as something entirely new, *an American*. It can be seen in the slogan on most American coins, *E Pluribus Unum*, which means "out of many, one."

The modernist quest for unity also can be seen in its architecture, in particular, at the International School of Architecture, founded by Walter Gropius in the 1920s. The school promoted the rectangular, unadorned glass and steel buildings that occupy the center of our major cities. International School architects believed that this uniform design would be liberating. In practice, it proved to be profoundly oppressive. The relentless boxes of modernist design were favored by Stalinist city planners and by the planners of Nazi concentration camps. Unity, in the modernist sense, led to relentless uniformity and a depressing tedium, which exterminated not only beauty, but also human beings.

Thomas Oden summarized the results of modernity's triumph as "a moral spinout." Oden's words are a bracing correction to anyone who wishes for a return to modernism:

> The bull's-eye definition of terminally fragmenting modernity . . . is as a disabling social malaise, a crash of the moral immune system, a collapse of virtue, *a moral spinout.* . . .
>
> The party is over for the hedonic sexual revolution of the period from the sexy '60s to the gay '90s. The party crasher is sexually transmitted diseases, with AIDS leading the way. We now have to learn to live with the consequences of the sexual, interpersonal, and familial wreckage to which this narcissistic money-grubbing, lust-enslaved, porn-infested, abortive self-indulgence has led us. Its interpersonal fruits are friendlessness, disaffection, divorce, and the despairing substitution of sexual experimentation for intimacy. Not a pretty picture![20]

In the next chapter we'll find out how postmodernism has come to not only critique but also to largely replace modernism.

Questions for Reflection and Discussion

?

1. Have you talked with someone recently who had utterly self-contradictory beliefs? If so, describe the conversation.

2. In your experience, whom have you found to be more optimistic about the future, the elderly or young adults? Why do you think this is?

3. Consider the way advertisements have changed in the past forty years. In the 1960s, actors in white lab coats spoke with "scientific authority" about a product. In the twenty-first century, products are advertised by associating them with fun or sexuality. What do you think accounts for this change?

4. Is it correct to say that if you cannot be *absolutely certain* about something, you should not believe it?

RECOMMENDED READING

Guinness, Os. *The Gravedigger File: Papers on the Subversion of the Modern Church.* Downers Grove, Ill.: InterVarsity Press, 1983.

Himmelfarb, Gertrude. *On Looking Into the Abyss: Untimely Thoughts on Culture and Society.* New York: Vintage, 1994.

Sire, James W. *The Universe Next Door.* Downers Grove, Ill.: InterVarsity Press, 1988.

Wells, David F. *No Place for Truth: Whatever Happened to Evangelical Theology?* Grand Rapids: Eerdmans, 1993.

3

Understanding the Postmodernist

"We create ourselves as a work of art," French philosopher Michael Foucault observed about the self. Many young adults seem to agree. "I really enjoy photography, so I worked for a newspaper for a couple of years. Then I designed Web sites for a company, but I couldn't hack the rat race. Now I'm working in landscaping, which I really like. I'm thinking about going back to school and getting my teaching certificate and teaching for a few years. What would really excite me, though, would be to pastor for a while and then maybe ..."

THE LOSS OF THE SELF IN POSTMODERNISM

As a pastor I've had literally dozens of conversations with young adults who sounded just like this. Roles no longer define who people are; rather they are to be tried on like clothing for a while and then taken off, based on opportunity, mood, or taste.

The same thing is true for many young adults in the area of sexuality. Studies indicate a great amount of fluidity in sexual behavior and significant changes in people's self-labeled sexual identities. This fluidity is also, of course, found in the popular phenomenon of "church hopping and shopping." "I was raised in a mainline church, but I got saved when a friend took me to his Baptist church. But I didn't like that real well, so I attended a large independent charismatic church for a while, but I missed a sense of rootedness. So I'm going to an Episcopalian church. I don't know how long I'll stay there ..."

What's going on? What's happening with so many young adults? It's part of a major shift in thinking called postmodernism. In the postmodern world, not only has the notion of nation and family disintegrated, but our understanding of the individual self has been evacuated of any core meaning. For this reason, postmoderns long for community through which to discover a group reference point for self-definition.

As we saw in the last chapter, modernity in many of its features was no friend to Christianity. Postmodernity may prove to be a not much better friend. But it has served the Christian cause in at least one respect: Postmodernity has, in God's providence, been used to kill arrogant, self-confident modernity.[1]

But what exactly are the differences between modernism and postmodernism? Cultural analyst Os Guinness describes the differences this way:

> Where modernism was a manifesto of human self-confidence and self-congratulation, postmodernism is a confession of modesty, if not despair. There is no truth; only truths. There is no grand reason; only reasons. There is no privileged civilization (or culture, belief, norm, and style); only a multiplicity of cultures, beliefs, norms, and styles. There is no universal justice; only interest and the competition of interest groups. There is no grand narrative of human progress; only countless stories of where people in their cultures are now. There is no simple reality or any grand objectivity of universal, detached knowledge; only a ceaseless representation of everything in terms of everything else.[2]

From Guinness, we can derive the following features of postmodernism:

- a mood of pessimism
- a celebration of diversity and fragmentation
- no absolute truth, just multiple perspectives
- tolerance as a supreme virtue

A Mood of Pessimism

There she was, running along the street, separated from her mother. She was a beautiful little Jewish girl, dressed in a red coat. She was fleeing from the Nazis who had invaded her village. In one of the most poignant scenes from Stephen Spielberg's *Schindler's List*, Spielberg focuses our attention on one child.

We have no capacity to comprehend, much less to empathize with, one million dead, two million dead. Who apart from God can respond to such a staggering amount of cruelty? But one child, one little girl filmed in color against a background of black and white—we can care about the fate of one child. Later in the film my heart broke as I saw the pile of Jewish bodies being readied for the crematorium. And there, on the top of the pile, the little girl dressed in her red coat.

The Holocaust is the major indictment of modernity's confidence in the power of human reason and the celebration of human progress. The perpetrator of the Holocaust was, after all, Germany, a society that reached its zenith at the beginning of the twentieth century. Germans held the bulk of Nobel prizes in science before World War II. German philosophers and theologians set the pace for these disciplines for almost two centuries. Likewise, German composers dominated the orchestral productions of the world's major symphonies. That a civilization as great as Germany could devote its industry, technology, medical resources, philosophy, and even theology toward the destruction of an entire race of people gave lie to the modern myth of humanity's inevitable progress.

In postmodern thought, there is a prevailing mood of cynicism, if not despair. Survey after survey has indicated that young adults are far more pessimistic about their own futures and the future of the planet than were their parents or grandparents at a similar age. Because today's world includes teen-on-teen violence, drug abuse, AIDS, and the destruction of our ecosystem, young adults do not share the modernist's conviction that human ingenuity will solve all of our problems. Indeed, human ingenuity is often seen as the cause of our problems.

Many young adults feel they are not inheriting a great civilization, but rather the hedonistic excesses of their parents. One young adult, in reflecting on the difference between his generation and the generation of the baby boomers said, "They partied on the beach and believed in sex, drugs, and rock and roll. When we go to the same beach, we cut our feet on broken bottles and used hypodermic needles, and swim in oceans polluted by human excrement."

We human beings have been humbled by the events of the twentieth century. We came into the twentieth century with big hopes, big plans, and big dreams. This was supposed to be the "Christian Century" (witness the mainline Protestant magazine by that name). But we have experienced two world wars, a Cold War, and now, localized ethnic wars. We ended the century very different from the way we entered it. We are now discouraged, cynical, and despairing of human potentiality.

A Celebration of Diversity and Fragmentation

Over against modernism's quest for unity and universal truth, postmodernism celebrates diversity. "All is different" could be the banner of a postmodernist newspaper. A person is no longer an American, he or she is a hyphenated American—German-Americans, Asian-Americans, African-Americans, Latino-Americans, and Native-Americans. Neither is a person's sexual orientation taken for granted. A person may be straight, gay, lesbian, bisexual, or transgendered.

The world is being retribalized. As a case in point, just try to follow the conflict in the Balkans, which involves ethnic Albanians, Orthodox Serbs, Muslim Bosnians, Catholic Croats, Communists, Fascists, and Democrats. One of the difficulties in generating Western sympathy for the enormous human tragedy in the former Yugoslavia was simply that the world could not keep track of the combatants without a scorecard. Retribalization has also affected Canada, as manifested in its French Separatist movement, Spain with its Basque Separatists, and such diverse places as Iraq, Armenia, and Sri Lanka.

Postmoderns don't live in a universe; they live in a multiverse! The postmodern preference for diversity can be found in its art and architecture. Modern art sought unity by reducing everything to pure colors and repeated shapes. Postmodern art, according to post-modern philosopher Jacques Derrida, does not seek for purity or unity, but rather is characterized by the collage, a juxtaposition of various elements and images.[3] One finds the use of collage in MTV videos, in advertisements, even in publications with different type-faces spread across the page, with no apparent meaning or purpose.

Modernist architecture with geometrically perfect glass and steel boxes has given way to postmodern buildings that are more playful and less uniform. Buildings are now designed with unusual ornamentation and features that have no utilitarian purpose. For example, one building at a state university near my home has a stair-case that ends abruptly in a wall. The skeleton of the building is on the outside rather than on the inside, and there are no 90-degree angles in any of its interior walls. You might call it a testament to diversity.

Wexner Center for the Arts, The Ohio State University. Used with permission.

No Absolute Truth, Just Multiple Perspectives

The old view of truth believed in an absolute truth toward which we were aiming, however fallible our attempts and relative our perspectives. The presupposition of the postmodernist is that there is no absolute truth to aim at, nor even any partial contingent truths. Since it is impossible to obtain such truths, it is absolutely silly to even try. According to postmodernism, there is no bull's-eye, because there is no target. "Shots going up, down, north, south, east, and west are . . . equally accurate. . . . Everyone's opinion is as good as anyone else's. The main criterion . . . becomes how you, as an individual, feel about it."[4]

To the postmodernist, there is no grand overarching story of humanity (what they like to refer to as "metanarrative"). The only narrative is the story of one's own community. A consistent postmodernist will never evaluate the truthfulness of a person's argument. Rather, he or she will instead be interested in who is making the statements—from which community they come. For example, is the statement being made by a Christian-Right Republican, an animal rights activist, or a feminist?

Christians would say that many of the stories of different communities contain some of the truth. But as Christians, we would strongly disagree with the notion that there is no single metanarrative, no single story that encompasses all people at all times. We believe in the existence of one Grand Story: the story of God's activity in human history. We believe in the metanarrative that begins with God's creation, and in the unity (as opposed to diversity) of the human race that derives from one original set of parents. Our original parents rejected God's purpose for themselves and the rest of humankind, and as a result they fell, losing paradise with all its benefits. But God purposed to save humanity and to redeem his original creation through the life, death, and resurrection of the incarnate Son of God.

Christians recognize that our apprehension of this Grand Story (metanarrative) is only partial. We should not worship our particular interpretation or theology about this Grand Story. But we do believe in the existence of the metanarrative that embraces all people at all times.

Because postmodernists maintain that there is no absolute truth, but just multiple perspectives, news coverage demands multiple perspectives, so that one community or person doesn't assert its version of the truth over another community or person. Not even the pope may offer the final word anymore on Roman Catholic tradition or faith. The media cover papal pronouncements as though the pope were simply expressing his personal views on a particular issue. Reporters will typically turn to other viewpoints—the viewpoints of other Roman Catholic laypersons or certain theologians—to determine how they feel about the issues of contraception or the ordination of women or abortion. Since there is no absolute truth, all perspectives are equally valid in determining what good Catholics should believe.

Consider the media's coverage of the O. J. Simpson trial. To newscasters, the issue never boiled down to whether O. J. Simpson was innocent or guilty of his wife's murder. Rather, much of the coverage dealt with the difference of perspectives between African-Americans and Caucasian-Americans regarding Simpson's guilt or innocence. Is even the crime of murder now just a matter of the perspective of one's particular community?

In a world of multiple perspectives, with no absolute truth or standard to which everyone can appeal and no outside authoritative source of information, poll taking reigns supreme. Virtually every story that covers a controversial issue will discuss the issue in terms of the latest poll. Appeal is not made to the Scriptures or to Western tradition or to a particular philosopher. Rather, the final court of appeals in a world without absolutes is what the ever-shifting majority agrees to at a particular moment in history.

Tolerance As a Supreme Virtue

One of the most prominent features of postmodernism is the exaltation of tolerance and open-mindedness to a place of supremacy in our hierarchy of virtues. Many postmoderns believe that what has gotten us into trouble in the past is the claim by some of possessing the truth. For the postmodern, tolerance requires that every community give up their claim of possessing the truth. The virtue of tolerance, therefore, is undergirded by a commitment to the absolute relativism of all truth claims.

Years ago, Allan Bloom, a University of Chicago professor, wrote a best-selling book titled *The Closing of the American Mind,* in which he stated the following in his introduction:

THE LOSS OF ABSOLUTE TRUTH IN LITERATURE

One aspect of postmodernism that has been much debated is deconstructionism. This critical method of interpreting the written word declares that the identity and intention of the author of a particular text is irrelevant to the interpretation of that text. Because no text has a fixed or absolute meaning, all interpretations are equally valid—or equally meaningless. One of the founders of the deconstructionist school, Stanley Fish, once said that the demise of objective truth "relieves me of the obligation to be right ... and demands only that I be interesting."[5]

Since there is no "right" interpretation, the opportunities to be "interesting" are unlimited. Historian Gertrude Himmelfarb describes it this way: "Since novels and poems are simply 'texts' (or 'pretexts') that are entirely indeterminate and therefore totally malleable, they can be 'textualized,' 'contextualized,' 'recontextualized,' and 'intertextualized' at will. The result is a kind of free-floating verbal association, in which any word or idea can suggest any other (including, or especially, its opposite), and any text can be related in any fashion to any other."[6]

Technology has exacerbated this problem. We live in a world of hypertext links in which words in a text can, with a click of a mouse, be decontextualized and reconnected to other texts that were wholly unimagined by the author of the original text. Former president Bill Clinton, who has often been called our "first postmodern president," demonstrated the loss of fixed meanings in any text during the Monica Lewinsky scandal with his famous words, "It depends on what the meaning of the word 'is' is."[7]

In literary criticism, consider, for example, J. Hillis Miller's analysis of one of William Wordsworth's poems, "A Slumber Did My Spirit Seal." The poem is only eight short lines and reads as follows:

A slumber did my spirit seal;
I had no human fears:
She seemed a thing that could not feel
The touch of earthly years.

No motion has she now, no force;
She neither hears nor sees;
Rolled round in earth's diurnal course,
With rocks, and stones, and trees.

The poem has traditionally been read as a memorial to a girl who died at a tragically young age. Traditional interpretations have centered on the contrast between life and death, present and past, youth and age. Miller, a deconstructionist, found in this brief poem a series of other contrasts, including "male as against female," and "mother as against daughter or sister, or perhaps any female family member as against some woman from outside the family—that is, mother, sister, or daughter against mistress or wife, in short, incestuous desires against legitimate sexual feelings."[8] He goes on to explore what he finds as "an obscure sexual drama," with the child in this poem representing "the virgin child" and the missing mother a "virgin thing," who is "sexually penetrated while still remaining a virgin." His interpretation moves further and further away from anything Wordsworth could have imagined or intended. But that doesn't seem to be a problem, since deconstructionists look into the mirror of a particular text and see not the author or the author's intention, but only their own faces.

There is one thing a professor can be absolutely certain of: Almost every student entering the university believes, or says he believes, that truth is relative.... The danger [my students] have been taught to fear from absolutism is not error, but intolerance. Relativism is necessary to openness; and this is the virtue, the only virtue, which all primary education for more than fifty years has dedicated itself to inculcating. Openness—and the relativism that makes it the only plausible stance in the face of various claims to truth and various ways of life and kinds of people—is the great insight of our times. The true believer is the real danger.[9]

In other words, if people would just give up the idea that they or anyone else possess absolute truth and, if instead, they would be tolerant of a diversity of ideas and opinions, the world would be a far better place.

How should biblical Christians respond to the absolutizing of tolerance as a virtue?

First, we must ask what is meant by the demand to be tolerant. Tolerance can often simply be a euphemism for not believing in anything strongly enough to object to a contrary idea. A Jewish talk show host, Dennis Prager, once said:

Liberals are always talking about pluralism, but that is not what they mean. In public schools, Jews don't meet Christians, Christians don't meet Hindus. Everybody meets nothing. That is, as I explain to Jews all the time, why their children so easily intermarry. Jews don't marry Christians. Non-Jewish Jews marry non-Christian Christians. Jews for nothing marry Christians for nothing. They get along great because they both affirm nothing. They have everything in common, nothing.[10]

G. K. Chesterton, the Christian writer, once said much the same thing when he remarked that tolerance is the virtue of those who don't believe in anything. There is, after all, a difference between tolerance, which may mean patience and grace toward those with whom I strongly disagree, and utter indifference.

Second, we must recognize that no moral person tolerates everything. Even those who absolutize relativism and preach tolerance as a supreme virtue find themselves marching against apartheid or Nazism or vocalizing strong opposition in classroom debate to homophobia, racism, or chauvinism.

Third, it is commonplace to experience the preachers of tolerance as among the most intolerant when it comes to opinions they find objectionable. Dr. Laura Schlessinger, who hosts one of the most listened-to radio call-in shows in America, has commented on the hate mail she receives for being so intolerant as to believe there is something like moral absolutes in the world: "The irony is that those people are mad because I made a judgment about somebody's behavior, and while they may admit that there is more than one possible opinion about the morality of any particular action in life, mine is obviously not one of them."[11]

Tolerance is often a cover to silence legitimate debate. When I attended law school, I sat under a lesbian feminist professor who viewed any disagreement with her perspective to be the mark of Neanderthal, bigoted, ignorant, straitlaced, prudish, puritanical, and intolerant thinking. A few years ago the school board in our city proposed an antiharassment policy in which they said (among other things) that hate speech against people with different sexual orientations would not be tolerated in the public schools by students, faculty, or administrative staff. If hate speech was engaged in with regard to sexual orientation, the speaker would be subject to discipline and potentially to expulsion from school.

After one public meeting I spoke with a school board member about the meaning of "hate speech." I asked her, "Would the policy that the school board is passing cover nonderogatory, nonpejorative speech in which a student raised the question about the morality of homosexual behavior during classroom discussion or debate? In other words, if a student during a high school classroom debate took a position that homosexual sex was immoral, would that be considered hate speech under the new policy?"

Without hesitating, she responded, "Absolutely, it would be! That kind of speech has no place in public schools, in my opinion. There

POSTMODERN SCIENCE

A few years ago, a physics professor at New York University named Alan Sokal and a physics professor in Belgium named Jean Bricmont jointly wrote a book called *Fashionable Nonsense,* in which they took excerpts from scholarly journals where postmodernists critique scientists by employing the multiple-perspectives, deconstructionist methods. Here is an example from their book:

> Is E = mc a male chauvinist equation? Perhaps it is. Let us make the hypothesis that it is, in so far as it privileges the speed of light over all other factors that are vitally necessary to us. What seems to me to indicate the possibility of the male chauvinist nature of the equation is not directly its use in creating nuclear weapons, rather it is the male perspective of privileging what goes fastest.[12]

In other words, because men like to drive fast, they have come up with this equation $E = mc^2$. The authors of Fashionable Nonsense respond: "Whatever one might think of 'other factors that are vitally necessary to us,' the fact remains that the relationship of $E = mc^2$ between energy and mass is experimentally verified to a high degree of precision, and it would not be valid if the speed of light were replaced by something else."

Alan Sokal was so incensed by the attack on science by what he called "nonsense science" that he submitted an article called "Transgressing the Boundaries: Toward a Transformative Hermeneutics of Quantum Gravity" to a scholarly journal dominated by postmodernist scientists. In the article, Sokal endeavored to write pure nonsense. Page after page was filled with buzzwords, absurdities, and non sequiturs, as well as appeals to authority rather than to logic and reason. In fact, Sokal said he tried deliberately to write not one intelligible, true thought. He appealed to emotion, prejudice, and class distinctions.

As Sokal predicted, the article was not only accepted for publication, but also praised by the journal's editorial board. Having lost the vision of truth, these postmodern academics could not even distinguish between sense and nonsense, between inane babbling and the capacity to actually say something. Consistent with postmodern sensibilities, some weren't even bothered by Professor Sokal's little ruse. When truth disappears, apparently so does the capacity to be offended.

is no room for that kind of thing. We ought not to allow students to call into question the morality of someone's sexual orientation or sexual practices."

The virtue of tolerance was used by our local school board to trump even students' or faculty's First Amendment rights of free speech in a public school setting. Apparently, however, as long as one marches in step with a perspective considered progressive at this moment in history, it is perfectly OK to be intolerant to those who are out of step.

Chuck Colson argued in an article titled "The Ugly Side of Tolerance" that he was once confronted by a reporter who rejected his "exclusivist" language in favor of an "all roads lead to heaven" message. Colson asked the reporter if he approved of Mother Teresa. Of course the reporter did. Colson asked, "Do you know why she helps the dying?" The reported responded, "Because she is a great humanitarian?" Colson answered, "No, it's because she loves Jesus—the One who says he is the only road to heaven. And that's why I do the work you like in the prisons. I wouldn't do it for a moral teacher."[13]

Colson's point was that many people love the benefit of the social good that Christians do, but they reject the spiritual (exclusivistic?) convictions that motivate the activity.

The truth is, to be motivated enough to actually expend oneself requires deep personal conviction about the worthwhileness of one's activity. It is not a lack of conviction or the belief that any conviction is equally valid that leads to good deeds. Rather, good deeds are the product of a passionate intolerance toward what one perceives as evil, married to an equally passionate commitment to work for what one perceives to be good and true.

WHAT IS GOOD ABOUT POSTMODERNISM?

Having critiqued certain features of postmodernism, I'd hasten to add that there is actually a great deal that biblical Christians and their postmodernist friends can agree on. It is a good thing to be despairing of human potential and cynical about human progress. The Bible doesn't hold out much hope for humanity apart from God. When speaking with a postmodernist, agree with the cynicism and despair, but add this kind of statement: "I've found a basis for being hopeful. It has nothing to do with confidence in humanity's ability to solve the world's problems. May I share with you the basis of my hope?"

Postmodernists have also done a tremendous service to the cause of Christ by opening up the modernist's closed universe. The Bible is a story about an open universe in which the supernatural (God, spirits, both good and bad, curses and blessings) is real and regularly intervenes to shape the material world of our existence. No one could be a biblical Christian and hold on to the closed, naturalistic world of modernism.

Postmodernists have further done immense service to the cause of Christ by restoring community to a central place and demoting the individual from its role as the ultimate criterion for making value judgments. The postmodernists have also challenged modernism's exclusive reliance on human reason as the only instrument for arriving at the truth. Biblical Christians believe in suprarational (*not* irrational) means of arriving at the truth. Suprarational means may include such things as spiritual gifts (prophecy, the message of wisdom, and the message of knowledge), dreams and visions, even intuition, or what one author calls "emotional intelligence."

Sharing Your Faith with a Postmodernist

We Need a Gospel Accompanied by the Power of the Holy Spirit

Postmodernists know that something is wrong with their lives. They know they are broken and have experienced brokenness in relationships (often through their parents' divorce, their own divorce, or through multiple failed dating relationships). They know the pain that comes through promiscuous sexuality. Postmodernists are looking for real change. They want to know that God is real, not just an idea. Postmodernists, more readily than modernists, will respond to the Holy Spirit's power to break addictions, to heal, and to offer a sense of spiritual reality.

Recently I was sipping a cappuccino in a Starbucks coffee shop (where I spend a lot of my free time). One of the servers was complaining that she hadn't slept in months because she suffers from horrible insomnia. I offered a few words of sympathy and retreated to my table to work and to drink my cappuccino. But I felt pressed by the Holy Spirit to go back to this woman and ask if I could pray for her to be healed of her insomnia.

I obeyed that leading and engaged her in a conversation that went something like this:

"You mentioned that you can't sleep and that you haven't slept for months. I'm a Christian pastor over at the Vineyard near here. Would you mind if I prayed for you that you might be able to get a good night's sleep?"

She said, "Vineyard? Man, all of your people come in here. I've watched you guys grow. You must be doing a great thing. But I haven't been in church for years."

I said, "I don't think that really matters now. Would it be OK if I prayed for you to be able to get to sleep?"

She said, "That'd be fine. It's very nice of you to offer to pray for me."

I said, "No, I mean right now. Would it be OK if I prayed for you right now, right here?"

She flushed a little bit and said, "Well, I guess so."

I said, "Well, you'll need to come out from behind the counter so I can pray for you."

Hesitating, she walked out from behind the counter and said, "You know I haven't been in church for years."

I said, "I know. You said that before. But it really doesn't matter to God. I'm still able to pray for you." I asked her right there in the center of Starbucks if it would be OK if I put my hand on her while we prayed.

She said, "That would be fine."

I prayed very simply that God, who loves her, would come and heal her body, calm her mind, and allow her to sleep. A week later I walked into Starbucks. Her entire countenance had changed. She ran out from behind the counter and said, "Rich, I've been looking for you. Let me give you a hug." She threw her arms around me and said, "I've been healed. I've never felt better in my life. The night after you prayed for me I had the best night's sleep I'd had in months. I feel like a totally new person. I can't tell you how good I feel. Thank you."

I said, "You know it wasn't me who healed you. It was God."

She said, "Yeah, I think I believe that. I think it was God."

I then asked her if she would come to church. She laughed and said, "You know I told you I hadn't been in church for years. But here's the deal. I promise you that in the next couple of weeks I'm going to come to church."

What that server from Starbucks needed is what many postmodernists need. They don't need a clever argument or a canned evangelistic approach. They need a touch from God and an experience that communicates that God is real and that he loves them enough to answer their prayers.

We Need Community, Not Just an Individualistic Gospel

I've mentioned throughout this chapter that postmodernists have suffered the loss of natural community. They have seen families (their own and others') break up. They may be living a thousand miles from their parents and may not have spoken with cousins or aunts and uncles for decades.

The television show "Friends" centers on a small group of young adults who share two apartments across the hall from each other. They hang together, laugh together, hurt together, cry together, and support one another in good times and in bad. The community they experience with one another gives meaning to their lives. The message of this show is captured in its theme song, "I'll Be There for You." The song promises that each of the friends will "be there" for each other, and it ends with the responding promise that the other person will "be there for me too."

Christian love has often been called the final apologetic. Christian writer Francis Schaeffer called Christian love "the mark of the Christian." Community not only tells the world that we are different, it also tells the world that we Christians have what they are looking for—not just words or a meeting or a set of beliefs. (We do offer words, meetings, and a set of beliefs, but that's not all we offer.) We offer community with the triune God and with people who will "be there for you!"

We Need to Proclaim a God Who Understands and Feels Our Pain

Pain is a big deal to postmodernists. The big stumbling block that keeps many postmodernists from coming to faith is the problem of pain. It seems that every other person I meet has been abused either sexually or physically, or through neglect has been left to fend for himself or herself. Postmodernists want to meet a God who feels and understands their pain.

We Christians worship such a God. Our Jesus is not like Buddha, who sits serenely with closed eyes meditating while people starve. He is not like the Hindu god who suggested that if a girl is sexually abused by her father, it must have been the result of some bad karma she inherited from a former life.

The Christian message to the postmodernist is this: *Our God understands pain.* He had nails driven through his hands. Our God knows what it's like to lose a loved one. The Father lost his Son at the cross; the Son lost his Father at the cross. The Bible tells us that God suffers when his people suffer. We can say with great theological accuracy, "Let me tell you where Jesus Christ was when those kids were being shot at Columbine High School. Jesus was there in the library, in the hallways, suffering with his people."

We Need A Metanarrative, Not Just Four Spiritual Laws

Postmodernists reject metanarratives and any all-embracing story, but they can't live well without one. Sharing four spiritual laws may have worked for the modernist, who was acquainted with the story line of Christianity and just needed key gospel facts on which to make a decision for Jesus Christ. But postmodernists (who are usually ignorant of the biblical story line) need to hear the entire biblical message, beginning with creation and the loss of paradise and ending with God's plan of redemption and our return to the Garden.

This kind of extended discussion of a grand story, of course, will not happen in one brief gospel encounter. But the need to see how the fragmented pieces of life all fit together and to figure out where one fits into the overall scheme of things is a need postmodernists acutely feel. Our church offers all-day seminars that tell the story of the Bible from beginning to end. These are immensely popular, and they help postmodernists understand the all-embracing story that encompasses everyone everywhere.

We Need to Articulate a Fuller Doctrine of Sin

Historically, much of conservative Christianity has severely truncated the biblical doctrine of sin, focusing almost exclusively on individual acts of sin (primarily sexual). This has left many young adults utterly unmoved. The attitude often is "Yeah, I hear what you're saying about sex with my boyfriend being wrong. But frankly, I don't feel guilty in the way you think I should feel guilty."

What do you say after you show someone what the Bible teaches about a certain sin and she shrugs her shoulders and says, "That's interesting, but I'm not at all convinced or inclined to change?" Postmodernism actually offers an approach that can be used on postmodernists themselves. According to postmodernist philosopher Michael Foucault, we must engage in a process that he calls "the Archaeology of Knowledge." We must dig up and expose the rules that govern any particular assertion of truth. In other words, we must get below the surface and uncover the foundations for a particular claim. Once we do that, according to Foucault, we will find that at the core, every truth claim is simply an assertion of power.

In the case of a promiscuous friend who asserts her right to have sex outside of marriage without guilt, we Christians can announce a full doctrine of sin. We can observe that the problem is not a disagreement about this or that activity. Rather, as we engage in our "Archaeology of Knowledge" regarding this sexual practice, we find that her justifications are rooted in her rebellion against God. She is simply claiming to have power above that of God.[14]

Campus Crusade for Christ staff workers Jon Hinkson and Greg Ganssle put it this way:

> While the modernist imagines herself a perfectly fit arbiter and neutral judge of any gospel claim put forward, it is a truism for postmodernism that we know or judge nothing neutrally. A postmodern thinker will not be surprised at the biblical teaching that her determination to preserve her rebellious autonomy skews her spiritual judgment and incites her to deploy her rationality evasively in the face of God's sovereign claim. I have often said to students, 'Let me tell you why, if the biblical story is true, you will hear it threateningly, and why you ought to apply a hermeneutic of suspicion to that very reaction.' In this way a key biblical truth is related to their familiar grid and this point of contact helps the gospel be heard more fruitfully.[15]

Postmodernism moves the discussion beyond the modernist tendency to reduce everything to words and ideas, as opposed to the congruence of one's life and ideas. We should, therefore, seize the opportunity to focus attention on the totality of life when communicating the Christian doctrine of sin. For example, it may not be relevant to the modernist that the preeminent philosopher of postmodernism, Michael Foucault, was a promiscuous homosexual who died of AIDS or that the progenitor of the current assault on truth, Friedrich Nietzsche, died in an insane asylum after a bout with venereal disease. Their ideas could be analyzed neutrally apart from their lives. But to the postmodernist, our philosophies are rooted in our personal interests and lifestyles.[16] The way we actually live becomes profoundly relevant to our claims of truth. This is a very Christian notion.

We Need Positive Apologetics

Positive apologetics point out the uncomfortable fit that unbelievers experience in their belief structure when they deny Jesus Christ. Francis Schaeffer, in his classic book *The God Who Is There*, described an encounter he once had at Cambridge University with a young practicing Sikh.

The Sikh strongly objected to Christianity. Schaeffer asked him if, according to Sikhism, cruelty and noncruelty were ultimately equal. The Sikh agreed. A student in the room seized the opportunity presented by this philosophy by picking up a boiling kettle of water and held it over the Sikh's head. The man looked up and yelled, "What are you doing?" The student answered, "I'm demonstrating that there really might be a difference between cruelty and noncruelty."[17]

It is not difficult to push postmodernists to the logical (or illogical) consequences of their beliefs. In another recent encounter in a coffee shop, I was listening to one of the servers loudly proclaiming her belief to another server that there was no such thing as absolute truth.

While I shifted uncomfortably in my seat, my wife said to me, "Why don't you just get up and talk with her already? You are driving me crazy."

I got up and went over to the server, and I said, "I heard you sharing the very interesting idea that there is no such thing as absolute truth."

She said, "That's right."

I said, "So you believe that all truth is relative, is that right?"

She said, "Yeah, it's all just a matter of opinion." (She was not a great philosopher!)

I said, "Let me understand what your position is. Are you saying that there is nothing that is absolutely wrong?"

She said, "That's right. Right and wrong just depend on the community we find ourselves in."

So I responded, "Well, let me ask you a couple of questions. Do you think that it was OK for the Nazis to herd Jewish families into gas chambers during the Holocaust?"

She said, "Well, of course, I don't think that was OK."

"But they were just following the story of their community. What about the way that the Afrikaners treated blacks for so many years in South Africa? Do you think apartheid is OK?"

In a very short time, the server admitted that there were in her mind some things that were absolutely right and some things that were absolutely wrong. She further admitted that there might be a standard that applies to everyone everywhere at all times. From there it wasn't very difficult to talk with her about the One who created the standard.

Rather than defend Christianity from postmodern assaults through "negative apologetics" (that is, rather than defend Christianity through rebuff attacks), why not assist postmodernists to experience tension points within their own belief systems? To do so can lead to very fruitful discussions in which an alternative explanation of reality is offered—the Christian gospel!

We Need to Take Courage

Most of my conversations do not resolve themselves as quickly or turn out as positively as my conversation with that young woman in the coffee shop. Salvation is by God's Spirit. If it is true that a postmodern unbeliever is "dead in [his or her] transgressions and sins"[18] (and it is true), then unaided by God's Spirit we cannot give that person life. It is important to read, to pray, to attend conferences, and to seek to know the mind-set of postmoderns as clearly as you can, so that you might speak the language of postmoderns.

But I'm concerned that some who are not philosophically minded could become overly intimidated by the task at hand. I'm also concerned when postmodern philosophers, such as Foucault and Derrida, are mentioned more often at Christian conferences than are the names of Paul or Isaiah. When all is said and done, it is still God who brings the dead to life—and not how much or how little we know about postmodernism.

I often say to the young adults I am mentoring, "Read as much as you can. Love as best you can. But rely totally on God for the results." Don't be discouraged!

We Need a God Who Is Presented in an Attractive Way to the Postmodernist

We must explain to postmodernists that our God is not Caucasian, male, or a conservative Republican or a member of a fringe third party! The God of Christianity does not hate gays or minorities. Our God is not a bigot, nor is he intolerant of diversity. Rather, our God is profoundly on the side of the postmodernist who is looking for a basis for morality. God offers us moral values that give meaning and dignity to human existence.

To the postmodernist who is longing for spirituality, our God is able to satisfy the deepest human longings. To the postmodernist who is searching for love (often in many of the wrong places), our God offers an overwhelming experience of love through the Holy Spirit and an unimaginable demonstration of love through the death of Jesus Christ. To the postmodernist who is having trouble making sense of the world, our God offers a framework for interpreting life and holds all the fragmented pieces of truth together in his own person. To the postmodernist who experiences life as hopeless, pointless, and fruitless, our God offers an inspiring hope—hope for change, hope for improvement, and hope for healing.

Postmodernists need an attractive God, and we know such a God. His name is Jesus.

Questions for Reflection and Discussion

1.   How would you respond to the statement, "Believing in Christ is just your perspective. But it's not necessarily my story"?

2.   Christians are often accused of being "intolerant and judgmental" because they, for example, object to two consenting adults who sleep together without first obtaining a marriage license. How would you respond to the charge of intolerance that is raised when you, as a Christian, assert a particular moral position?

3.   How do you feel about the author's story of praying for the server at Starbucks to be healed? What would you do if you overheard a stranger talking about how terrible he or she was feeling?

4.   What is the difference between the gospel presented for a community of people and the gospel presented in an individualistic way?

5.   How can the gospel be presented (as the author suggests) as "a metanarrative" and not merely as "four spiritual laws"?

RECOMMENDED READING

Carson, D. A. *The Gagging of God: Christianity Confronts Pluralism.* Grand Rapids: Zondervan, 1996.

Carson, D. A., ed. *Telling the Truth: Evangelizing Postmoderns.* Grand Rapids: Zondervan, 2000.

Dockery, David, ed. *The Challenge of Postmodernism: An Evangelical Engagement.* Grand Rapids: Baker, 1995.

Erickson, Millard J. *Postmodernizing the Faith: Evangelical Responses to the Challenge of Postmodernism.* Grand Rapids: Baker, 1998.

Grenz, Stanley J. *A Primer on Postmodernism.* Grand Rapids: Eerdmans, 1996.

Newbigin, Lesslie. *The Gospel in a Pluralist Society.* Grand Rapids: Eerdmans, 1996.

Norris, Christopher. *What's Wrong with Postmodernism: Critical Theory and the Ends of Philosophy.* Baltimore, Md.: Johns Hopkins Univ. Press, 1990.

4

Today's Diversity

Before my wife and I moved to Columbus, Ohio, so I could enroll in law school, we attended a large evangelical church in another city. We very much enjoyed the church and loved the pastor's preaching. We became involved in an adult Sunday school class that on one particular week was studying the Parable of the Good Samaritan.

Halfway through the class session, the teacher said something like this to the almost fifty adults sitting in front of him: "Look here at the way this poor fellow was treated by the Jewish priest and the Jewish Levite. Have any of you had negative experiences with Jews?"

I couldn't believe it! This teacher had turned Jesus' story completely on its head. For the rest of the class, rather than discuss how we as followers of Christ fail to be good neighbors, everyone gave vent to their deep-seated feelings of anti-Semitism. One man bitterly reported that his Jewish neighbors never raked their yard and allowed their leaves to blow into his yard. Another man related a story about purchasing a car from a Jewish car dealer many years before—a car that turned out to be a lemon. The anti-Semitic comments continued, because apparently the Christian folks in that room believed it was safe for them to share their prejudices and unhealed anger. They must have thought, "Well, this is a church, and there couldn't possibly be any Jews here."

What they didn't realize was that there *was* a Jew present in the room—me, a 19-year-old, brand-new follower of Jesus, who was coming out of a conservative Jewish background. I was terribly shaken that day by what I heard. It made me doubt the reality of the faith of people who could speak so hatefully about Jews, especially when Jesus their Lord was himself a Jew and the Bible they studied was written by Jews.

Over the years, unfortunately, what I experienced at that church proved not to be unique. On another occasion I was about to get into my car with my wife when a man at our church walked up and for no reason said, "You know, you can always tell a Jew."

"Really? How's that?" I asked.

He answered, "Because Jews always wear squeaky shoes."

What a profoundly ignorant comment, I thought. I said to him, "Do you know that I'm a Jew?"

All the color drained from his face. He stammered and then stumbled away. He didn't know what to say. I walked after him and said, "You know, I'm not angry with you. But I believe the Lord allowed this exchange to take place in order to show you your heart."

One of postmodernism's major themes mentioned in the previous two chapters is a celebration of diversity. Many Christians seem threatened by diversity, whether it's about relating to people of a different religion or race, or to people who have differing perspectives on politics and life. Some Christians oppose diversity simply because of its continued connection with "politically correct" thinking. So it may come as a surprise to some that within certain clearly defined limits, God is the greatest supporter of diversity in the universe. Indeed, God created diversity, and we can honestly say that God loves diversity!

DIVERSITY IS A FACT OF LIFE

The other day I stood at the counter and ordered a grande decaf nonfat cappuccino at a local Starbucks coffee shop. (Starbucks itself is a paradigm of diversity, allowing every single coffee drinker in the world to be differentiated from every other coffee drinker.) I noticed that the server was wearing a pentagram around her neck. Feigning ignorance, I said to her, "Gee, that's a pretty star you have around your neck. What's that all about?"

She very warmly replied, "Oh, thanks for noticing. I wear this because of my religion." (She was a practicing pagan!)

Before I had an opportunity to engage her in conversation, another woman working there said, "Look, I wear my girlfriend's ring around my neck." Still another server said, "I have a [unpronounceable name] around my neck. She's the Egyptian goddess of fertility."

All three shared about their respective necklaces (and beliefs) without a hint of either embarrassment or hostility. Diversity has become a fact of life.

By diversity I mean the sheer number of differences of race, culture, language, heritage, and religion in Western nations as a whole and in America in particular. The golfer Tiger Woods calls himself a "Cablinasian," which he coined to reflect his Caucasian, Black, American Indian, and Asian heritage. Millions of Americans complain that the current system of racial classification in the census form forces them to deny their heritage by requiring them to choose either a single race or check the box called "Other." The number of mixed marriages in the United States has grown from 150,000 in the 1960s to more than 1 million in 1990. And the number of racially mixed children now exceeds 2 million. Several states, including California and New Mexico, have become majority minority states. Diversity is a fact of American life in the twenty-first century.[1]

In the 1950s, religious sociologist Peter Berger could accurately write that the American religious landscape consisted of "Protestant, Catholic, and Jew." In the year 2000, Muslims outnumbered Presbyterians in the United States. They are also likely to soon approach the size of other groups such as Methodists, Lutherans, and Jews. The United States is now home to an estimated 1,200 mosques, with at least one in every state. In the past seven years, the number of mosques has grown by 25 percent; on average, there are more than 1,625 Muslims associated in some way with the religious life of each mosque. The mosques themselves are ethnically diverse. A recent study revealed that 93 percent of all mosques are attended by more than one ethnic group.[2]

As America's ethnic diversity grows, more television programs are broadcast in Spanish and other non-English languages. Unlike the early days of television where Ricky Ricardo was the only Hispanic on television, TV is slowly changing to reflect our more diverse society. With the growth of cable, several mass-marketed stations are now available, such as the Black Entertainment Television Network (appealing to African-Americans), Univision (focusing on Hispanics), and Lifetime (exclusively for women). "In-language" cable offerings include The Filipino Channel, Native American Nations, TV Asia, and World African Network.[3]

Of course, the United States is not the only nation facing dramatic changes in its ethnic makeup. In 1951, the total population of Caribbean and South Asian people in Britain was 80,000, most of them living in a handful of cities and ports. Twenty years later, it had reached 1.5 million. The 1991 census put the ethnic minority population at over 3 million. Diversity is now a fact of life in cities like London, Leicester, and Birmingham. By 1998, white children had become a minority at secondary schools in inner-London, and in the suburbs they made up only 60 percent of the secondary school population. Over one-third of inner-London's children do not have English as their first language. The fact that England is becoming increasingly multicultural is also seen in the mix of its fast food cuisine. Traditional English fast food, fish and chips, now ranks below Indian and Chinese restaurants in the number of outlets present in England.[4]

Even such democratic societies as France and Germany have experienced great turmoil over the recent pace of ethnic immigration. In 1989, a furor arose in France over a few Moroccan girls who wore headscarves to school. Political leader Jean-Marie Le Pen capitalized on this through a right-wing attack on what he described as a French surrender to "the Islamic assault on French culture and identity."[5] Tensions between ethnic groups in multicultural societies, while new in certain countries, have long histories in places such as the Balkans, South Africa, and Indonesia. The 1990s witnessed violent attacks by racist skinheads on Turks in Germany, ethnic cleansing by Serbs of Albanians in Kosovo, and rioting against ethnic Chinese in Indonesia.

GOD LOVES DIVERSITY

To the overwhelming evidence of growing diversity in America and other Western nations, we must add the fact that God seems to love diversity. Any person who opens up his or her Bible or looks out at creation will quickly be forced to the conclusion that *God loves diversity*.

Diversity in Creation

God has shown us a marvelous diversity in his creation. When he said, "Let the water teem with living creatures,"[6] he wasn't exaggerating. He created more than 20,000 different species of fish alone. Anyone visiting an aquarium realizes that Disney has nothing on God when it comes to creative imagination. This includes a fish that is actually shaped like a shovel and is appropriately named a "shovel fish." An "oarfish" can grow to 50 feet long and has two tentacles hanging from its bottom that look like oars; "hatchet fish" look like hatchets; "manta rays" look like gigantic bats; "smalltooth sawfish" look like fish with saber saws attached to their noses; "trumpet fish" have a trumpetlike mouth (I think they look more like a clarinet than a trumpet); and "umbrella mouth gulper eels" (two-foot-long eels) consist mostly of a mouth that opens like an umbrella.[7] Suffice it to say you would not like to find one of these in your backyard hot tub.

Not only are there 20,000 different species of fish, but God also decided to cause the sea to teem with 2,500 species of coral alone. One of the most enjoyable days I've ever spent with my son was when we went exploring a large coral reef while snorkeling at an underwater national park off the Florida Keys. I had no idea there was literally a rainbow coalition of types of coral: blue coral, hot pink coral, yellow coral, black coral, coral that looked like a human brain (called "brain coral"), coral with long tentacles, and dozens of other varieties. And swimming through the coral were schools of brilliantly colored fish of every shape and size imaginable.

To appreciate God's love of diversity, consider his creation of insects. Well over a million different known species of insects inhabit the world. Some experts estimate that there may be as many as 10 million varieties still unclassified. One out of every four animals on the planet is a beetle. And not every insect is tiny. Stick insects extend more than a foot. (Imagine seeing something like that as you step into the shower!) Or consider that 10 percent of the entire mass of animals in the world are ants and that a further 10 percent are termites.[8]

But if insects are not your thing, perhaps you can appreciate God's love of diversity by considering the hundreds of amazingly different breeds of dogs. For example, the Chinese Shar-Pei puppy has wrinkled skin that looks as though he is wearing his daddy's coat. The Puli (forgive me if this offends Puli owners) looks like the end of a mop or, to choose a more flattering description, a dog with dreadlocks and a little black nose. And what shall we say about little powder-puff dogs like Pekingese or Pomeranians, except that God and people who breed dogs apparently love diversity.

Of course, God's love for diversity is not limited to the animal kingdom alone. One could easily speak of the marvelous diversity that exists in the various climates of the world, ranging from the polar ice caps to tropical rain forests. In the same way, the plant kingdom and the heavens themselves declare that God loves diversity.

And when we consider human beings we find further evidence of God's love of diversity. What married person has not at one time or another stood back in awe (and utter frustration) at the discovery that his or her spouse not only possessed a different gender, but also a different (and often wrong) way of thinking. Americans have become fascinated by the exploration of these gender differences, as witnessed by such best-sellers as *Men Are from Mars; Women Are from Venus* by John Gray and the series of books authored by sociolinguist Deborah Tannen, such as *You Just Don't Understand.*

Fascination with diversity in America goes beyond gender and includes temperament and spiritual gifting. Whereas Americans a century ago would have described another person by character qualities such as honesty, diligence, or thriftiness, it has become commonplace to hear someone classify an acquaintance by his or her Myers-Briggs letters ("She is such an ENFJ") or, in some Christian circles, by Gary Smalley's four animals ("The problem in our marriage is that I'm a lion-otter and my wife is a beaver-retriever").

God's Love for Diversity Is Found in the Great Commission

In that most famous of all charges Jesus gave to his disciples, we read the following words:

> Then Jesus came to them and said, "All authority in heaven and on earth has been given to me. Therefore go and make disciples of all nations, baptizing them in the name of the Father and of the Son and of the Holy Spirit, and teaching them to obey everything I have commanded you. And surely I am with you always, to the very end of the age."[9]

One of the most helpful developments in the area of Christian missions in the last twenty-five years is a deeper understanding of what Jesus was referring to when he used the phrase *all nations.* Jesus was clearly not referring to the modern nation-state, such as Italy, which didn't even exist until the mid-nineteenth century, or to the group of countries that make up the United Nations. The Greek phrase for "all nations" is *panta ta ethnē,* which missions specialists tell us almost always refers to people groups. People groups were defined by the Lausanne Strategy Working Group as

> a significantly large grouping of individuals who perceive themselves to have a common affinity for one another because of their shared language, religion, ethnicity, residence, occupation, class or caste, situation, etc., or combination of these.... [It is] the largest group within which the gospel can spread as a church planting movement without encountering barriers of understanding or acceptance.[10]

The basic thrust behind "people group" thinking is the recognition that within various modern nation-states, there may be dozens or even hundreds of separate people groups. Thus, the political country of India is actually a composite of at least three thousand "nations" or people groups—the *ethnē* of the Great Commission—that Jesus commanded us to disciple.

The U.S. Center for World Missions in Pasadena, California, estimates that there are about 24,000 distinct people groups in the world, 16,000 of which are currently being discipled. The other 8,000, mostly among Muslim, Han Chinese, Hindu, Buddhist, and tribal cultures, don't have access to the gospel of Jesus Christ within their own culture.[11]

Diversity Will Last Forever

I don't know what your picture of heaven is, but the biblical picture of heaven is not a crowd of Caucasian, suburban, baby boomer, and Gen-X Americans, wearing clothing purchased from an L. L. Bean catalog or The Gap, all speaking English and singing contemporary worship songs before God's throne. To put it even more plainly, God's ultimate plan for the ages is not to turn everyone into a homogenized version of evangelical Americans. Most evangelical Americans probably need to experience a paradigm shift regarding what heaven will look like, because it will certainly not look like the vast majority of our churches on Sunday morning. In contrast to America's traditional response to ethnic diversity—requiring either assimilation or exclusion—the book of Revelation pictures the scene in heaven as follows: "After this I looked and there before me was a great multitude that no one could count, *from every nation,* tribe, people and language, standing before the throne and in front of the Lamb."[12] In heaven, people are going to maintain their diversity!

God loves diversity so much that I believe people are going to look different in heaven. This passage from Revelation seems to indicate that we are going to speak different languages and dress differently. Apparently khakis and wide-legged jeans will not be mandated for all of heaven's residents. Somehow we will be able to understand each other, and therefore love each other, but the growing diversity we are now seeing in the United States will mark eternity. Part of the unchanging purpose of God is that representatives of every people group in the world will one day sing what is called a "new song" before the throne, saying: "You [Jesus the Lamb] are worthy to take the scroll and to open its seals, because you were slain, and with your blood you purchased men for God from every tribe and language and people *and nation.*"[13]

Ten chapters later we read about the song of the Lamb that is going to be sung in heaven by followers of Christ, which contains the words, "Who will not fear you, O Lord, and bring glory to your name? For you alone are holy. *All nations* will come and worship before you, for your righteous acts have been revealed."[14]

Why Does God Love Diversity?

Why is it God's desire to have representatives from every ethnicity, class, caste, and language group worshiping him before his throne? John Piper, in his powerful book titled *Let the Nations Be Glad: The Supremacy of God in Missions*, brilliantly points out that the fame and greatness and worth of an object of beauty increases in proportion to the diversity of those who recognize its beauty.[15]

To illustrate, if the only person in the world who thinks you have a good singing voice or that you have musical ability is your mother, it's probably a safe bet that your voice isn't very good and that you're not very musical. Likewise, if the only people who appreciate a certain group (like the Hansons) are all under the age of twelve, or who appreciate a certain conductor (like Lawrence Welk) are all over the age of seventy-five, you would have to admit that those particular musical forms are not very great. But if you could find a type of music that everyone appreciated, now that would be great music! If not only white Americans, but also the Buddhist Brao of Cambodia, the Muslim/Nomadic Fezara of the Sudan, the Shamanistic Ulchi of Russia, African-Americans, residents of Tokyo and Mexico City, and the Muslim Qashqa'i of Iran all said in unison, "We love this music," then there would be something really special about it. God's greatness is magnified in direct proportion to the diversity of people who recognize his greatness.

Piper also points out that the greatness of a person's gift of leadership is directly related to the range of people impacted or influenced by that person.[16] Thus, if the only person you are able to lead is your five-year-old (and even she doesn't follow you very well), one could legitimately conclude that you have a small gift of leadership. If you are just able to lead people who are exactly like you—who are exactly your age, who have your level of education or your economic status, then, again, one might conclude that you have a limited gift of leadership. But if your leadership is recognized by people from every ethnic, language, occupational, educational, age, and religious group, then we could conclude, "Here is a person whose gift of leadership is exceedingly great!" God's glory is expressed when there is a diversity of people who come under the leadership of Jesus Christ. When people from every people group ("all nations") willingly submit themselves to Jesus Christ's leadership, God receives more glory than he would have if the same number of people bowed under his leadership, but they were all from one single ethnic group.

GOD'S SPIRIT AND DIVERSITY

In 1906, God moved dramatically in a Los Angeles meeting place on a street called Azusa. Known as the "Azusa Street Revival," these meetings were held on and off for seven years, morning, noon, and night. They were led by an African-American pastor named William Seymour and gave birth to the worldwide Pentecostal, Charismatic, and Third Wave (Empowered Evangelical) movements, now totaling approximately 27 percent of all Christendom.[17]

But the relatively unknown story of the Azusa Street Revival was the importance Seymour placed on racial reconciliation. Seymour held that love, as the primary evidence of the Spirit's baptism, was more important than tongues. It must "make all races and nations into one common family."[18] In the very first issue of *The Apostolic Faith*, Seymour stated, "Multitudes have come. God makes no difference in nationality. Ethiopians, Chinese, Indians, Mexicans, and other nationalities worship together." Three months later, in December 1906, he wrote, "The people are all melted together ... made one lump, one bread, all one body in Christ Jesus. There is no Jew or Gentile, bond or free, in the Azusa Street Mission.... He is no respecter of persons or places." And in the third issue of *The Apostolic Faith*, Seymour wrote, "No instrument that God can use is rejected on account of color or dress or lack of education. This is why God has built up the work.... The sweetest thing is the loving harmony."[19]

My experience of the outpouring of the Holy Spirit would confirm Seymour's description of racial reconciliation. Wherever I have seen the Holy Spirit poured out, there I have found Jews reconciling with Germans, Native-Americans reconciling with European-Americans, whites reconciling with blacks, and women reconciling with men. God loves to break down dividing walls, and he does so by pouring out his Spirit. Diversity is not our enemy; our enemy is our *fear* of diversity!

WHAT ARE THE LIMITS ON GOD'S LOVE OF DIVERSITY?

Acts 10 contains a wonderful biblical illustration of the scriptural balance between God's love of diversity and the limits he places on it:

> At Caesarea there was a man named Cornelius, a centurion in what was known as the Italian Regiment. He and all his family were devout and God-fearing; he gave generously to those in need and prayed to God regularly. One day at about three in the afternoon he had a vision. He distinctly saw an angel of God, who came to him and said, "Cornelius!"
>
> Cornelius stared at him in fear. "What is it, Lord?" he asked.
>
> The angel answered, "Your prayers and gifts to the poor have come up as a memorial offering before God. Now send men to Joppa to bring back a man named Simon who is called Peter."[20]

This text contains a beautiful description of the biblical position regarding diversity. The Bible doesn't teach that non-Christians are all bad people, or that if you are not a Christian you probably cheat on your wife, cheat in business, or are almost certainly uncharitable. Consider the biblical description of Cornelius as "God-fearing," though he was not yet a Christian.

When the Bible says that Cornelius feared God, at the very least it seems to indicate that Cornelius believed he was going to stand before God in judgment one day and be held accountable for his actions and his words. He was almost certainly a man of integrity who was scrupulous in his business dealings and honest in his communication. Moreover, Cornelius was not alone in his fear of God, because his entire family was devout.

Christians are sometimes shocked to discover that people of another faith often enjoy a healthy family life. I've noticed a tendency among some of my Christian friends to be puzzled by the apparent solidness of the Muslim, Mormon, or Jewish family that lives down the street. But the Bible unashamedly (and without qualification) suggests that Cornelius had a great family.

In addition, Cornelius was charitable, giving generously to the poor. The fact that he was not yet a Christian in no way rendered him a stingy person. (Consider that the practice of charity is central not only to Christianity, but also to the Jewish and Muslim faiths.) Indeed, his spirituality went beyond his horizontal relationships with his fellow humans and extended to his vertical relationship with God. The book of Acts tells us that he prayed regularly. One might say that, in terms of behavioral characteristics, Cornelius was a role model many Christians would aspire to be. I know many pastors who would say, "I'd love to have people in my church who would be like Cornelius (who, keep in mind, didn't yet know Christ)—people who were God-fearing, who had a great family, who were generous in their giving and who prayed regularly. How do I produce folks like Cornelius through my discipleship program?" In the neighborhood where I grew up, I knew a number of men like Cornelius—orthodox Jewish men. They had great families, were models of integrity, and walked to the synagogue every morning, regardless of whether it was snowing, raining, or freezing cold, to say their morning prayers—good people who were not Christians.

WHO IS BEING ARROGANT?

In considering the biblical limits on diversity, it is important that we be careful not to make those limits more restrictive than the

Bible itself makes them. A biblical Christian should have no problem saying that, within most religions of the world, there are people of true morality and real goodness—despite the fact that they are not Christians. Many of the values and ethical standards taught by Jesus in the Sermon on the Mount or elsewhere in the New Testament also can be found in the teachings of Buddha, Plato, Confucius, and Muhammad.

Moreover, at least some truth can be found theologically in religions outside of Christianity. As Arthur Holmes, philosophy professor at Wheaton College, is fond of saying, "All truth is God's truth." Thus, the biblical Christian is not standing against the world's religions on all matters. When arguing with the modern secularist, the biblical Christian can point out that the Christian stands with 99 percent of the world's population for 99 percent of history in declaring that the central concern of life is a relationship with God. "It is true," the Christian can say, "that I differ with my Muslim or Hindu friend regarding the nature of God and how it is that one finds salvation with God. But you, modern secularist, are the intolerant one when you suggest that the mass of humanity for the bulk of history has been entirely misguided by an irrational and superstitious concern about a relationship with a God who doesn't exist. And if God does exist, it is you, not we, who suggest that he is entirely irrelevant to conduct in the public square." The Christian stands with most of humanity for most of history by affirming that the human race is right in the importance they place on religious pursuits. We do not stand over against humanity, as does the modern secularist.

Recall our discussion of centered-set theory from chapter 1. We said there are other ways to look at people than in exclusively "in-out" terms. Centered-set theory opens up the possibility that a person who is far away from Christ may be moving toward him. As we speak to individuals who are not yet Christians, we may often address them as "seekers after truth" and not merely as "wrong." They may, indeed, be wrong regarding God, but through conversation and listening, you may discover that with a little bit of help this "seeker" might head in the direction of being "right."

Lesslie Newbigin confronts the arrogance of the modern secularist, who often compares religious differences to the parable of the blind men who touched different parts of an elephant. "Religious differences may seem irreconcilable," says the secularist, "but they can be harmonized as different perspectives of the same greater reality."

Newbigin's responds to the secularist this way:

> In the famous story of the blind men and the elephant, . . . the real point of the story is constantly overlooked. The story is told from the point of view of the King and his courtiers, who are not blind but can see that the blind men are unable to grasp the full reality of the elephant and are only able to get hold of part of it. The story is constantly told in order to neutralize the affirmations of the great religions, to suggest that they learn humility and recognize that none of them can have more than one aspect of the truth.
>
> But, of course, the real point of the story is exactly the opposite. If the King were also blind, there would be no story. The story is told by the King, and it is the immensely arrogant claim of one who sees the full truth, which all the world's religions are only groping after. It embodies the claim to know the full reality which relativizes all the claims of the religions.[21]

In other words, the secularist is at least as arrogant as the Christian is alleged to be. The secularist claims to see the big picture, while the Christian (along with every other religion) supposedly sees only part of it. But what special revelation do secularists have that allow them to take the unique and privileged position of the King, who alone sees truth?

WHAT WAS THE MESSAGE PETER WAS SENT TO DECLARE?

There are limits on the extent to which the biblical Christian can affirm diversity. In the Acts account, Cornelius was told by God to "send men to Joppa to bring back a man named Simon who is called Peter."[22] Why did God (through his angel) command Cornelius to find the apostle Peter? Was it so Peter could announce to Cornelius and his family, "Cornelius, God wants you to know that you are already in the right with him. Cornelius, you may not realize it, but you are already saved, even though you have not yet heard or believed in the gospel! Cornelius, you will be declared innocent before God on the Day of Judgment because it is enough that you are a God-fearer, that your family is devout, that you are charitable, and that you pray regularly"?

The answer is emphatically, "No!" When Peter retells the story later, he reports, "[Cornelius] told us how he had seen an angel appear in his house and say, 'Send to Joppa for Simon who is called Peter. He will bring you a message through which you and all your household *will be saved.*'"[23] In other words, Peter was not sent to bring Cornelius the message "you are already saved" or "your sins are already forgiven." Peter was sent to bring a message through which, in the future, if Cornelius believed it, *he would be saved.*

THE IMPORTANCE OF THE NAME OF CHRIST

Here's the biblical limit on diversity: No matter how good, devout, prayerful, or God-fearing a person is, he or she must believe the gospel message in order to be saved. That was the message Peter preached to Cornelius. Peter affirmed it in his speech to Cornelius saying, "All the prophets testify about [Jesus] that everyone who believes in him receives forgiveness of sins *through his name.*"[24]

How is it that one receives forgiveness of sins? By believing in any name? Any God? Any message? By just being sincere? God-fearing? Charitable? The limits of diversity are that we receive forgiveness only through believing in the name of Jesus Christ.

The New Testament conveys this message, and in particular, the apostles in the book of Acts convey this message. Recall that the apostles did not as a general rule preach to a pagan audience, but primarily to Jews and God-fearers. In other words, the apostles regularly spoke to people who were going to the temple in Jerusalem or who were in attendance in a local synagogue. Their audience was chiefly made up of people who regularly prayed, gave alms, and who, in large measure, were like Cornelius. What did they preach? Not "you are already OK with God as you are." The apostles were not sent throughout the Roman Empire to announce a salvation that people *already* possessed but just didn't know about. Rather, their message was, "Salvation is found in no one else, for there is *no other name* under heaven given to men by which we must be saved."[25]

The point at which Christ confronts diversity lies here: There is only one way of salvation, namely, conscious faith in Jesus Christ. John Stott puts it well when he writes, "Our claim, then, is not just that Jesus was one of the great spiritual leaders of the world. It would be hopelessly incongruous to refer to him as 'Jesus the Great,' comparable to Alexander the Great, Charles the Great, or Napoleon the Great. Jesus is not 'the Great'; He is *the only*. He has no peers, no rivals, and no successors."[26]

The New Testament teaches that Jesus is the *only Savior:* "For there is one God and one mediator between God and men, the man Christ Jesus."[27] It also teaches that Jesus is *the only way* to find God: "I am the way and the truth and the life," [said Jesus]. "No one comes to the Father except through me." The New Testament teaches that failure to believe in the one and only Son of God results in eternal condemnation: "Whoever believes in him is not condemned, but whoever does not believe stands condemned already because he has not believed in the name of God's one and only Son."[28]

THE NARROWNESS OF THE CHRISTIAN GOSPEL

These assertions about Jesus aggressively confront the religious diversity that is so valued in the current Western world. One can hear the objections: "How can you be so narrow? How dare you be so intolerant? So smug? What gives you the right to condemn everyone else's religion?"

We must keep in mind that the confrontation between the exclusive claims of Christ and our pluralistic culture is not just a modern phenomenon. We are not the first people in world history to be rejected because we assert that there is only one way to God. Why were the early Christians martyred? Why was every apostle, other than John, put to death for his faith? Why did the Romans herd Christians into the Colosseum and feed them to lions or pierce them with gladiators' swords? The violent opposition early Christians met at the hands of the Romans was not simply the result of Christians preaching Jesus. The Romans would have quite happily added Jesus to their pantheon of other gods. What created the violent opposition against Christians in the early centuries was their assertion of the exclusive claims of Christ. Early Christians preached Jesus as *the only way*.

Throughout history, few people have been bothered by the "private faith" of others. Even in the former Soviet Union under the rule of Communism, the Soviet constitution guaranteed "freedom of religion." By this guarantee they meant freedom to believe as you wished—as long as you did not take your faith into the public square. Today in America many people consider it entirely inoffensive, although a bit irrational, to assert faith in Jesus Christ. "Hey, if that's what works for you, no problem!" Faithfulness to the apostles' message, however, demands that we Christians not only proclaim that "Jesus works for me." Rather, the message must affirm "not only do I believe in Jesus, but you, dear friend, must also believe in Jesus in order to get right with God. For there is no other way, no other name, no other means by which you can be saved other than through conscious faith in Jesus *the one and only*."

IS IT IMPORTANT THAT WE GET THE NAME RIGHT?

Is it really necessary that we come to God in the name of Jesus? What about other names, such as Krishna, or Buddha, or Allah? We have already seen from the book of Acts that the name Jesus is important to God. We read the apostles' claim that "there is *no other name* under heaven given to men by which we must be saved."[29] And also, "All the prophets testify about him that everyone who believes in him receives forgiveness of sins *through his name*."[30] Paul tells us that "everyone who calls on *the name* of the Lord will be saved."[31] He also writes, "[God] . . . gave [Jesus] *the name* that is above every name, that at the name of Jesus every knee should bow, in heaven and on earth and under the earth, and every tongue confess that Jesus Christ is Lord, to the glory of God the Father."[32]

Why is the name Jesus so important to God? First, in the Bible, a person's name was more than just a label. One's name stood for the full character of a person in all that he or she was and did. But even though a name is more than a label, it is not less than one either. It is important to God that we use the proper label for his one and only Son.

Consider this analogy from my marriage. My wife's name is Marlene. Imagine that I rolled over in bed one evening, looked at my wife, and said, "*Betty,* you are really beautiful. I love you, *Betty.* Come over here and give me a kiss." It is highly unlikely that my wife would say in response, "Marlene, Betty, it makes no difference what you call me. Sure, I'm in the mood to kiss." Rather, I would expect my face to be slapped and Marlene to scream at me, "WHO'S BETTY!? Why did you use *that name* when you were talking to *me*?"

God invested much in the name of his Son. He sent an angel to Joseph in a dream to make sure that Joseph gave Mary's baby the name Jesus (the LORD saves), "because he will save his people from their sins."[33]

BUT ISN'T IT ENOUGH THAT A PERSON IS SINCERE?

We often hear the argument that as long as a person is sincere, he or she will be accepted by God. Is sincerity enough? Certainly a person must be sincere in order to be saved. God isn't going to save someone who is insincere, who has a "veneer" faith a millimeter deep. A person can't just verbally agree with a set of doctrines, keep his or her heart far from God—and hope to be saved. God will never save a person who, every time he or she is faced with a tough decision, chooses against Christ, saying, "Not your will, but *my* will be done." Sincerity is necessary for salvation, but it is not sufficient.

What an oddity that sincerity is considered enough only when we are speaking about God. Is it enough that soldiers defending your country are sincere? Don't we also want them to know how to fire a gun? Is it enough that the plumber who installs the gas line for your new stove is sincere? What about the pilot who is flying the 747 with your children on board? Is sincerity all you're looking for in a surgeon? Are you content with sincerity as the exclusive qualification for the coach of your favorite football team? What about the engineer who works at the nuclear power plant in your city? If sincerity won't save us in a time of war, keep us from a gas line explosion, keep a plane in the air, help your football team, or prevent a nuclear accident, why does anyone think that sincerity will save them from God's judgment?

Suppose for a moment that the biblical narrative is true—that a real God exists who, in love, created people in his image. Suppose further that the people he created rebelled against him and rejected his rule over their lives. Now imagine that God formulated a way to rescue people and sent prophet after prophet to announce his way of rescue. But people continued to reject his message and his messengers. Now imagine that this real God went ahead and executed the rescue according to plan by coming to earth in the person of Jesus Christ. But instead of accepting Jesus, people took him and hung him on a cross. Now suppose that God turned the tables on this rebellious race and used Jesus' death to actually pay the price for their rejection and rebellion. Finally, suppose that God raised Jesus from the dead and declared him to be Lord of the universe. Would it make any sense for God to have gone through all of this (actually he did much more than this brief summary suggests) if a person could get into heaven simply by being sincere? Why would God allow his Son to die a bloody death on a wooden cross or allow his prophets to be stoned and beaten if it didn't matter whether people submitted to God's way of salvation or not? If sincerity alone was sufficient, then God went to a lot of trouble for nothing.

WHAT KIND OF SALVATION DO YOU WANT?

When the average person in the Western world asserts that "all roads lead to God"—and ultimately to salvation—what he or she likely has in mind are roads leading to a *Christian* concept of God and a distinctively *Christian* understanding of salvation. In other words, the assertion that "all roads lead to God" commonly means that a person would enter eternity with a supreme being who loves them and accepts them, no matter what they believe about God, Jesus, the cross, or the resurrection of Christ. Many people don't realize that the world's religions do not offer the kind of salvation offered in Christianity. The question can justly be posed to the proponent of the "all roads" philosophy, "What kind of salvation do you want?"

Do you want a salvation offered by the Hindu scriptures (the Upanishads)? They state that since all things are ultimately the Existent, individual differences are no more significant than are the individual rivers that in the end flow together to make the single ocean: "When all beings finally come to the One, they will no longer remember or care about their individual existence. They will know only That, and they will become fully That, because they always have been and always can be That."[34] If you desire to have your individual existence obliterated, you will find such a salvation in Hinduism, but not in Christianity.

The Jains (at least Jain monks) believe that salvation is obtained by going about naked and exposed to sun, wind, and cold, gradually cleansing from one's soul the impurities of innumerable lifetimes. In the final state of purification, the ascetic remains totally inactive to avoid the accumulation of further karma. When finally restored to purity, the soul remains eternally free and independent in a state of inactive omniscient bliss.[35] Does the "all roads" supporter wish to have the salvation of the Jains? If the Jains have the salvation you want, then you must follow a path of nakedness, exposure, and inactivity.

Or perhaps the salvation offered by the Buddhists is what is desired. According to one branch of Buddhism, salvation (Nirvana) simply means the blowing out or extinction of one's self, thus freeing the self from subsequent rebirth. Are you seeking complete extinction and the obliteration of yourself?

If a person wants to permanently retain his or her individuality and exist in a loving personal relationship with the kind of God described in the Bible, then there is only one person who offers that kind of salvation: Jesus.

Why do so many assert an "all roads lead to God" philosophy? In part, it is because of ignorance regarding what the world's religions actually teach about salvation. The Christian philosopher Blaise Pascal suggested that the answer also lies in our pride:

> Pride tells us we can know God without Jesus Christ, in effect that we can communicate with God without a mediator. But this only means that we are communicating with a God who is the [prideful] result that comes from being known without a mediator. Whereas those who have known God through a mediator know their own wretchedness. Not only is it impossible to know God without Jesus Christ, it is also useless.... [For] knowing God without knowing our wretchedness leads to pride. Knowing our wretchedness without knowing God leads to despair. Knowing Jesus Christ is the middle course, because in Him we find both God and our wretchedness.[36]

DON'T ALL ROADS LEAD TO GOD?

Perhaps you've heard people say, "There are many paths to God. Why can't you Christians see that?" The reason why a committed follower of Jesus can't see this is because it is a direct contradiction of Jesus' teaching. He never spoke about many roads up a mountain, but about *two roads*—one narrow road that leads to eternal life and an eternal relationship with God, and another broad road that leads to eternal damnation and an eternal separation from God.[37]

In the physical realm, all roads don't lead to the same place. Our church building is located in central Ohio. If people traveled east from our church building they would never end up in Florida, no matter how long they drove or how sincere they were. This same kind of objective reality exists in the spiritual world. Just because we are dealing with God doesn't mean that objective reality ceases to exist. If there is a real God (assuming that all religions are not just a gigantic fraud), then there is a real way to get to God. The road to God is not created by people; rather, people discover it, or more precisely, God reveals it.

IS CHRISTIANITY NARROW OR BROAD?

It is as important for Christians to assert the *inclusivity* of Christianity as it is for us to defend its exclusivity: "Salvation is found in no one else, for there is no other name under heaven given to men by which we must be saved."[38] And it is also undeniable that the only assured means of salvation is conscious faith in Christ's name.[39]

Nevertheless, we must continually remind our friends (and ourselves) that the Christ we proclaim is not some local deity embraced only by politically conservative Western Caucasians. The vast majority of the world's Christians are Latinos, Africans, and Asians, who do not look, dress, or worship in the style of Western Caucasian Christians. Jesus Christ is bigger than politics, than nationality, than race or gender, and than any other way we may choose to divide the world. The love of diversity did not originate in the second half of the twentieth century. It originated with God.

Further, it is essential that conservative churches move beyond a defective evangelical spirituality that entirely emphasizes the rational and has no place for the emotional or mystical components of faith. We must frankly acknowledge that many people, in the West at least, have turned to Eastern religion because they are seeking a fuller spirituality than the one offered by modernistic, rationalistic churches in America. Regaining a more full-orbed, more biblical approach to God that includes our emotions, an experience of the Holy Spirit, a sense of community, and the reality of mystery (in other words, the admission that we don't exhaustively understand everything) gives us an evangelical spirituality worth taking to the marketplace.

Finally, as we make it a priority to listen to our neighbors, friends, and family, we will hear themes that eventually point to Jesus Christ. For example, if our friends are ardent feminists, their passion for justice is embraced by Christ. If they are Buddhists or New Agers, their passion for spirituality, as well as their rejection of secular modernism as horribly materialistic and reductionistic, is also affirmed by Christ. Of course, in all philosophies there are differences from Christianity that cannot be bridged or minimized. My point is that, in any discussion, the Christian, after listening and learning, should be able to affirm the longings that have been placed in each of us as image bearers of God.

The Christ whom Paul preached was not a little, narrow Christ. He differed from the philosophies and gods of the Greco-Roman world not by being *smaller* than them, but by being *infinitely greater!* Thus to the magical, polytheistic, occult-laden city of Ephesus, Paul preached Christ who is "seated . . . at [God's] right hand in the heavenly realms, far above all rule and authority, power and dominion, and every title that can be given, not only in the present age but also in the one to come."[40] And to the Christians in Colosse, who lived in a city that fostered many beliefs similar to those held by the contemporary New Age movement, Paul declared, "the mystery of God, namely, Christ, in whom are hidden all the treasures of wisdom and knowledge."[41] To use current jargon, Paul was saying to all of the competing claims of truth in a pluralistic culture that "my story is not smaller than your story. My story is bigger than your story and swallows up the truth of your story by its incredible vastness."

Questions for Reflection and Discussion

?

1. In light of the growing diversity across the North America, do you find you have much contact with people who are different from you? If so, discuss.

2. The author asserts that God creates and loves diversity. Do you agree with his perspective? If so, in what ways can you positively affirm God's love of diversity at your church or in your classroom at school?

3. It's been said that the most segregated hour in America is 11:00 A.M. on Sunday morning. People seem to prefer to worship God with others who are just like them. How diverse is the church or fellowship where you worship? If it is not diverse racially, ethnically, or age-wise, why do you think it isn't? What do you think makes a church appealing to diverse groups of people?

4.   The author states that Christianity is meant to be both inclusive and exclusive. What does he mean by this? Do you agree? How can you as a Christian strike the right balance on this issue?

5.   Perhaps the most unacceptable intellectual position today is the conviction that one possesses "the truth." Such a position is seen as intolerant, arrogant, and completely indefensible. Christians, however, are called to affirm Jesus Christ as Lord and as the only way to God. Which of the author's approaches do you think is most effective in communicating Jesus as the only way? Which do you think is least effective?

RECOMMENDED READING

Carson, D. A., ed. *Telling the Truth: Evangelizing Postmoderns.* Grand Rapids: Zondervan, 2000.

Newbigin, Lesslie. *The Gospel in a Pluralist Society.* Grand Rapids: Eerdmans, 1989.

Piper, John. *Let the Nations Be Glad: The Supremacy of God in Missions.* Grand Rapids: Baker, 1993.

Part 2

Is the Feminist My Enemy?

5

Was Jesus a Feminist?

During my law school days, I enrolled in a class taught by a woman professor who happened to be a staunch feminist and radical lesbian. Her class turned out to be a semester-long diatribe against men. Any viewpoint other than the one she advocated was viewed as "hopelessly Neanderthal and representative of a patriarchal system that needs to be torn down." As a man, I found myself completely turned off by her class. But beyond that, she became the lens through which I viewed all feminists. I began to believe that all feminism was shot through with male bashing, radical pro-abortion stands, bizarre feminist spirituality, hatred of heterosexual marriage, and the general meanness of temperament that so characterized my professor.

Against the backdrop of my experiences with self-styled feminists such as my law professor, I adopted a basically antifeminist viewpoint. But in the last decade, as I've spent more time studying Jesus' words about and practices toward women, and as I've studied the treatment of women in world history and the history of modern feminism, I've been forced to rethink many of my positions. My conviction is that many Christians view feminists as their enemies not because they have thoughtfully considered all of the issues, but because they have encountered radical feminists such as my law school professor.

Let's explore a different definition of feminism from the one offered by my professor. To be a feminist simply means to treat women as human beings—not lesser human beings, not dumb, lazy, frivolous human beings, not human beings to be made fun of—just human beings.

In her best-selling book *Wild Swans*, Jung Chang tells the story of three generations of Chinese women growing up in twentieth-century China—her grandmother, her mother, and herself. Her grandmother was subjected to the thousand-year-old practice of foot binding:

> My grandmother's feet had been bound when she was two years old. Her mother, who herself had bound feet, first wound a piece of white cloth, about twenty feet long, around her feet, bending all her toes except the big toe inward and under the sole. Then she placed a large stone on top to crush the arch. My grandmother screamed in agony and begged her to stop. Her mother had to stick a cloth into her mouth to gag her. My grandmother passed out repeatedly from the pain.[1]

How could families allow such treatment of women? Supposedly the sight of women teetering on bound feet was designed to produce an erotic effect on men. As they viewed female vulnerability, they felt a protective impulse. Listen to the author's poignant description of her grandmother's ongoing torment for the benefit of men:

> The process lasted several years. Even after the bones had been broken, the feet had to be bound day and night in thick cloth because the moment they were released, they would try to recover. For years my grandmother lived in relentless, excruciating pain. When she pleaded with her mother to untie the bindings, her mother would weep and tell her that unbound feet would ruin her entire life, and that she was doing it for her own future happiness.[2]

In China, mothers-in-law would examine the feet of the prospective bride. If they were normal, the mother-in-law would reject her, and the young bride would experience the disdain of the community and her new family.

HOW WOMEN ARE TREATED TODAY

A recent *New York Times* article reported that a woman came into a Kabul hospital with burns over 80 percent of her body. An official of the Taliban, the fundamentalist group that rules most of Afghanistan, prohibited the doctor from undressing her. The doctor said she would die if he didn't treat her. "Many Taliban die on the battlefield," replied the official. The woman, untreated, died.

Since the Taliban took power several years ago, their decrees have narrowed the world for women. Women may no longer work or go to school. They may not leave their houses without an approved reason. They may not talk to men or ride in a vehicle alongside men who are not relatives.[3]

Another young woman who tried to flee Afghanistan with a man who was not her relative was stoned to death on orders from the country's militant Islamic rulers. Recent reports come from Kabul of cases where men have beaten women for wearing white socks or plastic sandals with no socks—attire that Taliban zealots said was likely to provoke "impure thoughts" in men. One Taliban official said, "Some women want to show their feet and ankles. They are immoral women. They want to give a hint to the opposite sex."[4]

Taliban treatment of women, however, was characterized as good by one Muslim cleric, who stated, "The outside world, in conjunction with our enemies at home, have unleashed a false propaganda against us, that we are violating women's rights. But the reverse is true: the world should take lessons from us. By strictly observing the Sharia law, we have given great honor and dignity to our women."[5]

While not nearly as oppressed as women in Afghanistan (and many Muslim countries today), most women above the age of 40 can share personal stories of their own gender-based discrimination. For example, a female relative of mine worked in a business office for many years. Her skills and work habits were excellent, and she regularly received high scores on her evaluations. However, when a job opened up for which she was clearly qualified, the company would not advance her because she was a woman. Instead, they brought in a younger, less experienced man whom she had to train for the job that should rightfully have been hers. That experience left her understandably bitter. She eventually joined a feminist political organization and worked tirelessly for laws ensuring equal treatment for women in the workplace.

It would be impossible to overstate how miserable the position or how negative the view has been toward women throughout world history. Whether we are talking about female circumcision in twenty-first–century Africa, the raping of Muslim women by Serb soldiers during the Bosnian War, or the reduction of women to the possession of particular genitalia in Western Internet pornography, it is fair to say that women have rarely received equal treatment to men in either ancient or modern culture.

. To adequately appreciate how liberating the message of Jesus is toward women, one must read his words and observe his practice against the backdrop of world cultures and particularly against the backdrop of the centuries immediately before and after the New Testament era. This background will pave the way to look at how Jesus adopted a thoroughly revolutionary perspective on women.

HOW WOMEN WERE TREATED IN ANCIENT ISRAEL

Realize that no monolithic viewpoint existed toward women in ancient Judaism. Women's positions differed widely, based on social class distinctions. Judaism was made up of various sects, including the Pharisees, the Sadducees, and the Essenes. Even within these sects, there were differing rabbinic schools. Positive, as well as negative, statements from the rabbis can be deduced from reading ancient sources. Nevertheless, the overall tenor of the rabbinical writings about women before and after the time of Jesus was extremely negative.

If you look in the Apocrypha of a Roman Catholic version of the Bible, you will find the book of Ecclesiasticus, or the Wisdom of Jesus ben Sirach. His writing profoundly influenced later rabbis and is frequently quoted in the Talmud and other rabbinical sources. Yet, his view of women is so uniformly pessimistic that one author labeled ben Sirach "Male Chauvinist #1."[6]

Jesus ben Sirach considered women to be the prime example of all evil: "For from garments comes the moth, and from a woman comes woman's wickedness. Better is the wickedness of a man than a woman who does good; it is woman who brings shame and disgrace."[7] Sirach regards women as a lustful sex, in need of careful restriction, lest they seduce men. Whereas the New Testament regards Adam as primarily responsible for the historical origin of sin, Sirach, together with other rabbis, regards Eve as the origin of sin through whom we all die.[8]

Baby girls fare no better in Sirach's world. Daughters are regarded as little more than painful burdens:

> A daughter is a secret anxiety to her father, and worry over her robs him of sleep; when she is young, for fear she may never marry, or if married, for fear she may be disliked; while a virgin, for fear she may be seduced and become pregnant in her father's house; or having a husband, for fear she may go astray; or, though married, for fear she may be barren. Keep strict watch over a headstrong daughter, or she may make you a laughingstock to your enemies, a byword in the city and the assembly of the people, and put you to shame in public gatherings.[9]

Sadly, Jesus ben Sirach was not alone among rabbinic writers in castigating women. We encounter patent misogyny in *The Testaments of the Twelve Patriarchs,* composed sometime between 109–106 B.C. Women are portrayed as evil and lead the essentially good man down the path to evil. The author warns, "For evil are women, my children; and since they have no power or strength over man, they use wiles by outward attractions, that they may draw him to themselves. And whom they cannot bewitch by outward attractions, him they overcome by craft."[10] Women spread their evil "by means of their adornment . . . and by the glance of the eye instill the poison, and then through the accomplished act, they take them captive. For a woman cannot force a man openly, but by a harlot's bearing she beguiles him."[11] The logical conclusion drawn by the author is that all women should reject attractive clothing, jewelry, and cosmetics: "Command your wives and daughters, that they adorn not their heads and faces to deceive the mind: because every woman who uses these wiles has been reserved for eternal punishment."[12]

According to *The Testaments of the Twelve Patriarchs,* it seems that every woman is a potential nymphomaniac. Again we read in *The Testament of Reuben,* "concerning them [women], the angel of the Lord told me, and taught me, that women are overcome by the spirit of fornication more than men and in their heart they plot against men."[13]

The view of women, however, is not uniformly negative in intertestamental writings (the Jewish writings authored between the second century B.C. and the birth of Christ). Even in Sirach, the good wife is praised, and wisdom is portrayed in feminine terms. More important, the book of Judith, written about the same time as Sirach, portrays a woman as the heroine of the nation (although there is some ambivalence here because she accomplishes her end by exploiting her physical beauty and seducing men). Nonetheless, a fair reading of the rabbinic literature before the time of Christ would lead one to conclude that the prevalent attitude among many Jewish people in the centuries immediately preceding Jesus was essentially negative toward women.

HOW WOMEN WERE TREATED BY SOME IN THE YEARS FOLLOWING CHRIST

The negativity toward women continued in the centuries following Christ. Josephus (a Jewish historian who wrote in the first century A.D.) observed, "The woman, says the law, is in all things inferior to the man." The law, of course, says no such thing. But his harsh attitude is echoed in the most widely known rabbinic threefold daily prayer still found in some twentieth-century Jewish prayer books: "Praise be to God that he has not created me a gentile! Praise be to God that he has not created me *a woman*! Praise be to God that he has not created me an ignoramus!"[14] In the Babylonian Talmud, this prayer is attributed to Rabbi Meir, who lived in the first part of the second century A.D. and claimed to be faithfully passing on what he learned from Rabbi Akiba. This prayer, thus, may reflect Pharisaical attitudes toward women near the time of Christ. The fact that this statement is not simply a teaching, but rather a prayer, considerably increases its significance. Moreover, it wasn't simply recommended as an occasional prayer, but rather was said as a *daily* prayer, and it has been used by some ever since.[15]

Women's Portrayal in the Talmud

The Jewish Talmud is composed of two distinct parts: the Mishna, completed under the direction of Judah ha-Nasi (Judah the Prince, or Judah the Patriarch) in about A.D. 200, and the Gemara, which offers commentary on the Mishna. The Gemara was written by two different academies—one located in Palestine and the other located in Babylon. It was completed in A.D. 499.

The reason it is important to consider what the Talmud teaches about women is because it contains oral traditions that date back to the time of Christ. Even though the Talmud was composed several centuries later, its viewpoints fairly represent the general Pharisaical viewpoint at the time of Christ.[16] To adequately appreciate how revolutionary Jesus' approach toward women was, we must explore at some length the prevailing attitude toward women in Jesus' day. As we will see, almost every rabbinic perspective was contradicted by the explicit teaching and practice of Jesus.

In a work as vast as the Talmud, it would be impossible to arrive at *the* Talmudic view of women. C. G. Montefiore attempted to sum up the rabbis' view of women as recorded in the Talmud: "Women were, on the whole, regarded as inferior to men in mind, in function, and status."[17]

Women are the subject of numerous rabbinic put-downs. For example, the rabbis said, "Four qualities are ascribed to women: they are gluttonous, eavesdroppers, lazy, and jealous. They are also querulous and garrulous. . . . As regards the last mentioned characteristic of excessive talkativeness, it was unkindly said that ten measures of speech descended to the world; women took nine and men one."[18]

No unanimity existed regarding a woman's intellectual capacity, but we do read, "Women are light-minded," and, "It is the way of woman to remain at home and for man to go into the marketplace and learn intelligence from other men."[19] Women were also chastised for their love of finery and concern about their personal appearance: "The things which a woman longs for are adornments," and "A woman's thoughts are only for her beauty."[20]

One charge consistently leveled against women was their supposed partiality toward the occult. The Talmud claims that "women are addicted to witchcraft" and "the more women, the more witchcraft" and "the majority of women are inclined to witchcraft." For that reason, the Talmud argues the scriptural command "Do not allow a sorceress to live"[21] is in the feminine gender.[22]

It may come as a surprise, then, that the rabbis in the Talmud had a very positive view of marriage. Indeed, to marry and rear a family was a religious command, and to be single was viewed with great horror by the Talmudists: "The unmarried person lives without joy, without blessing, and without good." It is further said that an unmarried man is not a man in the full sense, because, quoting Genesis, "Male and female, created he them, and blessed them and called their name Man."[23]

According to the rabbis, marriages were made in heaven. A classic story illustrating this belief begins: "A Roman lady asked a rabbi, 'In how many days did the Holy One (blessed be he) create the universe?' 'In six days,' he answered. 'What has he been doing since then up to the present?' 'He has been arranging marriages.'"[24]

But despite this high view of marriage, many rabbis permitted men to divorce their wives for a good reason, a bad reason, or no reason at all. The more lenient opinion of the Hillelite disciples (disciples of Rabbi Hillel, a near contemporary of Christ) prevailed and was adopted as the generally accepted perspective in the Talmud. Even under the more strict school of Shammai, a woman was not permitted to divorce her husband, but a husband alone could divorce his wife. Thus, the Talmud said: "A woman may be divorced with or without her consent, but a man can only be divorced with his consent."[25]

To ameliorate this regarding a woman's inability to obtain a divorce, Jewish courts would sometimes bring strong pressure to bear upon a husband until he said, "I am willing to grant my wife a divorce." But if a man was stubborn, no court could force a divorce. Even desertion, no matter how long it lasted, didn't give a woman grounds for divorce. A woman could potentially find herself stuck in social limbo for decades without any resolution to her situation. Only if trustworthy testimony came that her husband had died was she allowed to remarry.[26]

The negative perspective toward women is also evident in the rabbinic preference for sons over daughters. For instance, there is a peculiar rabbinic interpretation placed on the biblical statement: "The LORD had blessed [Abraham] in every way."[27] When asked, "What does it mean that Abraham was blessed in every way," one rabbi answered, "That he had no daughter." A story was also told about a rabbi's wife who gave birth to a daughter. He was very upset about it. His father, to cheer him, said, "Increase has come into the world." But another rabbi told him, "Your father has given you empty comfort; for there is a rabbinic dictum: the world cannot exist without males and females, but happy is he whose children are sons and woe to him whose children are daughters."[28]

The same thought is contained in the explanation of the words of the priestly benediction, "The LORD bless you and keep you."[29] The rabbis said that this means to be blessed with sons and to be kept from daughters because daughters need continual and careful guarding.[30]

Finally, consider the rabbinic attitude about the education of women. As a general rule, the Jewish community placed a very high value on education. Schools were established in every Jewish community. School began at the age of six or seven. The greatest dignity was attached to the profession of teacher, and they were held in highest esteem. The Talmud, in fact, says that Jewish law gives the teacher precedence even over a parent, because the parent only brings the child life in this world, whereas the teacher brings him the life of the world to come.[31] Sadly, this priority on education was for boys alone and did not extend to girls.

Should girls be taught Torah? One teacher declared, "A man is obliged to have his daughter taught Torah." But this statement is immediately followed by the opposing view: "Whoever teaches his daughter Torah is as though he taught her obscenity." Rabbi Cohen suggests that this latter opinion was the one more generally held and practiced. For instance, notice was taken of the fact that in the biblical exhortation "Teach your children," the Hebrew word for *children* more literally denotes "your sons" and so excludes daughters. Indeed, one rabbi went so far as to state, "Let the words of the Torah rather be destroyed by fire than be imparted to a woman." It was also said that when a woman put a question to a rabbi in connection with the golden calf, he derisively responded: "A woman has no need to learn except in the use of the spindle."[32]

HOW WOMEN WERE TREATED IN ROME AND GREECE

People held widely different perspectives regarding women's status or roles in the Greco-Roman world. In general, a woman's rights were directly related to her social status. In late Republican Rome in the second century B.C., upper-class women could manage their own businesses and financial affairs, as well as own, inherit, and dispose of property.

Yet even upper-class women were second-class citizens in ancient Rome, as I discovered on a recent visit I took with my wife to Rome. As we explored the Colosseum together and read about its history, we found that women were not permitted to sit on the lower levels of the Colosseum with the men. Rather, even the wives of senators were confined to standing on the very upper level of the Colosseum, along with prostitutes, beggars, and non-Roman citizens. What a vivid picture of discrimination. Roman men, in effect, said, "No matter how wealthy, well-educated, or honorable you may be, you women must stand in the back, along with all of the rest of the people we regard as human garbage."

In ancient Athens, women lacked all independent status. They could not enter into any transaction worth more than one measure of barley. They also could not own any property, with the exception of their clothing, personal jewelry, and personal slaves. At all times they had to be under the protection of a guardian. If they were unmarried, the guardian was their father or closest male relative. If they were married, the guardian was their husband. If widowed, the guardian was their son or a male relative by marriage or by birth. At all times the woman belonged to a family and was under the legal protection of its head.[33]

Just like ancient Judaism, the Greeks also had a tradition of seeing women as the source of the world's evil. In keeping with this theme, Pandora, the first woman, is a deceptive, hollow imitation of the goddesses she was made to resemble. Her opening of a box became the source of death and disease among humankind.

Women were also seen as the embodiment of negative characteristics. The Greek poet Simonides wrote a poem about women's tendencies toward laziness, uncontrolled appetite, slovenliness, gossip, and adultery. Each type of woman reflects the characteristics of its animal origin. For example, Simonides writes about

- the pig woman, who wears unlaundered clothing and sits unwashed among the dunghills, becoming fat.
- the donkey woman, of whom it is impossible to get her to work.
- the mare woman (the aristocratic woman), whose husband finds her tastes too expensive.

He sums up the poem with this statement: "Women are the biggest single bad thing Zeus has made for us; a ball and a chain; we can't get loose since that time when the fight about a wife began the Great War, and they volunteered, and went to hell."[34] Hipponax, a poet famed for his vicious satire, said, "The two best days in a woman's life are when someone marries her and when he carries her dead body to the grave."[35]

While Plato argued in favor of equality for women (suggesting that men and women do everything together, including war and guard duty),[36] Aristotle had a relatively low estimation of women. In Aristotle's view, women are suited by nature for their private role in the household, and because they are naturally inferior to men, they must be trained to obey their husbands and fathers. Not only are men more fit to rule, thought Aristotle, but he believed that different qualities are distributed to the soul in the case of men and women. In this vein, Aristotle wrote, "For rule of free over slave, male over female, man over boy are all different, because while parts of the soul are present in each case, the distribution is different. Thus the deliberative faculty in the soul is not present at all in a slave; in a female it is present but ineffective, in a child present, but undeveloped."[37]

JESUS THE REVOLUTIONARY

In stark contrast to both the general attitude of rabbis toward women and the Roman and Greek perspectives, both before and after the New Testament period, is the perspective of Jesus of Nazareth. His statements and practices were nothing short of revolutionary.

Jesus and Divorce

Jesus redefined the rabbinic perspective on divorce in both a more permissive and a more protective direction for women. Unlike the rabbis, who taught that only a man could sue for divorce, Jesus gave implicit permission for women to dissolve their marriage bonds.[38] Where the Hillelite school permitted men to divorce their wives for such minor infractions as burning their supper, Jesus underlined the permanence of marriage, saying, "I tell you that anyone who divorces his wife, except for marital unfaithfulness, and marries another woman commits adultery."[39]

Jesus and Women's Equality to Learn

It was Jesus' willingness to teach women Torah and to accept women as spiritually equal to men that Jesus showed himself to be truly revolutionary. Recall that it was generally accepted rabbinic opinion that women should be barred from learning Torah.[40] In striking contrast, we have the story of Jesus teaching Torah to his disciple Mary as recorded in the book of Luke.[41] Martha, Mary's sister, is doing what was culturally expected of a woman in her day who had invited a famous rabbi into her home. She was busy preparing a meal for the rabbi. But her sister, Mary, was doing what was absolutely forbidden. Mary was found sitting at Jesus' feet, listening to him teach her in Torah (because Jesus was a rabbi, everything he spoke would have been considered Torah). Mary's posture at Jesus' feet was not simply the posture of adoration (as though she were gazing lovingly up at her Master without a thought in her pretty little head). Rather, Mary was taking the position of a disciple who in that day would always be found sitting at the feet of his or her Master, receiving instruction.

Jesus and the Choice of Disciples

Women were regularly found among the disciples of Jesus.[42] The fact that Jesus chose twelve men to be apostles does not necessarily demonstrate a preference for exclusive male leadership in the church, as is often suggested. It could be a deliberate attempt by Jesus to fulfill the Old Testament typology of the twelve patriarchs of Israel. In creating a new Israel, Jesus built his new community on twelve new patriarchs (apostles).

Many argue, however, that Jesus' choice of twelve new patriarchs demonstrates a privileged position in the church for men, even if it were being done in fulfillment of an Old Testament pattern. But the twelve apostles were also all Jewish. Does this mean that Jewish believers should be given a privileged place in the body of Christ over Gentiles when we choose leaders? The apostles were also young, and all hailed from Judea and Galilee. They also were not seminary trained. Why do we focus on their maleness as being paradigmatic, but not their Jewishness, youthfulness, or lack of formal academic training, when arguing against women's potential ordination? Perhaps it is because, at this crucial point of nondiscrimination, Christians are far less radical than our Lord himself.

Jesus and What He Doesn't Say

What is most startling about Jesus' relationship to women, though, is what he doesn't say. Jesus never made women the butt of his jokes. In remarkable contrast to the rabbis (and modern Christian followers), he did not portray them as more lustful, lazy, vain, or irrational than men in his stories. He never suggested in his teachings that women were more prone to witchcraft or theological error than men, nor did he ever suggest that women were less intelligent or less capable than men. Indeed, a case could be made that Jesus gave a privileged place to women over men.

Jesus and Firsts for Women

Consider the following "firsts." The first news of the incarnation went to a woman.[43] The first miracle was performed for a woman.[44] The first Samaritan convert was a woman.[45] The first person clearly told by Jesus that he was the Messiah was a woman (and a Samaritan woman at that).[46] The first Gentile convert was a woman.[47] The first resurrection teaching was given to a woman.[48] The first to witness the resurrection was a woman.[49] The first witnesses to the resurrection were women[50]—and this in stark contrast to a culture that said women could not give legal testimony.

Dorothy Sayers, the Christian writer and close friend of C. S. Lewis, summed up Jesus' attitude toward women:

> Perhaps it was no wonder that women were first at the Cradle and last at the Cross. They had never known a man like this Man. There never has been such another. A prophet and teacher who never nagged at them, never flattered or coaxed or patronized; who never made sick jokes about them ... who rebuked without querulousness and praised without condescension; who took their questions and arguments seriously; who never mapped out this sphere for them, never urged them to be feminine or jeered at them for being female; who had no ax to grind and no uneasy male dignity to defend; who took them as he found them and was completely unself-conscious. There was no act, no sermon, no parable in the whole gospel that borrows pungency from female perversity. Nobody could possibly guess from the words and deeds of Jesus that there was anything "funny" or inferior about woman's nature.[51]

WOMEN IN THE HISTORY OF THE CHURCH

The contributions of women in the history of the church would fill a library of books. Some were famous contemplatives such as Teresa of Avila and Teresa of Lisieux. Others were famous missionaries such as Lottie Moon, Mary Slessor, Amy Carmichael, Elisabeth Elliot, and Annie Armstrong.

Still others were powerful Bible teachers such as Maria Woodworth-Etter and Phoebe Palmer. In the history of the church, it seems that when the church experiences the renewing presence of the Holy Spirit, we see women exercising all the gifts of the Spirit, including leadership and teaching. However, when the church goes through a period of institutionalization, women's roles become restricted. Thus, in early Pentecostalism, many of the most powerful leaders flowing out of the Azusa Street Mission were women, including Julia Hutchins, Neely Terry, Jennie Moore, Agnes Ozman, and Florence Crawford. They preached from pulpits, in storefronts, and in tents. Women went from house to house looking for people to pray for, anointing them with oil and healing them in the name of the Lord.

Affirming women's leadership, William Seymour, the leader of the Azusa Street Revival, once declared, "Before Jesus . . . organized his church, he called them all into the Upper Room, both men and women, and anointed them with the oil of the Holy Ghost, thus qualifying them all to minister in this gospel. On the day of Pentecost, they all preached through the power of the Holy Ghost. In Christ Jesus there is neither male nor female, all are one."[52]

William Seymour was actually preceded in this perspective by Phoebe Palmer, a powerful teacher and theologian who was a founder of the Holiness School of Teaching in the nineteenth century and whose book *The Way of Holiness* appeared in fifty editions by 1867. Phoebe Palmer was once met by a woman who said that she desired to live a holy life, but an obstacle hindered her. One of the conditions Phoebe Palmer had established for "receiving entire sanctification" was to give public witness to this "blessing." This woman belonged to a denomination that barred women from speaking in the church. What was she to do?

Phoebe Palmer responded, "At Pentecost the Holy Spirit was poured out upon all those who gathered in the Upper Room, both men and women, and they were empowered to testify to Christ." According to Phoebe Palmer, women were not only *allowed* to speak, but were *compelled* to do so by the very Spirit of God. Palmer detailed her viewpoints on women's ministry in a four-hundred-page book titled *The Promise of the Father.* One of Phoebe Palmer's statements in the book needs to be added to contemporary discussions about women's roles. She wrote, "We believe that hundreds of conscientious, sensitive Christian women have actually suffered more under the slowly crucifying process to which they have been subjected to by men who bear the Christian name than many a martyr has endured in passing through the flames."[53]

THE ACHIEVEMENTS OF MODERN FEMINISM

It has become commonplace for evangelical Christians to bash modern feminism. Yet, almost all Christians, both men and women, would find it virtually unthinkable to set the clock back to the situation as it existed for women even as recently as seventy-five to hundred years ago. What was it like to be a woman at the beginning of the twentieth century?

In the workplace the better-paid positions were mainly barred to women. Only 553 women doctors practiced medicine in Great Britain by 1912. Women were excluded from the upper ranks of civil service, law, and the accounting professions.[54] A century ago, the typical female worker in America was young, single, an immigrant or the daughter of immigrants, and working as a domestic servant. A young woman working as a domestic servant had very little autonomy, did the heaviest jobs in the household, worked very long hours, and typically had only a half day off each week.[55]

The second most common job for women was in the garment industry. Women toiled in small, filthy old buildings with grime-coated windows that blocked out sunlight and denied access to fresh air because the windows were often nailed shut. The noise from mechanical looms and shuttles was deafening. The average woman earned about six dollars a week and was at the mercy of her shop foreman, who fined the women for talking, laughing, singing, or accidentally staining or tearing the fabric on which they worked.[56] The tragic and infamous fire at the Triangle Shirtwaist Factory building in New York City, which resulted in so many women's deaths (due to their inability to escape because the fire exits were locked and chained), helped to end the oppressive working conditions of female garment workers.

The only profession open to educated women was teaching. Henry Finck, in *The Independent* of April 11, 1901, voiced a typical perspective that included the following prophecy:

> Having once discovered the charm of the eternal womanly, men will never allow it to be taken away again, to please a lot of half-women who are clamoring for what they illogically call their "rights." [One day] they will try to take the place of our soldiers, our sailors, our firemen, mail carriers, and policemen. All employment, which makes women bold, fierce, muscular, brawny in body or mind, will be more and more rigidly tabooed as unwomanly. Woman's strength lies in beauty and gentleness, not in muscle.[57]

Newspapers frequently ran stories mocking women's attempts to advance themselves in men's professions. The *New York Times* said of "pretty" Mamie Frey, the only woman watchmaker in Chicago, "She is acknowledged to be an expert, but women ... prefer to trust their timepieces to a mechanic of the other sex. That is why she is so unhappy."[58] Another story reported a meeting of a women's club that was discussing the future of American international relations when a Chinese merchant showed up with colorful samples of his silk goods. The *Times* reported, "All the important debating points were said to be forgotten in the excited rush to peruse and purchase."[59]

Education was thought by many to be unhealthy for young women on the grounds that its cerebral challenges strained their abilities, and even wore them out physically. Nathalie Dana complained that her parents would not allow her to attend Bryn Mawr because a cousin had died after graduation, even though, as Nathalie reported, "Her death was caused by typhoid fever and occurred a whole year after she left college."[60]

At the beginning of the twentieth century, there were a number of outstanding women's colleges throughout the United States, but few offered courses in engineering, advanced science, advanced economics, or other studies that were preparing men for successful careers at the highest levels of the professions, industry, or government. In fact, the number of women college graduates at that time was less than twenty for every one hundred men with degrees.

Legal restrictions on women are even more shocking to our contemporary sensibilities than the vocational and educational limits placed on women. As a general rule, women could not sue in court, serve on juries, vote in national elections (only four or five states permitted women to vote in state elections), or run for elected office. Women did not gain the right to vote in the United States until 1920, in Great Britain until 1918, and in France, Italy, Romania, and Yugoslavia not until after World War II. Only in 1971 did Switzerland allow women to vote in federal and most cantonal elections.[61]

In the family, thought to be the province of women, rights were restricted as well. A mother's right to custody of her children took second place to that of their father. A child was considered "the property" of the father, but not of the mother. A married woman could not have her own bank account, get a bank loan, establish credit in her own name, enter a contract without her husband's signature, or keep the income she earned.[62]

Eventually, women's rights advocates lobbied for a spate of civil rights legislation guaranteeing, among other things, equal pay for equal work, nondiscrimination in employment, equal access to credit, equal access to higher education, and prohibition of sexual discrimination in federally funded educational institutions.

WHO WAS SUSAN B. ANTHONY?

She was the first woman to be portrayed on a circulating United States coin. Susan B. Anthony was born in Adams, Massachusetts, in 1820 and was brought up in a Quaker family that had a strong devotion to Christ and, as a result, to causes of justice. After teaching for fifteen years, she became active in the Temperance Movement and attempted to draw attention to the effects of drunkenness on families. Campaigning for stronger liquor laws, she and Elizabeth Cady Stanton petitioned the New York State legislature to pass a law limiting the sale of liquor. The legislature rejected the petition because most of the 28,000 signatures were from women. Anthony then realized that women would never be taken seriously unless they were given the right to vote. And so she became a leading suffragist for the next half century.

But Susan B. Anthony did not simply advocate for the rights of women. She also campaigned tirelessly for the abolition of slavery and for the full citizenship of blacks, including their right to vote. In the newspaper she published from Rochester, New York, Anthony regularly denounced lynchings and racial prejudice. She was an outspoken critic of abortion, calling it "child murder," and she worked to pass laws outlawing abortion. As an educational reformer, she argued for coeducation and claimed there was no difference between the minds of men and women. She worked for child labor legislation and for the rights of women in the workplace. All the while she was ridiculed, lampooned, and opposed by legislators, newspapers, business owners, educators, male workers, and, sadly, by many pastors and Christian writers.

From a century's distance, we can appreciate Susan B. Anthony for what she was—a true follower of Jesus who stood firmly in the social justice tradition of the Christian church.

A Question for People Who Dismiss Feminism

I would ask this question of those who dismiss feminism as being completely anti-Christian or who make feminists the butt of jokes or the objects of disdain: Would you want your daughters to grow up with the opportunities afforded women in 1920? It seems to me that instead of bashing feminists or viewing them as enemies, men and women ought to get down on their knees and thank God for the achievements of feminists—some of whom were devoted Christian sisters and brothers. Seldom do I find myself quoting the actor Alan Alda, but I really like his definition of being a feminist. He said, "I am a feminist insofar as I believe that women are people."

We could say the same thing about Jesus. He valued women, spent time with them, never viewed them as uniquely vain, dumb, lazy, or frivolous. He never made fun of women, but was friends with them, hung out with them, taught them, and preferred them at the most significant moments of his life. He liberated them, and he healed them. Jesus spat in the eyes of the culture's view of women. And if you accept Alan Alda's definition of feminism, then Jesus was a feminist!

Questions for Reflection and Discussion

?

1. Do you find yourself in agreement with feminist thinking? If so, in what ways? In what ways are you in disagreement with modern feminism?

2. Have you or a woman you know ever experienced the kind of mistreatment the author described at the beginning of this chapter?

3. What surprised you the most about the first-century view of women from the perspectives of Judaism, Greek, and Roman culture?

4. What do you find was Jesus' most dramatic statement and/or action with respect to women?

5. If the church today were to treat women the way Jesus did nearly two thousand years ago, what would it look like?

RECOMMENDED READING

Chang, Jung. *Wild Swans*. New York: Anchor, 1991.

Cohen, Abraham. *Every Man's Talmud*. New York: Schocken, 1949.

Foster, Richard. *Streams of Living Water: Celebrating the Great Traditions of the Christian Faith*. New York: HarperCollins, 1998.

6

What Should We Think of Feminists?

In the last chapter, I told you about a negative experience I had with a self-professed feminist law professor. She was a male basher and an absolutizer of abortion rights (the belief in abortion through the ninth month of pregnancy), as well as someone who held strongly anti-Christian views when it came to the matter of spirituality.

In subsequent years, I've had many similar experiences with graduates of Womyn's Studies departments (women is spelled "womyn" to eliminate any reference to "men"). My wife refuses to call herself a "feminist" because modern feminism has become so identified with a pro-abortion perspective. (Interestingly, it was early Christian feminists, such as Susan B. Anthony, who campaigned for America's first anti-abortion laws. These laws were seen as protective not only of unborn children but also of women.). My wife also grew weary of explaining why she, the holder of a bachelor's degree with honors from a major university, chose to take a decade out from career pursuits in order to be a full-time mother of our children. She has had innumerable conversations with women and men who seem to question her intelligence when they say with feigned sincerity, "Oh, you stay home with your kids. How nice!"

SECOND-WAVE FEMINISM

Isn't the reason some Christians refuse to reexamine the roles of women in the church and in society due to their negative experiences with what I'll call "second-wave feminism"? We do not merely struggle with Jesus or Paul or other Scripture writers when considering the roles of women, but also with second-wave feminists. If we can determine which aspects of feminism ought to be rejected by biblical Christians and which ought to be affirmed, I believe we will be in a position to hear the words of Scripture with fresh ears, untainted by our negative experiences. We would very likely also find more common ground with feminists than we ever thought possible.

If feminism simply meant treating women as people, then there ought to be little for the biblical Christian to object to in the feminist movement. Unfortunately, the first wave of feminism (1850–1970), which fought for such things as the end to workplace discrimination, the right to vote, equal educational opportunities, and equal pay (and was led, in part, by some fervent Christians), was followed by a second wave of feminists who thought that equality with men was not enough. This second wave, or New Feminism, believed that women's identity needed to be blown to bits and rebuilt from the ground up.

Germaine Greer spoke for many second-wave feminists when she attacked traditional roles for women and femininity in her best-selling book called *The Female Eunuch*. She felt that femininity and, indeed, womanhood, itself, is life-denying and dehumanizing. Consider these excerpts from her book:

- Any . . . aim is likely to be followed in a "feminine" way, that is, servilely, dishonestly, inefficiently, inconsistently.
- The female's fate is to become deformed and debilitated.
- We can, indeed, we must, reject femininity as meaning *without libido*, and therefore incomplete, subhuman.
- Every girl whose upbringing is "normal" . . . is a female faggot.
- Woman is never genuine at any period of her life.
- Women cannot love.
- Women must be frigid.
- The ignorance and isolation of most women means that they are incapable of making conversation.
- Women are always precipitating things of violence in pubs and dancehalls.[1]

It would be hard to come up with a more virulent attack on women in even the most extreme male chauvinist writings. But Greer's bashing of femininity and women serves to support her premise that womanhood and femininity need to be thoroughly reconstructed.

In a similar vein, Betty Friedan attacked traditional female values and modes of coping by making frequent use of an analogy between Nazism and contemporary American culture. "We are committing, quite simply, genocide," Friedan wrote, "starting with the mass burial of American women and ending with the progressive dehumanization of their sons and daughters."[2] According to Friedan, the home was a "comfortable concentration camp" whose prisoners were housewives who had been brainwashed by femininity. Such women were not "fully human."[3]

Another second-wave feminist writer, Kate Millett, attacked marriage and family as being thoroughly corrupted by its "crass and exploited economic basis." She even rejected romance as a basis for male-female relationships, saying, "The concept of romantic love affords a means of emotional manipulation in which the male is free to exploit." For Millett, heterosexual love always works against women; nowhere is this more apparent than in the institution of marriage, where Millett describes wives as "domestic servants and slaves."[4]

WEAKNESSES OF SECOND-WAVE FEMINISM

Let's consider four weaknesses of second-wave feminism that rightly trouble Christians.

Demeaning Motherhood and Homemaking

Biblical Christians would likely strongly object to the second-wave feminist attempt to reconstruct women's identity (and, indeed, all of society). In particular, biblical Christians reject excessive attacks on women who choose the roles of mother and homemaker, saying that these attacks are both shame-creating for many women and harmful for many children. Full-time mothers and homemakers when asked by someone, "So, what do you do?" commonly respond apologetically, "Well, I just stay home." Many women feel pressured to go back to work after having children, because they never hear the message that full-time mothering is a worthwhile vocation. Indeed, while "choice" was the banner under which first-wave feminists marched, second-wave feminists blatantly deny women the right to choose. According to Betty Friedan, "No woman should be authorized to stay home and raise her children.... Women should not have that choice precisely because if there is such a choice, too many women will make that one."[5]

Women who attend the church I pastor have regularly commented on how liberating it is to be in an environment where raising a child to responsible adulthood is affirmed as one of the most valuable and worthwhile things a human being could devote themselves to. I recall one woman who graduated at the top of her class in law school, but who chose to homeschool her kids, commenting, "Right now I could be spending every day working on the filing of Form 10Ks with the Securities and Exchange Commission on behalf of some corporation. I can't believe that God has given me the privilege to not only have children, but to get to teach them at home."

I am not suggesting that a woman who chooses to pursue a career outside the home rather than in it has necessarily made a bad choice. What many women, including my wife, object to is the anti-homemaker and antichild-rearing message of many second-wave feminists. Consider what Kate Millet, whom *Cosmopolitan* magazine called the "silver-tongued spokesperson for the feminist movement," wrote in her book *Sexual Politics:*

> The care of children is infinitely better left to the best trained practitioners of both sexes who have chosen it as a vocation, rather than to the harried and all-too-frequently unhappy persons with little time or taste for the work of educating young minds.... The collective professionalization (and consequent improvement) of the care of the young would further undermine family structure while contributing to the freedom of women.[6]

The real agenda of second-wave feminism is thus announced: to undermine family structure, which encourages women to be nurturing mothers and supportive wives, and to turn the raising of children over to the professionals.

An article in *Glamour* magazine warns mothers not to wait too long after the birth of their children to get back to work. Why should they not wait, you might ask? Apparently, because a delay might result in so great a bonding (love?) between the new mother and her baby that the new mother will find it too painful to leave. The editors write, "Babies are hard to resist once they are at this stage, and mothers can sometimes find it difficult to 'break away' if they delay too long."[7]

Why is it assumed that mothers *should* break away from the hugely important task of raising their children? Why do second-wave feminists regularly display a knee-jerk reaction to the woman who chooses home and family over a career? When First Lady Barbara Bush was invited in 1990 to give the commencement address at Wellesley College, hundreds of angry coeds protested. They argued that Mrs. Bush wasn't a suitable role model for young women because she had spent her life raising children rather than pursuing a career for herself. According to second-wave feminists, it is not enough to communicate career as an option. One must aggressively attack traditional roles for women (wife and mother) as stultifying and dehumanizing—a product of being brainwashed by a patriarchal society.[8]

It would be difficult, if not impossible, to square the devaluation of the role of wife and mother with such biblical counsel as "train the younger women to love their husbands and children, to be self-controlled and pure, to be busy at home, to be kind."[9] While this is hardly the only thing said about women in Scripture, it is part of biblical wisdom and in no way corresponds to the view of the home as "a comfortable concentration camp."

Despite decades of feminist teaching to the contrary, many women apparently do not agree with this radically negative assessment of domestic life. *Ms.* magazine reported the findings of the Center for

Gender Equality, a think tank funded and led by Faye Wattleton, former president of the Planned Parenthood Federation of America. The report found that nearly half the women surveyed (48 percent) said, "It is better for society if a woman stays home to take care of the family while a man is the achiever outside the home."[10] Not surprisingly, *Ms.* found this statistic "troubling" and "a throwback to prefeminist days" (or, more accurately, pre-second-wave feminism days). *Ms.* further reports that Faye Wattleton was so disturbed by this and other findings that she said, "Something is happening. We have to find out what's going on inside women's heads."[11] Maybe what is going on "inside women's heads" is a profound love for and bond with their children. Many women are not persuaded that the only valuable things in life are those things for which there is financial compensation—things found in a career and in climbing the corporate ladder.

Creating a Counterfeit Spirituality

It would take a complete chapter or even an entire book to begin to scratch the surface of the problems with much of second-wave feminist spirituality. Christians who are sensitive to the history of female oppression by men have done some excellent work in pointing out the misogynist nature of some historic male theology and church practice. Feminist church historians have recovered long-neglected stories of great women of faith in Christian history.

But serious issues must be addressed in much of feminist theology and spirituality. For example, biblical Christians might take issue with the unusual redefinition of sin that has been proposed by certain feminist theologians. They suggest that a focus on pride as the cause of the Fall betrays a perversely male perspective of the human condition. It is suggested that rather than pride or willful rebellion against God, women's root sin is acquiescing to domination by men and failing to be self-actualized.[12]

Three simple criticisms can be offered to this redefinition of women's root sin. First, it is demeaning to women to suggest that their failure to reach God's destiny is rooted in victimization and not in willfulness. Don't women (like men) exercise their wills when they sin? Don't women (like men) frequently *choose* to rebel and to live self-centered rather than Christ-centered lives?

Second, while it may be true that some women are not as boastful as men, the fact that pride may take on a different appearance in men than in women does not negate feminine pride as a viable source of women's sins.

But most fundamentally, neither "acquiescing in male domination" nor "the failure to self-actualize" are categories the writers of Scripture would have ever used. They seem to be almost entirely the result of feminist ideology and are not the product of deep reflection on biblical paradigms or thought forms.

Some feminists have also sought to redefine Christ and God in ways that radically deviate from historic Christian orthodoxy. Daphne Hampson, who was a lecturer in systematic theology at the University of Saint Andrews in Scotland, describes herself as *post-Christian* inasmuch as she believes that Christianity and feminism are incompatible and that "the Christian myth is untrue." She chose, therefore, to reconceptualize God in ways "that would not carry so many patriarchal myths or that hurt women."[13] In a similar vein, Rosemary Ruether dismisses the classic definition of Christ's person found in the Chalcedonian Creed, saying, "Once the mythology about Jesus as Messiah or divine Logos, with its traditional masculine imagery, is stripped off, the Jesus of the synoptics can be recognized as a figure remarkably compatible with feminism."[14]

Goddess worship has permeated some mainline churches as seen in Re-imagining conferences that celebrate communion by substituting "feminist elements of milk and honey" for traditional male elements of bread and wine. *Sophia,* the Greek word for wisdom, is invoked as the one presiding over the table. Many Christian observers of these conferences believe that the participants have called on a deity distinct from the triune God. Bible scholar Elizabeth Achtemeier voiced these sentiments after attending a Re-imagining conference: "Some women have reacted [to injustices to women] with justifiable rage, but what they are really doing is constructing a new church, a new religion. It is an entirely different religion than the Christian faith."[15] In another writing she said, "[By rejecting God's transcendence] worshipers of a Mother Goddess ultimately worship the creation and themselves rather than the Creator."[16]

Donald Bloesch perhaps best summarized the evangelical critique of radical feminist theologies: "When a theology becomes consciously ideological, as in some forms of feminist and liberation theologies, it is bound to lose sight of the transcendent divine criterion, the living Word of God, by which alone it can determine the validity of its social valuations."[17] It seems that the feminist ideology, not the Bible or the historical faith of the Christian church, has become the criterion for shaping recent feminist theology.

Asserting That Men are Dispensable

Gloria Steinem is credited with this oft-quoted maxim about the necessity of men: "A woman without a man is like a fish without a bicycle." Many well-known Hollywood actresses have chosen to adopt children without the benefit of marriage. Who needs men? Who needs fathers?

Hallmark now offers a line of greeting cards that celebrate divorce as liberation. One card reads, "Think of your former marriage as a record album. It was full of music—both happy and sad. But what's important now is . . . You! The recently released Hot, New, Single! You're going to be at the Top of the Charts!" Another card depicts two female praying mantises. Mantis One says, "It's tough being a single parent." Mantis Two responds, "Yeah . . . maybe we shouldn't have eaten our husbands."

People Magazine celebrated Joan Lunden's divorce with this headline: "After the painful end of her 13-year marriage, the Good Morning America co-host is discovering a new life as a single mother—and as her own woman!" Divorce is not a cause for depression or a sign of failure. No—it is a step toward independence and liberation. The story tells us that, following her divorce, Lunden "leased a brand-new six-bedroom, 8,000-square-foot house" and then went to Bloomingdale's, where she bought, among other things, seven televisions and rooms of fun furniture that were "totally unlike the serious traditional pieces she was giving up."[18] Divorce is seen not only as independence, but also as a home-decorating option. How very modern we have become!

But studies of children of divorce suggest that divorce is not just the occasion for another newly created greeting card or for redecorating one's house. Rather, according to Judith Wallerstein's study of the long-term effects of divorce on children, "Divorce is deceptive. Legally it is a single event, but psychologically it is a chain—sometimes a never-ending chain of events, relocations, and radically shifting relationships strung through time, a process that forever changes the lives of the people involved."[19] Even ten or fifteen years after a divorce (at a time when most experts predicted that the effects of divorce would have long since passed, like a bad cold), children of divorce were underachieving and drifting, as well as having a significantly difficult time establishing strong love relationships of their own.

Most often, the major loss in a child's life that follows the divorce of his or her parents is the absence of a father. Fatherless homes fare badly on all measurable criteria. More than 70 percent of all juveniles in state reform schools come from fatherless homes. One study, summarizing the relationship between crime and one-parent families, stated, "The relationship is so strong that controlling for family configuration erases the relationship between race and crime and between low income and crime."[20] This conclusion shows up time and time again in the literature.

Another sociologist, David Popenoe, said, "I have found few other bodies of evidence that lean so much in one direction as this one: on the whole, two parents—a father and a mother—are better for a child than one parent."[21] Here is what he concluded:

- Two-parent families are the best antipoverty program ever devised.
- Almost all of the income difference between whites and blacks disappear if fathers are present in the home.

- Children who grow up with their mothers alone are two times as likely to drop out of high school and two and a half times as likely to become teen mothers as children who grow up with both parents.
- Fathers' involvement is strongly linked to improved quantitative and verbal skills, improved problem-solving ability, and higher academic achievement.
- Fathers' involvement is directly related to a child's ability to manage his or her own emotions and exercise self-control.
- Children who grow up in two-parent homes delay their first sexual experience and suffer far less child abuse. Most child abuse is from a non-relative child-care provider.[22]

Charles Ballard, an African-American social worker, has seen firsthand the civilizing effect of fathering on young men. Since 1982 he has reunited thousands of absent, unwed fathers with their children through his Institute for Responsible Fatherhood and Family Revitalization. Ballard observes the following:

> I can take you to any street in the city of Cleveland and we could walk down the street together and I can tell you just by looking at the front of a house if that house has a dad in it or not. Because if there is a dad in the home, the grass will probably be mowed, the screen door will be fixed. You might see a man standing out front playing catch with his son. You won't see a group of aggressive boys standing out in front of the house because dad will deal with them. If dad is in the home you will see a home that is well managed, fixed-up and sons who are under control.[23]

While we are all aware of exceptions to Ballard's observations, his experience is that calling men to be responsible fathers will motivate them to go on to finish school and find work. What a man needs first of all is to be a responsible dad—not to have a good job, as is popularly asserted.

And contrary to the Hallmark line of divorce greeting cards and to Gloria Steinem's expressed opinion, society does away with the role of men and dads to its extreme detriment.

Eliminating All Gender-Based Distinctions

Second-wave feminists such as Kate Millett have argued for years that socialization, not biology, best explains human behavior. "Patriarchy," she said, "takes the blank slate of an infant and encourages young men to develop aggressive impulses, and the female to thwart her own or to turn them inward."[24] She claims that there is no biological basis for sexual differentiation in role or temperament. Wherever gender differences exist, most second-wave feminists insist they are the product of "patriarchal society."

Social science literature, however, does not support this extreme claim that there is no basis in "nature" (biology) for gender-specific behavior. The current debate is no longer about nature versus nurture. Rather, it poses the question, To what extent does nature account for behavior or to what extent does nurture account for behavior? Almost all of the current work in the social sciences now suggests that these two (nature and nurture) work together.

Consider some of the findings in the literature. Bear in mind that these findings refer to averages and patterns, so it is always possible to discover individual uniqueness that deviates markedly from the norm. Some males will score above the average female with regard to nurturance, and some females will score above the average male with regard to aggressiveness. A warning is also in order as one examines the findings: *Christians ought to reject the biological determinism that some Christian literature tends to promote.* Even though biological factors predispose the average male or female in certain directions, God can overcome predispositions and tendencies.

Physiological differences between men and women include the following: Men generally have

- a faster basal metabolic rate.
- more muscle mass.
- denser, stronger bones, tendons, and ligaments.
- more sweat glands.
- a higher peripheral pain tolerance.

Women generally have

- a thicker layer of subcutaneous fat.
- a more acute sense of touch.
- a finer sense of perception.
- a more acute sense of hearing, taste, and smell.
- better color discrimination.[25]

These tendencies play into the universal pattern of woman as primary caregivers and child rearers and men as providers and protectors. In advanced technological societies like ours, however, gender differences that remain in our biology may be less important in defining appropriate roles.

Other interesting biological differences include a much larger amygdala in men—the brain center for aggressiveness. Men also are more responsive to external stimuli (food, sex, threats) because of testosterone-produced neurotransmitters in the brain.

Further studies indicate that men and women use communication very differently. Often men communicate to convey information and display knowledge. Women have a tendency to communicate to connect emotionally with other people. In Deborah Tannen's words, "Men tend to engage in *report* talk and women tend to engage in *rapport* talk."[26]

Experts have discovered many other interesting biological and sociological differences that could be cited in support of the simple proposition that men and women are biologically different. But anyone who has raised both a boy and a girl could probably have told us that without the benefit of the studies.

A friend of mine decided he and his wife were going to take a nonviolent, gender-neutral approach to raising their children. They chose not to give their son toy guns or toy swords, but instead to give him stuffed animals similar to ones they gave their daughter. They told me their son had turned every stuffed animal into a gun and was walking around the house shooting people with his teddy bear. Their daughter, on the other hand, was always trying to nurse the teddy bear, and she would rock it to sleep.

While gender differences are interesting and self-evident, it is the interpretation and application of these differences that sometimes get us into trouble. In some Christian books today about the roles of women, biological and sociological differences are cited to support the proposition that men are better suited for leadership in the church than women because of their created design. To me, this is simply nonsense. There is nothing in any of the current biological evidence that would suggest a role of leadership for men over women in the church.

While it is true that a larger amygdala in men (the brain center for aggressiveness) may explain why men gravitate toward competitiveness in life situations, it is not the case that competitiveness is necessarily a virtue for Christian leadership. Indeed, women's tendency toward cooperativeness may be closer to Jesus' ideal of servant leadership than the male tendency of one-upmanship. Nor is there anything in *report talking* rather than *rapport talking* that would incline one to believe that men are better suited for leadership than are women.

In short, biological differences may incline us toward different roles in early child rearing (I believe they do), but they should not incline us toward differing roles or destinies in the body of Christ. I am particularly disturbed when I read the arguments of certain conservative Christians that sound biologically deterministic. Does not our theology tell us that God is bigger than biology? An awareness of gender differences can be helpful in assisting men and women as they attempt to sort out child-rearing roles, especially in a society that gives no direction whatsoever to young married couples. But biological determinism is positively harmful and unchristian when it steals from women the revolutionary liberation that Jesus came to offer.

TALKING WITH A SECOND-WAVE FEMINIST, AND THE JEWISH PARALLEL

One of the major problems Christians have in getting a fair hearing for the claims of Christ is the association of Christianity with a negative personal experience in the past. As one who comes from a Jewish background, I can tell you that many Jews reject Jesus not

RAPE CRISIS CENTERS AND SECOND-WAVE FEMINISTS

According to the United States Department of Justice, somewhere in America a woman is raped every two minutes. In 1996, 307,000 women were victims of rape, attempted rape, or sexual assault. Much abuse against women and young children (both boys and girls) occurs within the family.

Most often it has been second-wave feminists who have raised the most vocal and practical opposition to violence against women and children, particularly domestic violence. It is generally second-wave feminists who run Rape Crisis hot lines around the country and who operate Rape Crisis Centers. Similarly, many second-wave feminists have raised money and operate shelters for battered women and their children.

Tori Amos, the singer-songwriter, who is herself a rape survivor, founded the Rape Abuse and Incest National Network (RAINN) and writes movingly about receiving a letter from a 13-year old girl in Paris whose stepfather had been molesting her for years. The girl wrote, "If I had known a phone number that would have been able to help me, I certainly would have dialed it. But I want you to never forget, Tori, that every day some other daughter loses their dignity!"[27]

because they've wrestled with the New Testament and dismissed it, but rather because of the pain they've experienced at the hands of those who claim to represent Christ.

In Auschwitz, Jews were led to gas chambers while their "Christian" guards celebrated Christmas and sang Christmas carols over the loudspeakers. Many Catholic priests and Lutheran pastors in Germany supported the Nazi regime or were silent in the face of massive persecution of Jews. During the Crusades, Jews were herded into synagogues by "Christian" crusaders and were burned alive. The catalog of crimes against Jews at the hands of Christians is a long one. The most basic task of a Christian who wants his or her Jewish friend to consider Jesus as the Jewish Messiah is to exorcise the demons of Christian-Jewish historical relations. Such an exorcism can begin to take place as a Christian frankly acknowledges the many problems that institutional Christianity has historically created. Cover-up or minimization of the church's sin simply bars the door to Jewish people's entrance into Christ's kingdom.

Along with this acknowledgment, a frank statement regarding the power of sin even in the Christian's life would be warranted.[28] You might say something like this to a Jewish friend:

> I want you to know that it's difficult for me to talk with you about the person who is most important to me, namely, Jesus. It's not because I'm embarrassed about him. I'm not. But I am, frankly, embarrassed about the way that we Christians have represented him. My little bit of reading about Christian-Jewish relations over the centuries causes me to want to hide my head in shame. Have you personally had any negative experiences at the hands of people who call themselves Christians?

This is the time to listen and not say anything.

If you come to find that a Jewish person has had a negative experience, you might say something like this:

> I am so sorry that that person who called himself a Christian represented Jesus so badly. I apologize on his behalf. I guess it points out to me the reality of what the Bible talks about regarding the power of sin in people's lives, even people who claim to have a relationship with God. For myself, I hope to represent my faith better to you than what you've experienced in the past.

I don't know any Jewish person who would not be touched by that honest display of humility regarding one's Christian faith.

The reason I briefly discuss historic Christian-Jewish relations is because many of the same kinds of issues exist between Christians and women. In short, for many women, Christianity represents a nearly unbroken history of patriarchy and oppression. It does no good to merely point out all of the benefits brought to women by the church. Such a discussion may come later, once the air is cleared. At the front end, I've found it extremely helpful to frankly acknowledge that the church has done a horrendous job in modeling the love of Jesus toward women.

After confession, I try to talk about the way that Jesus interacted with women, based on my own research of the Scriptures (you may want to review the chapter titled "Was Jesus a Feminist?"). This typically solicits a lot of interest. Moreover, I've been able to defuse some of the hostility that women have toward the church by pointing to the treatment of women in the church I pastor. The relationship of women and the church (in particular, the roles that are open to women in the church) is the subject of the next chapter.

Questions for Reflection and Discussion
?

1. Are you personally aware of the demeaning of the roles of wife and mother by second-wave feminists? How would you counsel a young married pregnant woman about God's will for her life?

2. Consider the evidence that the author presents regarding the negative effects of divorce and fatherlessness on children. How can these findings be shared in a way that doesn't cause despair to a single parent?

3. Does your life experience confirm or deny the significant biological differences between men and women? How would you translate these differences into appropriate family or work roles for men and women?

4. Have you considered the issue of the negative historical association of Christianity and an oppressed group? How can this awareness help you in your witness?

RECOMMENDED READING

Davidson, Nicholas. *The Failure of Feminism.* Buffalo, N.Y.: Prometheus, 1988.

Grenz, Stanley R., and Roger Olsen. *20th-Century Theology.* Downers Grove, Ill.: InterVarsity Press, 1992.

Roe, Earl O. *Dream Big: The Henrietta Mears Story.* Ventura, Calif.: Regal, 1990.

Sommers, Christina Hoff. *Who Stole Feminism?: How Women Have Betrayed Women.* New York: Simon & Schuster, 1994.

Whitehead, Barbara Dafoe. *The Divorce Culture.* New York: Knopf, 1996.

7

What Roles Are Open to Women in the Church?

I taught business law at a state university that used to be visited by an open-air preacher and his wife. His wife wore high-collared, long-sleeved dresses that went down to her ankles, even on hot summer days. She looked like someone who would have been out of fashion in the 1890s! She never spoke publicly, but rather nodded approvingly when her husband finished his tirade about modern women with the statement, "My wife always submits to me. I don't respect any man whose wife doesn't submit to him in everything!" It would be impossible to overestimate the hostile reaction of the crowd, both male and female, to this preacher and his wife. I was literally heartbroken as I watched these two individuals reinforce prejudices against Christianity that already existed in the media-saturated minds of the students in attendance.

Sadly, prejudice against Christianity gets reinforced by the activities and practices of local churches and denominations. When a major denomination was reported to have allowed a woman to address its convention from the floor but not from the platform, what message is sent to women across America? Is it not that Christianity considers women to be inferior to men and permits women to speak to men only from a position literally lower than the position accorded to men?

One of the major stumbling blocks in the relationship of the church and feminists is the position taken by many churches that women may not be ordained or serve in the role of senior pastor.

WOMEN IN THE CHURCH

While whole forests may not have been felled in generating books and articles on the roles women should play in the church, the logging industry has been kept busy, as have most denominational conventions, concerning this controversial issue.

The most widely debated Scripture passage regarding women's roles in the church is found in 1 Timothy 2:9–15.

> I also want women to dress modestly, with decency and propriety, not with braided hair or gold or pearls or expensive clothes, but with good deeds, appropriate for women who profess to worship God.
>
> A woman should learn in quietness and full submission. I do not permit a woman to teach or to have authority over a man; she must be silent. For Adam was formed first, then Eve. And Adam was not the one deceived; it was the woman who was deceived and became a sinner. But women will be saved through childbearing—if they continue in faith, love and holiness with propriety.

THE PLAIN MEANING APPROACH

Many people wonder, Why not just obey the plain meaning of 1 Timothy 2:12, where the apostle Paul said, "I do not permit a woman to teach or to have authority over a man; she must be silent"? Does not allowing women to teach or lead men in church signal a compromise with the feminist spirit of our age and an unwillingness to hold on to God's clear Word despite its unpopularity?

Yet consider a couple of challenges. It is not at all plain what Paul meant to communicate to his original readers, plus it is even less plain how Paul's words should be applied today.[1] I know of no text that has been more variously interpreted than this one. My files include at least fifteen very different interpretations of 1 Timothy 2, and I have a bookshelf of books on the subject that fall far short of being exhaustive.[2]

The fundamental issue is simply this: Does 1 Timothy 2:9–15 create a *universal* prohibition against women teaching and leading men, or is it merely *specific* counsel given by the apostle Paul for a particular church situation?

Another basic challenge with this text (apart from the challenge we have of applying first-century social roles to third-millennium urban settings) is lack of agreement regarding the correct translation of many words. For example, "I do not permit a woman to teach or to *have authority over* a man" (1 Timothy 2:12, emphasis added). That little phrase "have authority over" is one possible translation of the Greek word *authentein.* Unfortunately, this Greek word is used nowhere else in the New Testament. Some scholars say it refers to *any* exercise of authority or leadership by a woman over a man in the church. Other scholars say that the word *authentein* means "to domineer" or "to usurp authority from" a man. In other words, what is prohibited is a domineering use of authority. The problem is that the connotation of the word *authentein* changed from classical Greek usage (where it meant to "domineer over") to the time of the church fathers (where it meant merely "to have authority over"). We simply don't have enough information regarding what Paul meant, based on the word's contemporary usage in the New Testament era, to conclusively state what the plain meaning of *authentein* is.

Exactly what is the meaning of the word *silent?* "I do not permit a woman to teach or to have authority over a man; she must be *silent*" (1 Timothy 2:12, emphasis added). Some scholars say that a woman, according to this text, must be absolutely silent in the church, to have no vocalization other than, perhaps, to sing. Others would permit a woman to pray or to prophesy (à la 1 Corinthians 11), but would not permit a woman to teach or exhort a man. Still other scholars say that "silent" is a very bad translation of the Greek word *hēsychia* and insist that this Greek word instead suggests having a "quiet spirit" or learning with a "respectful attitude"—so that what is being enjoined here is learning in meekness before one presumes to correct a teacher, and not being absolutely silent in church.

Finally, no one agrees about the plain meaning of 1 Timothy 2:15: "But women will be saved through childbearing—if they continue in faith, love and holiness with propriety." Other translations read: "But women will be saved through the birth of the child (not through childbearing, but the birth of the Child—meaning that women will be saved through the birth of the Christ-child.)[3] Thus, this second translation would suggest that through the Man born of woman (Christ), women (and men) will be saved.

In keeping with the first translation, a few scholars suggest that the verse's background is the Jewish myth that women were particularly susceptible to demonic attacks during childbirth. Paul was thus merely giving a word of assurance to Christian women that they (through faith) would be "saved"—protected from demonic attacks during childbirth. A modification of this view is that women will be "saved" or protected from the curse of Eve, namely, difficult childbirth, by their faith. Others suggest that women will be saved as long as they adopt the role appropriate to them, namely, childbirth and domesticity. To summarize, there is no common agreement on what these individual words mean in 1 Timothy 2:9–15.

As we attempt to apply 1 Timothy 2 to third-millennium urban settings, it's important to remember that the New Testament opened doors of opportunity to women. First Timothy 2 is the *only* explicit teaching that seems to restrict a woman's capacity to teach or lead men in the church.[4] Women are given the gift of the Spirit and are called to prophesy under the new covenant.[5] Women are found laboring alongside Paul—women, such as Priscilla, actually instructing male teachers (Acts 18). Have you noticed that Priscilla is usually mentioned before her husband (husbands at that time, like today, were generally mentioned before their wives)? Priscilla was probably the more prominent leader of the two, and she is called a "fellow worker" with Paul.[6]

In a much-debated text in Romans 16:7, another woman named Junia is classed as an apostle.[7] Indeed, in Romans 16, women are commended nearly twice as often as men for working hard in the Lord.[8] Euodia and Syntyche were apparently women who labored with Paul in the gospel.[9]

WHY SO FEW BIBLICAL EXAMPLES?

Some people are troubled by the rarity of examples in the Bible of women leading men, and thus conclude that it is normative for men to lead, while allowing for some exceptions in unusual circumstances. Seminary professor Craig Keener intelligently responds to the notion that, because most leaders in the Bible were men, most leaders in the church today should be men:

> This position has two serious weaknesses. First, it fails to take into account cultural conditions that anyone who observes the modern church would have to take into account today. If the percentage of a given gender (or race, culture, etc.) in one period should determine the norm for all periods, some other periods of church history leave men (and certain races, cultures, etc.) in a rather bad light. Many of the mission fields opened in the late nineteenth and early twentieth centuries were pioneered by single women; does that mean men are less capable missionaries, able only to take over after women have done the initial work? . . .
>
> The second problem with the view that male dominance in certain areas means that those are exclusively male areas is that its logic is severely distorted. No one would argue this analogy to make other points: for instance, to say that a certain mission field is dominated by Baptists, but includes a few Christian and Missionary Alliance workers is not the same as saying that this field *ought* to include only Baptists.
>
> Is it not possible that even today, the fact that men outnumber women in many ministries in the church is due, in part, to the limitations we have placed on women? . . . Perhaps some percentages remain skewed in

the body of Christ only due to unequal opportunity. If so, justice as well as faithfulness to the Lord of the harvest demands that we find ways to make opportunities more widely available.[10]

THE PLAIN MEANING RULE AND ITS APPLICATION PROBLEMS

Many Christians read the Bible without any sensitivity to cultural differences. Perhaps you've seen the bumper sticker that reads, "If the Bible says it, then I believe it, and that settles it!" But the Bible enjoins many things that we don't necessarily do because of differences in culture. For example, Paul commands women in the church at Corinth to wear head coverings.[11] Yet, most churches today (even the most traditional ones) don't require women to wear head coverings. Paul goes on to say that "if anyone wants to be contentious about this, we have no other practice—nor do the churches of God."[12] Apparently, head coverings were worn not only in Corinth, but in other Pauline churches as well.

On five different occasions the New Testament commands Christian men to greet each other with a kiss.[13] Yet, while men in Christian churches will often hug each other, it is very rare, especially in America, for men to follow the explicit teaching of Scripture by kissing each other.

We must admit that we all read the Bible with the understanding that New Testament culture is different from ours. Not every single statement is meant to be transcultural or universal in its application to all circumstances. Missiologists have talked for years about the principle of "contextualization," which says that one must analyze the *why* behind scriptural commands as well as the *what*. The *what*, namely, the specific practice, may change over time. The *why* is often transcultural and universal. Once we discover the "why," we can then apply the unique restrictions found in 1 Timothy 2 to a cultural situation vastly different from first-century Ephesus, namely, twenty-first–century Western society.

Not only is the meaning of 1 Timothy 2 not plain, however, but neither is the application. The most conservative perspective of 1 Timothy states that no woman may teach or lead any man above the age of puberty. Women can serve, pray, prophesy (in charismatic churches), teach other women, and teach boys—but they cannot teach a Sunday school class where there are teenage boys or men present, if their teaching involves "authoritative teaching" or is an exercise of church leadership. In many conservative churches, women may also not be ordained or exercise authoritative leadership over any male in the church who is a teenager or an adult. (This view has been variously labeled as "complementarian," "traditionalist," or "hierarchicalist." I've chosen the label "complementarian," but would not object to one of the other labels.)

As mentioned previously, some have suggested that any kind of compromise regarding a woman's restricted role in the church is simply accommodation to the feminist spirit of the age. But trying to analyze the motives of a person with whom one disagrees is a game that two can play. Perhaps the *refusal* to allow women to teach and the most complementarian interpretations of this text are simply the results of knee-jerk, reactionary chauvinism. Perhaps some men squeeze this text (1 Timothy 2) for all its worth in order to maintain male power and to bolster their sagging male self-esteem. Perhaps their insecurity leads them to be domineering. Of course, these charges are quite unfair, as is the complementarian charge that any alternative explanation of 1 Timothy 2:12 is a covert attempt to accommodate the feminist spirit of the age. We must get beyond name-calling and suspicion of motives in the church.

Yet even among those who have taken a highly complementarian position regarding women's roles in ministry, one can find grave inconsistencies in their actual practices that eventually eat up the rule. For example, some conservative churches forbid women from teaching, but allow them to "share insights" for thirty minutes from the Bible, with appropriate illustrations. Other churches allow certain kinds of teaching, for example, teaching in a conference setting but not on Sunday morning, or they allow teaching on marriage but not on doctrine. Still others permit women to teach on any topic as long as she is "submitted to a male leader as her head." Of course, nothing in this text requires it or permits it as an exception to Paul's rule.

Most often the inconsistency takes place on the mission field. If, indeed, Paul is announcing a universal rule that prohibits all women from teaching all men, then how can churches justify women preaching the gospel and instructing men in other nations, while not allowing them to do the same here? Many missions were pioneered in the nineteenth and twentieth centuries by women. Western churches are left open to the charge of implicit racism ("It's OK for people of other nations to be taught by women, but not OK for women to teach men in the civilized West!").

Finally some complementarian scholars say that women are allowed to *teach*, but they may not *lead* men by becoming an elder or senior pastor of a church. This position seems to be difficult to maintain as a matter of sound interpretation, since nothing suggests that the emphasis of Paul's prohibition falls more heavily on leading than on teaching. The attempt to separate teaching and leading is, in my mind, the least tenable exegetically.[14] One must choose between either the universal rule of no teaching and no leading of men or the view that Paul's restriction was due to a local first-century problem and is therefore inapplicable today.

EGALITARIAN POSITIONS: WOMEN MAY TEACH AND LEAD IN THE CHURCH TODAY

A whole range of opinions can be given why 1 Timothy 2:9–15 was not meant to be a universal prohibition against all women teaching or having authority over all men in all cultures for all time, but instead should be restricted to its immediate audience—the church in Ephesus in the first century A.D. Some would simply dismiss Paul's counsel here as being wrong or irrelevant because of the influence of his patriarchal culture. But this is not a viable position for an evangelical Christian who regards the biblical canon as authoritative.

WHO WAS HENRIETTA MEARS?

Dr. Henrietta Mears was called by Campus Crusade founder Bill Bright "one of the great women of the twentieth century and one of the greatest influences of my life. She directly discipled thousands of young men and women, whom God led into full-time ministry." Evangelist Billy Graham called Henrietta Mears "one of the greatest Christians I have ever known!"

Who was this extraordinary woman? Dr. Mears came from a rich spiritual heritage that went back several generations. Her father was an extraordinary man. Henrietta's mother once said about her husband, "If the Bible says that every man who bridleth his tongue is a perfect man, then your father is a perfect man. I have never heard him say an unkind word."

In tribute to Henrietta's mother, Dr. W. B. Riley, minister of the First Baptist Church of Minneapolis, Minnesota, wrote the following: "As a Bible teacher she had few equals in the city of Minneapolis. And in 'the practice of the presence of God' she had no superiors. Like Martin Luther of old, one and two hours a day she spent upon her knees." At the funeral of Mrs. Mears, Dr. Riley turned to Henrietta Mears and said, "I hope the spiritual mantle of your mother will fall upon you." It certainly did.

In 1928, when Henrietta Mears became director of Christian education at the First Presbyterian Church of Hollywood, California, they had 450 people enrolled. In two and a half years, the enrollment grew to 4,200. She demanded the very best of the Sunday school teachers who worked under her leadership. Henrietta also began Gospel Light Press as a publisher of Sunday school curriculum, the first Sunday school publisher to provide graded Bible lessons.

But her major impact was as a beloved teacher of college students. As a direct result of her teaching, over 400 young men and women went into full-time Christian service. Among them were Bill Bright, founder of Campus Crusade for Christ; Richard Halverson, chaplain of the United States Senate; and Paul Carlson, a missionary martyred in Africa.

Henrietta Mears also founded Gospel Light International, which helps missionaries with their Christian education literature needs, and founded the Forest Home Christian Conference Center, a camp at which thousands of young men and women made decisions for Christ. Forest Home was the camp at which Billy Graham settled his doubts about God's Word once and for all and dedicated himself to proclaim God's Word and "turn sinners to the Savior."

If Henrietta Mears had been restricted from teaching or leading men, millions may have gone to a Christ-less eternity not having experienced her ministry.[15]

Some opposed to the universal application of 1 Timothy 2 claim to have found evidence of a feminist cult operative in Ephesus, which involved the worship of various goddesses. By means of this text, some suggest, Paul was merely attempting to stamp out this feminist-cult teaching that had become popular in the Ephesian church among many women. Opinions vary wildly regarding whether evidence exists for the existence of this feminist cult in Ephesus at that time. My friend Wayne Grudem, a theologian, suggests that no external evidence exists of a feminist cult operating in Ephesus at the time of the writing of 1 Timothy, so how do we know that the apostle Paul was linking his prohibition to that particular problem? Moreover, if evidence external to the text can so radically alter the meaning of a text, then what hope does any nonscholar have of reading a biblical text accurately?

Other scholars believe that this text resulted from the social position of women in the first century. Women were not permitted to teach or to have authority because they were unlearned. What Paul was doing then was not *prohibiting* something so much as *permitting* women to learn. For these scholars 1 Timothy 2:11 is the key verse: "A woman should *learn* in quietness and full submission" (emphasis added). In other words, until a woman *learns*, she should not presume to be a teacher. This view, in my opinion, has some merit. Remember, many first-century rabbis considered it a sin to teach Torah to women. Thus, rather than being a restriction, Paul is actually contradicting contemporary rabbinical opinion and opening the door for women to learn.

Most convincing is the perspective that takes into account all of the Pastoral writings; it is probably best represented by the well-respected biblical scholar Gordon Fee.[16] Fee, along with many other scholars, states that the overall purpose of 1 and 2 Timothy was to combat false teaching. For example, we read in 1 Timothy 1:3–4: "As I urged you when I went into Macedonia, stay there in Ephesus so that you may command certain men not to teach false doctrines any longer, nor to devote themselves to myths and endless genealogies." First and 2 Timothy were written to direct Timothy to stamp out false teaching, because, it would seem, false teachers had infiltrated the church. Many influential women were listening to this false teaching and spreading it throughout the church like a virus:

> They [the false teachers] are the kind who worm their way into homes and gain control over weak-willed women, who are loaded down with sins and are swayed by all kinds of evil desires, always learning but never able to acknowledge the truth. Just as Jannes and Jambres opposed Moses, so also these men oppose the truth—men of depraved minds, who, as far as the faith is concerned, are rejected. But they will not get very far because, as in the case of those men, their folly will be clear to everyone.[17]

Because the women in the Ephesian church had become the carriers of this false teaching, Paul addressed them in 1 Timothy 5:13: "They get into the habit of being idle and going about from house to house. And not only do they become idlers, but also *gossips* and busybodies saying things they ought not to" (emphasis added). Fee suggests that "gossip" is a poor translation for this Greek word (*phlyaros*). The word is better translated "to talk foolishness," and it was mainly used in philosophical texts in the ancient Greek world to convey the idea "to communicate false teaching."

Against the backdrop of this threat of spreading false teaching through gullible women in the church, we must read Paul's prohibition to these Ephesian women, when he said, in effect, "I don't want you to teach, but instead to learn in silence."

Paul's argument is strengthened by his reasoning in 1 Timothy 2:14: "And Adam was not the one deceived; it was the woman who was deceived and became a sinner." What Paul was *not* saying is that women are inherently more deceivable or, as has sometimes been suggested, that women are always the source of heresy or Christian cults. Rather, following his chief concern, Paul argued that just as Eve became the one through whom false teaching spread to the man, so women in the Ephesian church are now the vehicle through whom false teaching is spreading. In other words, as Eve opened the door to Satan, women in the Ephesian church have become the open door to demonic teaching and therefore must be silenced.

ADAM CREATED BEFORE EVE?

Many complementarian scholars argue that the prohibition against women teaching or leading men is a transcultural prohibition that flows from Paul's reasoning in 1 Timothy 2:13: "For Adam was formed first, then Eve." He appeals to the example of Adam and Eve as an appeal to creation that is universal. Because a man (Adam) was created first, it is argued that men at *all* times and in *all* places and in *all* situations should teach and lead. Women, whatever their qualifications and education, should never teach or lead a man, because a woman (Eve) was created after a man.

Did Paul mean for us to have a practice in twenty-first–century churches that would promote less qualified men above more qualified and gifted women because this honors God's plan in creation?

I don't think Paul intended for us to adopt this utterly illogical perspective, because nothing in the creation account (Genesis 2) suggests that women necessarily were subordinate to men. Craig

Keener observes, "The Hebrew phrase 'helper suitable for him' (Genesis 2:20) denotes a role of strength ('helper' usually refers to God in the Hebrew Bible), and 'suitable' may mean 'corresponding to' or 'equal to' (so that the woman is not viewed as a superior helper like God, nor as an unmatched creation like the animals)."[18]

Along with Keener, I do not believe that Paul twisted Scripture to make his point, as some who dismiss Paul's reasoning have argued. A possible interpretation may spring from the principle of *primogeniture*. Paul may be arguing that women should not lead or teach (there in Ephesus), because men have the right of the firstborn to lead. In ancient Israel (as in many ancient cultures), the firstborn son had certain inheritance rights. Since man was born before woman, Paul might be arguing that men had the right of the firstborn.

But even if Paul was referring (albeit obscurely) to some principle of primogeniture, God frequently overrules the cultural laws of primogeniture. In many Old Testament contexts, those born first did not always have priority in God's plan. Jacob, for example, was given leadership over his firstborn brother, Esau. Isaac was given leadership over his firstborn brother, Ishmael. And David was given leadership over his older brothers. The rule of primogeniture, therefore, doesn't have to lead us to the conclusion that women ought never to lead in a church.

I think the most likely explanation is that Paul was making an *ad hoc* argument that he perhaps did not entirely fill out. Perhaps the Ephesian women were poorly educated in the church and (like Eve) were dependent on the men for teaching. The argument would go like this: "Eve depended on Adam for instruction regarding God's will, so you Ephesian women, likewise, must depend on your male leaders for instruction." Rather than making a transcultural argument, Paul was arguing *ad hoc,* using the Adam and Eve story for illustrative purposes only.

How Can We Summarize?

First, much debate has been stirred among sincere scholars regarding the true meaning of 1 Timothy 2:9–15, both in the appropriate translation of the passage and also in its interpretation and application. Many true brothers and sisters in Christ who are godly, learned, and sincere, differ on these matters. I, for one, find some complementarian views based on the supposed plain meaning of the text to fall short in their persuasiveness.

Second, the entire New Testament seems to be tilted toward giving women opportunities consistent with their gifting and calling before God. We see this in Jesus' practice and attitude toward women, in Paul's partnership with women leaders, and in such texts as Galatians 3:28: "There is neither Jew nor Greek, slave nor free, male nor female, for you are all one in Christ Jesus." The New Testament offers multiple liberating calls to women from the ways in which cultures have historically classified people. If 1 Timothy 2 is read as a universal restriction for all time on all women, despite their gifts or individual callings by God, then it stands entirely alone. I choose to read it in a manner congruent with the rest of the New Testament and to treat it as addressing a local problem in a first-century church. My conclusion is that women may teach and lead in the church today.

Third, refusing to read 1 Timothy 2:9–15 as a universal ban on women teaching or leading men in all situations for all time does not mean that we can call into question every divine command whenever the culture determines that it is no longer fashionable. A clear line of distinction falls between the *moral prohibitions* of the Bible and those pertaining to our *social relationships*. When the Bible calls something sin, it is always sin for everyone, everywhere, for all time. Homosexual sex, adultery, and premarital sex will always remain sin, despite the frequency of their practice in contemporary culture. It doesn't matter how much the culture shifts, the practice of sex outside of heterosexual marriage should always be rejected by biblical Christians.

Whether women should be in leadership or teach men, however, is not in the category of a *moral* command. If it were, God would not violate his own standards by ever allowing a woman to lead or to teach a man. God never violates his own holiness. But, without condemnation, the Bible does portray women teaching and leading men. While instances of women leading are admittedly rare in the Old and New Testament context, we do find clear examples of women leading with God's approval. Deborah led the nation of Israel as its judge and senior leader.[19] Huldah, a prophetess, provided leadership during the time of the divided monarchy, as she was sought out by King Josiah for counsel concerning the Book of the Law.[20] There is little doubt that Priscilla was a leader in the church.[21]

Don't fear we're teetering on a slippery slope if we say that certain commandments in the New Testament may not be universally applicable, but may be culturally relative. As I said earlier, everyone reads the New Testament that way; otherwise we men would greet each other with kisses, as the Bible commands five times.[22] All of us draw lines regarding social relations; otherwise we would insist that women never cut their hair or that they continue to wear veils today.[23]

But in my opinion, 1 Timothy 2 does *not* raise a transcultural barrier to women in either teaching or senior leadership in the church. Its prohibitions were designed for a particular church, namely, Ephesus, at a particular moment in history, namely, the first century.

THE PROMOTION OF THE GOSPEL

I must raise one reservation with regard to a thoroughly unrestricted practice of women teaching or leading men. This concerns the promotion of the gospel. I believe (along with Gordon Fee and many others) that the controlling principle behind 1 Timothy 2, as well as behind other Pauline commands about social relations, is the *promotion of the gospel*. Paul regularly called on people to limit their freedom in order to not hinder the spread of the gospel. Paul, for example, told women in Titus 2 to "be busy at home" and to take on certain domestic roles. Why? Is it meant to bar women from ever having a career or a ministry outside the home? Not at all. Rather, Paul's reason for requiring domesticity of women was "so that no one will malign the word of God."[24] In much the same way, Paul commanded slaves to obey their masters in Titus 2:9. Why? Because he approved of slavery and wanted this institution perpetuated forever? Of course not! He commanded slaves to be subject to their masters in order to "make the teaching about God our Savior attractive."[25] The promotion of the gospel was and remains the supreme criterion for judging behavior, according to the apostle Paul.

Paul commanded the Corinthians not to eat meat offered to idols so that they wouldn't put a stumbling block in someone's way regarding the gospel.[26] He similarly told people to give up their right to sue each other so that they wouldn't bring any shame to the gospel.[27] The promotion and reputation of the gospel undergird this particular text in 1 Timothy. If the gospel was at risk of being hindered, then Paul had no problem saying to a woman, "At this particular time, in this particular context, I want you to take on this role and not that one."

But Paul could be exceptionally flexible in different cultural settings regarding people's social relationships, as long as the gospel wasn't being hindered. He had coworkers who were women, and he let women teach men in different contexts. He often observed that women were a great value to him in spreading the gospel among men. Women even apparently exercised leadership in some of Paul's churches.[28]

The New Testament message to women concerning leadership roles in the church could be summarized as follows: "There is no biblical prohibition against you teaching or leading in the church. *All roles* are open to you, including those of senior pastor and elder, *if you are gifted and called by God.* But the role you choose depends on the culture you live in and whether your exercise of leadership or teaching would promote or hinder the gospel." To promote the gospel, the New Testament would permit enormous liberty, for example, in a university town or in a third-millennium Western urban area. In fact, the gospel would be hindered if it were communicated to twenty-first–century women that they were automatically barred from roles of leadership or authoritative teaching simply because of their gender. Social relations are cultural clothing that can change, but the gospel never changes!

On the other hand, if a woman exercised her God-given liberty in a village in India or in the Muslim world where the liberating message of Christianity has not penetrated and worked for generations, this would create a great stumbling block to the gospel. For the sake of the gospel, the New Testament would teach, "If you are working in India or in a Muslim culture, you women must limit your liberty."

A dear American friend of mine allowed herself to be veiled from head to toe while she was living as a missionary in Pakistan. Did she have God-given liberty to wear jeans and a T-shirt, as she did in the United States? Of course! Would it have been beneficial for the spread of the gospel? Absolutely not. She voluntarily took on a culturally restricted role so that the gospel would be promoted. Of course, men must do the same thing! The apostle Paul voluntarily gave up his right to financial support from the Corinthians in order to promote the gospel.[29]

A rule based on calling, gifts, and cultural acceptability is obviously a far more challenging rule than a so-called "plain meaning" rule based on a narrow reading of a lone biblical text. But the New Testament is not a rulebook on the exact manner for carrying out social relations in every culture. We need the ongoing leadership of the Holy Spirit to find our way through. What is appropriate in a university setting may not be appropriate in rural England. What is appropriate among 20-year-olds may not fit with 70-year-olds.

In a time of enormous cultural transition, we need great discernment to work these things out in practice. But the New Testament contains a strong note of liberation that operates in sharp contradistinction to all of the prevailing cultural attitudes toward women throughout the history of the world. In contrast to those attitudes, Jesus and the apostle Paul never made fun of women, never treated them as inferior, never patronized them, never said they were less competent or less intelligent than men. Women are given enormous liberty, a liberty found in the gift of the Holy Spirit. Women and men are equally gifted, and there is no biblical prohibition against a woman being called to any role in the church whatsoever.

But for the sake of the gospel, in certain settings, in certain places, at certain times, a woman might voluntarily limit her freedom because she loves Jesus more than she loves her right to exercise a certain role. In so doing, she follows the path of her Lord, who laid down his life in order to save the world.

AN APPEAL TO FELLOW PASTORS AND LEADERS

If you are convinced by the argument that women may be called by God to teach and lead, then I believe you must do more than simply wait for a woman to rise to the occasion. In other words, more is demanded of church leadership than simply a shrug of the shoulders and a perspective that says, "Women in our church are free to teach or lead. We simply don't have any women who desire to do that at this point." Because the teaching and leadership of men historically have not been options in many churches, many women simply read God's will through the lenses of the options that are available. It would be unusual for a woman who has excluded herself from the possibility of senior leadership in the church to be able to hear God calling her clearly to such a position.

Let me share with you my personal experience in this regard. As I have taught in seminars and in my own church about the Bible's liberating word to women, I have had many women (some of them in tears) say to me, "I've always struggled with the prevailing teaching about women in the church. Internally, I felt like I had something to offer. I felt God tugging me to teach or to lead. But I've always felt torn because I was told that this wasn't God's will. As a result, I've questioned myself a thousand times, wondering whether I was just selfishly ambitious or full of pride. You don't know how many times I've gone back over what I thought God was saying to me and doubted my ability to hear him."

I make an appeal with all my heart to fellow pastors and leaders: Do not allow women in your congregation to spend years wrestling like this—wondering whether they are full of pride and selfish ambition because they feel called to leadership or teaching. If you believe that the Bible does not prohibit women from leading or teaching, then boldly say so. Bless women in your congregations. Affirm their gifts. Actively work to promote them in various roles.

In your messages, use women as examples of leaders. In other words, don't just wait for a courageous woman to emerge. Look around the congregation for women who can be promoted. In so doing, you will be providing "a ministry of welcome" to all women and, in particular, to women of a feminist persuasion. And you will be following the path of your Lord, about whom Dorothy Sayers wrote, "Perhaps it was no wonder that women were first at the Cradle and last at the Cross. They had never known a man like this Man. There never has been such another."[30] Two millennia is enough time for women to meet other men who are like that Man.

Questions for Reflection and Discussion

?

1. According to the author, what aspects of 1 Timothy 2:9–15 are not plain? Does it trouble you that parts of Scripture are difficult to understand?

2. Are you aware of church practices we take for granted that have no biblical warrant? What might be some examples? Are you aware of biblical commands that almost no one in Bible-believing churches obeys? What might be some examples?

3. Have you seen inconsistencies between the teaching of your (or another) church or denomination regarding the role of women and its actual practice? How have you responded to the inconsistency?

4. Do you agree with the author's distinction between moral commands on the one hand and commands about social relationships on the other? Why or why not?

5. How would you counsel a woman who felt called to preach and lead regarding God's will for her life?

RECOMMENDED READING

Beck, James R., and Craig L. Blomberg. *Two Views on Women in Ministry.* Grand Rapids: Zondervan, 2001.

Grenz, Stanley J., with Denise Muir Kjesbo. *Women in the Church.* Downers Grove, Ill.: InterVarsity Press, 1995.

Grudem, Wayne, and John Piper, eds. *Recovering Biblical Manhood and Womanhood.* Wheaton, Ill.: Crossway, 1991.

Hurley, James B. *Man and Woman in Biblical Perspective.* Grand Rapids: Zondervan, 1981.

Keener, Craig S. *Paul, Women and Wives.* Peabody, Mass.: Hendrickson, 1992.

Tucker, Ruth. *Women in the Maze.* Downers Grove, Ill.: InterVarsity Press, 1992.

Williams, Don. *The Apostle Paul and Women in the Church.* Glendale, Calif.: Regal, 1977.

Witherington III, Ben. *Women in the Earliest Church.* Cambridge: Cambridge Univ. Press, 1988.

Part 3

Is the Homosexual My Enemy?

8

Judgment, Tolerance, and the Spread of Gay Rights

Matthew Shepard, a 21-year-old foreign-language student, wanted to become a diplomat. Toward that end, he attended the University of Wyoming in Laramie, a town where pickup trucks outnumber sport-utility vehicles and the start of the hunting season is celebrated by thousands of local hunters. Although Matt was short in stature (a mere 5'2"), he was tall in his language abilities, speaking both Arabic and German.

On the night of October 6, 1998, he sat down in a bar to have a beer when two men came up to talk. When Matt indicated that he was gay, the two men, Aaron McKinney and Russell Henderson, said they were gay also. Apparently they posed as homosexuals in order to lure Mr. Shepard out to Mr. McKinney's pickup truck. Once inside the truck, McKinney and Russell beat Matt, drove him to an isolated area of town, tied him to a fence, and pistol-whipped him with a .357 magnum handgun while he begged for his life. (Matt Shepard's relatives said he also suffered burns on his body.) After nearly beating him to death, McKinney and Russell stole his wallet and shoes and left him tied to the fence.

Eighteen hours later a passing bicyclist saw Matt Shepard's crumpled form lashed to the fence, but thought he was a scarecrow.

When he stopped, he found Matt's burned, battered, and nearly lifeless body. Matt Shepard died of his injuries five days later. His two assailants were tried and convicted of felony murder, aggravated robbery, and kidnapping. Both were sentenced to two consecutive life terms in prison without the possibility of parole.[1]

"There is incredible symbolism about being tied to a fence," said Rebecca Isaacs, political director of the National Gay and Lesbian Task Force in Washington. "People have likened it to a scarecrow. But it sounded more like a crucifixion."[2]

ACT-UP PROTEST AT ST. PATRICK'S CATHEDRAL

In the fall of 1989, several thousand AIDS and abortion-rights activists held a noisy demonstration outside St. Patrick's Cathedral in New York. Several dozen activists entered the cathedral to disrupt a Sunday worship service being conducted by Cardinal O'Connor, throwing condoms in the air, chaining themselves to pews, and screaming, "Stop killing us! Stop killing us! We're not going to take it anymore!" Placards read, "The cardinal lies to his parishioners," "Cardinal O'Connor won't teach safe sex," and, "Stop the murderous AIDS policy." Apart from the disruption of the mass, the protest was particularly infamous because of an incident in which a protestor smashed a communion wafer and ground it into the floor. This outraged many Roman Catholics, who believe the wafer to be the literal body of Jesus Christ.

GAY PRIDE PARADE IN NEW YORK

Gay pride parades have become annual events in most large cities in America. The parades began in 1969 as acts of defiance, but have become commercialized in the past several years. In San Francisco, the Budweiser Clydesdales parade among the marchers. In West Hollywood, more than 350,000 people participated in a two-day-long, twenty-eighth annual Gay and Lesbian Pride Festival. The West Hollywood gay pride parade is California's third largest annual parade behind the Rose Bowl Parade and the Santa Claus Lane Parade.

In June 2000, an editor for the *National Review* covered a gay pride parade in New York City and wrote a graphic description of what he saw and heard as the floats passed by. One float was sponsored by the Hellfire Club. Others included people whose behavior and appearance seemed designed to be cringe-inducing. One can't help but think of the words of the apostle Paul, who described the darkened human heart and mind this way: "Having lost all sensitivity, they have given themselves over to sensuality so as to indulge in every kind of impurity, with a continual lust for more."[3]

MASSACHUSETTS COURT RULES THAT A MIDDLE SCHOOL MAY NOT PROHIBIT A BOY FROM DRESSING LIKE A GIRL IN SCHOOL

In Brockton, Massachusetts, a fifteen-year-old boy identified himself as a girl and won a court case that would allow him to wear girl's clothing to school. In the case, brought by the Gay and Lesbian Advocates and Defenders (GLAD) on behalf of this fifteen-year-old student who was born male but claims to have a female gender identity, the court ruled that disciplining a biologically male student for wearing girl's clothing would violate "her" First Amendment right of free expression and constitutes sexual discrimination. According to GLAD's staff attorney Jennifer Levi, "This case confirms that a school may not exert its authority over a student simply to enforce stereotyped ideas of how boys and girls should look. Nor can a school's discomfort with the fact that a biologically male student has a female gender identity, justify enforcing a dress code in a discriminatory way."

The boy began wearing women's clothing and makeup to school in 1999 when he was in seventh grade. Sometimes the clothing included tight skirts and high-heeled shoes, and at one semi-formal dance a "slinky" black dress. This caused confrontations, school officials said. The boy was repeatedly sent home to change.

In court, school officials acknowledged that female students who dressed similarly were neither disciplined nor barred from attending. The school claimed that the boy was often disruptive in school. He would dance and yell in the halls, which they viewed as trying to draw attention to himself. Once he sparked a confrontation by blowing kisses at a male student. On another occasion he grabbed a male student's buttocks.

School administrators all the way up to the district superintendent believed they gave him every consideration, but they had to consider the educational needs of hundreds of other students as well. The Massachusetts Superior Court strongly disagreed, writing that "for her" wearing women's clothes is "not merely a personal preference, but a necessary symbol of her very identity." And to force her to do otherwise would mean "the stifling of a person's selfhood merely because it causes some members of the community discomfort."

"Rather than damaging the educational interests of other students," the court said, "exposing children to diversity at an early age serves the important social goals of increasing their ability to tolerate differences and teaching them respect for everyone's unique personal experience."[4]

Is this case a harbinger of things to come, or is it a curious anomaly on the American legal scene? How extensive is the spread of gay rights in the United States? What is the cultural context for any contemporary discussion of homosexuality?

SPREAD OF THE GAY RIGHTS MOVEMENT

The Spread in Counseling

In 1973, the American Psychiatric Association voted to strike homosexuality as a psychiatric illness from its diagnostic and statistical manual. Many believe that this decision was not the result of new scientific evidence, but "was instead an action demanded by the ideological temper of the times."[5] In recent years, "reparative therapy" (psychotherapy to eliminate an individual's sexual desires for members of his or her own sex) and "transformational ministry" (the use of Christianity to eliminate homosexual desires) have been severely attacked by the psychiatric, psychological, and social work communities.

A STORY OF TWO CHANGED LIVES

Two men in our church, whom I'll call Bill and Roger, were gay partners infected with HIV and living with AIDS. Bill had met some people who attended our church, and he began to ask spiritual questions. They invited him to their small group, where Bill began to clearly experience Christ's love for him.

Bill accepted Jesus as his Savior and took steps to walk in obedience. He left Roger and moved in with his parents. Roger would still come to see Bill occasionally, but he couldn't understand the change in Bill. Roger didn't like our church, because Bill would no longer live with him. He felt that we got in the way of their relationship. Eventually, Bill died of AIDS.

Roger was living in a nursing home (in Columbus) when a volunteer from Project Compassion (our church's ministry to victims of HIV/AIDS) came to visit him. He was slowly dying from AIDS and had hardened his heart toward God since "losing his partner to the church."

The Project Compassion volunteer decided to befriend Roger by taking him places and spending time with him. When Roger found out she was a member of our church, he told her why he didn't like us. She was patient and listened, and she showed him unconditional love.

Roger began coming to various Project Compassion parties and events held at our church and met other Christians who also loved him unconditionally. They also would visit him in his nursing home. Roger slowly became open to the Lord and eventually committed his life to Jesus. Both Bill and Roger died knowing Jesus as their faithful friend, their Savior, and their Lord.

We have witnessed several proposed changes to the code of ethics governing the various professional associations of mental health professionals.[6] For example, the National Association of Social Workers approved a policy statement that said, "The National Association of Social Workers (NASW) believes social workers have the responsibility to clients to explain the prevailing knowledge concerning sexual orientation and the lack of data reporting positive outcomes with reparative therapy. NASW discourages social workers from providing treatments designed to change sexual orientation or from referring practitioners of programs that claim to do so."[7]

The American Psychiatric Association came out foursquare against "reparative therapy":

> The potential risks of "reparative therapy" are great, including depression, anxiety and self-destructive behavior, since therapist alignment with societal prejudices against homosexuality may reinforce self-hatred already experienced by the patient. . . . The possibility that the person might achieve happiness and satisfying interpersonal relationships as a gay man or lesbian is not presented, nor are alternative approaches to dealing with the effects of societal stigmatization discussed.[8]

The American Counseling Association, likewise, adopted a position opposing the "promotion of reparative therapy as a cure for individuals who are homosexual."[9]

A movement is afoot not only to recommend that social workers, counselors, psychologists, and psychiatrists refrain from engaging in "reparative therapy," but also to discipline members of these various associations through the removal of their license to practice. Homosexuals who wish to change their orientation are seen as simply having internalized the "homophobic mind-set of the larger culture."[10]

In sum, professionals are being muzzled from offering homosexuals the hope of change. Homosexuals are being dissuaded from seeking change by being told that (1) change is impossible, and (2) their very desire for change is simply due to a sense of alienation derived from an unaccepting environment. The goal of therapy, according to the counseling associations, ought to be to allow "gay men and lesbians to become comfortable with their sexual orientation and understand the societal response to it."[11]

The Spread in Schools

Several states, including California, Minnesota, New Jersey, and Vermont, have state laws prohibiting discrimination based on sexual orientation in all of their state schools. Dozens of municipalities, including most of America's largest cities (such as New York, Los Angeles, Denver, Chicago, and Detroit) have passed local ordinances that prohibit discrimination against gays, lesbians, and transgendered people. Depending on the particular ordinance or state law, local schools sometimes will prohibit even a nonpejorative debate about the morality of homosexuality by either teachers or students because of its "discriminatory effect."

In Massachusetts, two fathers taped a graphic sexual talk during a workshop sponsored by a national gay organization, which included two members of the state's Department of Education's HIV/AIDS awareness program. The workshop, which was ostensibly about AIDS prevention, ended up offering extremely graphic discussions of homosexual sex. Teenagers as young as age fourteen participated in the workshop.

Cindy Beal, founder of Justice and Peace Consulting, defended the program:

> There were a couple of subjects in which they purposely avoided making or implying value judgments. The question when to become sexually active, what is fisting, and a question about sadomasochism were answered as factually as possible to avoid stigmatizing anyone in the room who participated in those behaviors, and to maintain the educational atmosphere that there is no shame in asking questions or talking about anything. Therefore, both Mr.

Gaucher and Ms. Ables [Mr. Gaucher was a consultant with the Massachusetts Department of Public Health; Ms. Ables was the coordinator of HIV/AIDS program for the Massachusetts Department of Education] described the practice of "fisting" in an accurate way.

In keeping with this nonjudgmental, values-neutral philosophy, the consultants answered a question from a teen about sadomasochism this way:

We made it clear that for some people that's what they're interested in, and for many people it's not what they want to be doing. But we didn't want people who engage in nontraditional activities to feel judged, but in no way did we say "go out and try this" because we wanted to make people who weren't interested in it to feel just as good and not judged.[12]

A firestorm erupted when tapes of the workshops began hitting the airwaves. The fallout cost two Department of Education employees their jobs. Some parents in Massachusetts demanded the firing of the education commissioner. The parents who taped the workshop had planned to release copies of the tapes at a statehouse news conference, but a gay legal defense organization (Gay and Lesbian Advocates and Defenders) won an emergency restraining order barring distribution of the tapes on the grounds that they violated state wiretap laws. The parents also face state criminal charges and civil lawsuits for alleged violations of teenagers' rights of privacy.[13]

Nearly a thousand gay/lesbian alliance clubs meet in high schools across the country, many of them partially federally funded. In addition, several states now require "sensitivity training" of school staffs with regard to homosexuality, taught by various homosexual groups.[14]

The Spread in Law

Literally hundreds of civil rights ordinances, policies, and proclamations from states, cities, and counties all over the United

States now prohibit discrimination based on sexual orientation. These would include everything from a federal executive order by the former president Bill Clinton barring discrimination in public employment with the federal government to laws prohibiting discrimination in private employment, credit extension, and public accommodations.

In my hometown, the city council attempted to pass a sweeping ordinance barring discrimination against sexual orientation in the workplace about fifteen years ago. Hundreds of people opposed to this ordinance jammed the chambers of the council and nearly threatened a riot. City council members, obviously attuned to the political implications of passing such an unpopular ordinance, decided to shelve the proposed changes.

Several years later, having learned from their prior experience, the city council passed the same ordinance in a closed-door midnight session that had minimal advance public notice. The mayor immediately signed the ordinance into law. The public did not even get wind of the change in law until a small column appeared in the newspaper several days later. By that time, the only possible course of action would have been a lengthy and expensive referendum drive. Friends in other cities tell me that ordinances have been passed in similar fashion (without public debate or comment) in their towns as well.

The most controversial laws have involved family relationships, specifically whether homosexual couples may adopt children and whether homosexual couples may marry. Through court decisions, a number of states have approved of private and agency adoptions by lesbians and gay men. Other states expressly prohibit such adoptions by state statutes. California governor Gray Davis, as one of his first acts as governor, engendered intense controversy when he signed an executive order mandating social service workers to consider homosexual couples (alongside heterosexual couples) when making recommendations on the adoption of children.

The most notable change in family law, however, occurred in Vermont when, on April 26, 2000, the state became the first to extend to lesbians and gay men a new marital status called "civil unions." Civil unions provide virtually all the state-sponsored protections, responsibilities, and benefits afforded through civil marriage. Beatrice Dohrn, former legal director of LAMBDA (the nation's oldest and largest gay legal organization), made this comment after the signing of this historic piece of legislation:

> Vermont has sent a signal to the entire nation that it is no longer tolerable to deny lesbian and gay couples the respect other couples take for granted. When other states follow suit, they will certainly be grateful to Vermonters for their leadership. Today is a day of celebration for lesbians and gay men in Vermont, and throughout this country. Of course, we continue to still look forward to the day when we win the freedom to participate fully in marriage itself.[15]

In response to the growing national trend of courts and states recognizing gay marriages and civil unions, Congress passed a federal law signed by former president Clinton in 1996, called the "Defense of Marriage Act." This act defined marriage "as the legal union between one man and one woman as husband and wife." In addition, the law says that individual states do not have to respect the laws or judicial proceedings of other states concerning relationships of same-sex persons that are treated as marriage. In other words, the state of Utah does not have to treat a gay couple who were "married" or joined in a "civil union" in Vermont as "married" or "united" for purposes of law in Utah. The constitutionality of the Defense of Marriage Act has not yet been decided.[16]

The Spread in Private Clubs

James Dale earned the rank of Eagle Scout, the highest honor in the Boy Scouts. The Boy Scouts found out through a newspaper article that Dale was gay. Dale, the co-president of Rutgers University's gay/lesbian alliance, had given a speech, which was the subject of the newspaper report. In 1992, he sued the Boy Scouts after one of their New Jersey councils rejected his application for adult leadership and subsequently fired him. Dale sued under New Jersey's antidiscrimination laws, which prohibited discrimination based on, among other things, sexual orientation in places of "public accommodation." The New Jersey Supreme Court held that the Boy Scouts illegally fired Dale, and it ordered the organization to reinstate him.

But in a 5–4 ruling, the United States Supreme Court decided that the New Jersey Supreme Court was wrong in forcing the Boy Scouts to accept James Dale. Chief Justice William Rehnquist wrote in his majority opinion that Boy Scout values are spelled out in the Scout oath and law, which required scouts to be "clean" and "morally straight."

The Boy Scouts assert that homosexual conduct is inconsistent with the values embodied in the Scout oath and law. Dale's presence in the Boy Scouts would, at the very least, have forced the organization to send a message, both to its young members and the world, that the Boy Scouts accept homosexual conduct as a legitimate form of behavior. The First Amendment protects those who refuse to accept these views.[17]

Reaction was swift in the wake of the Supreme Court's ruling. United Way agencies in various cities withdrew their funding of local Boy Scout troops. The borough of Manhattan (New York) banned its schools from sponsoring Boy Scout troops. A backlash against the backlash resulted in the United Way reversing its policy on funding cutoffs and local school boards across the country lifting school district bans on Boy Scout recruiting in schools.

Perhaps the case that most directly touches on Christian practice and liberty is one involving the Tufts University Christian Fellowship group, a local affiliate of InterVarsity Christian Fellowship. Julie Catalano was barred from a leadership position in TCF because she concluded, after several years of struggle, that her homosexuality was not in conflict with the Bible. After being barred from leadership, Ms. Catalano filed a complaint with Tufts University, alleging a violation of university and student government policy against discrimination based on sexual orientation. The Tufts

Community Union Judiciary met without a hearing, found TCF guilty of discrimination, and banished the group from campus, revoking $5,700 a year in student fees.

John Leo, a columnist for *U.S. News and World Report*, saw nationwide implications in the Tufts decision: "The politically correct left now relies far more on coercion than persuasion or moral appeal. The long-term trend is to depict dissent from the gay agenda as a form of illegitimate and punishable expression."[18]

On appeal, TCF was reinstated, even though the school judiciary found that they had discriminated against Catalano by holding her to different standards than a heterosexual senior leader. The importance of the Tufts case cannot be overstated, because it raises the very important question of whether religious groups have the right to use sincerely held religious beliefs about homosexuality when selecting leaders. Many Americans feel that religious convictions are not a justification for discrimination based on sexual orientation. For them, such discrimination is the moral equivalent of discrimination based on race, ethnicity, and gender.

RESPONDING TO GAY RIGHTS: IS IT ALL RIGHT TO DISCRIMINATE?

Many people, both inside and outside the church, believe that Jesus settled the issue of discrimination when he taught in the Sermon on the Mount:

> "Do not judge, or you too will be judged. For in the same way you judge others, you will be judged, and with the measure you use, it will be measured to you.
>
> "Why do you look at the speck of sawdust in your brother's eye and pay no attention to plank in your own eye? How can you say to your brother, 'Let me take the speck out of your eye,' when all the time there is a plank in your own eye? You hypocrite, first take the plank out of your own eye, and then you will see clearly to remove the speck from your brother's eye."[19]

Often when Christians raise objections to the view that homosexuality is a legitimate alternative to heterosexuality, or to the equating of homosexual marriage with heterosexual marriage, someone will immediately quote Matthew 7:1: "Do not judge, or you too will be judged." Is Jesus asking Christians to cease making moral judgments about all activities in life? Does Jesus want Christians to suspend their critical faculties regarding the rightness or wrongness of an activity such as homosexual sex? Is Jesus saying to the Christian that he wants us to approach the world with an easygoing, benevolent tolerance like that of an open-minded grandparent?

It is highly unlikely that Jesus wants Christians to refrain from making moral judgments, because if he did, he would be contradicting what he says just a few sentences later: "Do not give dogs what is sacred; do not throw your pearls to pigs. If you do, they may trample them under their feet, and then turn and tear you to pieces."[20] How are we to determine which people toward whom we are to exercise great discretion in speaking if we don't make some kind of moral judgment? If Christians are never to judge anything or anyone, how can we obey Jesus' warning to "watch out for false prophets"? "They come to you in sheep's clothing, but inwardly they are ferocious wolves. By their fruit you will recognize them."[21] Or how could a church ever exercise church discipline, which Jesus commands us to do in Matthew 18? If the Christian is not to judge, why did Jesus tell us in John 7:24 to make sure we use "right judgment"?

Apparently not all judgment is forbidden to the Christian by Jesus' command "Do not judge." What Jesus does prohibit is the kind of *self-righteous* judgment that religious people often engage in. He condemns the position of superiority in which a person stands above others and essentially says, "I'm better than you are. I'm not like you. You are dirty, and I am clean."

Christian judgment, in essence, requires a Christian to live on a tightrope. On the one hand, we may be pulled off to the left into a libertine position, "Oh, come on, live and let live. Who are you to call anything 'sin'? Don't exercise any discipline. Every lifestyle is equally valid! It's all just a matter of opinion and preference!" On the other hand, we may be pulled off the tightrope to the right into a self-righteous smugness and self-satisfied sense of superiority. In that posture, we may refer to other human beings in belittling, shaming, and condescending ways. Jesus warned us against both self-righteousness and libertinism when he said, "Watch out for the yeast of the Pharisees and that of Herod."[22]

On most issues, Jesus usually ends up on the side of maximum mercy and also maximum righteousness. It is always dangerous to imagine what Jesus might say about a particular issue. Based on what he did say regarding judgment, as well as on his support for heterosexual marriage, he might say this to the church today:

> "Do you want to speak out about homosexuality because you hate sin and wish to stand on the side of God and morality? I'm glad that you hate sin. All true Christians ought to hate sin. But if you really hate sin, why not start with the sin in your own life? This is what I meant by looking at the speck of sawdust in your brother's eye and not paying attention to the plank in your own eye. Stop beating up on Ellen DeGeneres [the 'out of the closet' comedienne] unless you've first made a searching inquiry concerning the sins that you are most guilty of. If you are a pastor, have you vehemently condemned greed in your church? After all, in the Gospels, I have repeatedly condemned greed, but said nothing about homosexuality. Have you gone after divorce, which is far more common in your church, even among your leaders, than is homosexuality?"

How extremely telling that Jesus used the image of *eye surgery* when he explained to the church how to deal with another's sin. The eye, of course, is one of the most sensitive organs in the body. If you've ever had anything lodged in your eye, you know that even the smallest speck can cause incredible pain. When I was in college, I was a part-time roofer. While working one day, a little piece of metal flew up and became lodged under my eyelid. I tried to get it out with my finger, but I couldn't remove it. The piece of metal began to scratch the surface of my eye, and it drove me crazy. My eyes filled with tears and my nose began to run. Like a groping blind man, I closed my eyes and climbed down a two-story ladder and then walked—my eyes almost entirely shut—to a student health clinic three blocks away. That three-block walk was torture. Arriving at the clinic, I blurted out, "I've got something in my eye. You've got to help me." Fortunately, a very kind doctor immediately ushered me into her office and told me to lie down on the examining table. Taking a little cotton swab as she peered under a magnifying glass, she gently pulled the piece of metal out. What an enormous relief when that speck was removed!

Whenever we approach someone about sin in any area of their life, we must remember that we are performing eye surgery. We are not removing a callus from the bottom of their feet or a sliver from their knees or hands. If people overreact to our correction, it's because we are dealing with their eyes, and not simply their hands or feet.

Therefore, if we are to engage in the correction or challenge of a homosexual practice, we must be exceptionally gentle and gracious, refusing to stand above people with an air of moral superiority. Instead, we stand on the same level, speaking out of our own experience of brokenness and healing. In the words of the classic phrase, we must be like "one beggar telling another beggar where to find bread." Every one of us, homosexual and heterosexual, needs to be saved from sin. How enormously gracious it can be to take a speck out of a person's eye (a speck that is killing them), just as it was a grace to me when a caring physician removed the speck from my eye. Yet, I say this in the full awareness that eye surgery needs to be carried out with extreme care.

More important, the church must *never* communicate in action or attitude that homosexuals are the worst of sinners. Scripture does not rank sins (which is more sinful—divorcing one's spouse of twenty years and breaking up a family of five, or two single men engaging in a homosexual act?). Suggesting that homosexuality is the worst of all sins makes the job of eye surgery much harder for redemptive Christian ministries.

WELCOMING INDIVIDUALS WITHOUT AFFIRMING THE GAY RIGHTS AGENDA

Churches, pastors, and individual Christians have been placed in a tricky position by the current climate of political discourse. Many simply refuse to allow for a position that warmly welcomes individual homosexuals while rejecting the political perspective that homosexual practice ought to be treated as the equivalent of heterosexual practice in all spheres of life.

Based on my experience as a former attorney who was involved politically and as a pastor who leads a church, I offer three principles to assist churches, pastors, and individuals through this precarious minefield.

A Church or a Christian Should Never Be Content to Merely Announce a Moral Position against Homosexuality to Satisfy One's Christian Duty

Christians are more than mere moralists or Pharisees. It is incumbent on Christians and churches to place the weight of emphasis on the hope of redemption for homosexual sinners, as well as for every kind of sinner. So that the hope of redemption is not mere rhetoric, churches would be wise to sponsor one of the many excellent Christ-centered healing ministries or to partner together with other local churches toward that end.[23]

Another way that churches can express love to individual homosexuals, and to the homosexual community in general, is by devoting a part of their resources toward befriending and caring for AIDS sufferers and those who carry the HIV virus. This kind of involvement by individuals and churches can be one of the most powerful ways of practicing the welcome of Christ toward the least, the last, and the lost. I have witnessed firsthand the power of this kind of ministry through my own congregation's involvement with hundreds of AIDS sufferers over the past decade.

We have been intentionally trying to model Mother Teresa's work in India to love people regardless of their politics, religion, or former sins. Treating each person with dignity has caused the doors of local hospitals, halfway houses, and prisons to be thrown wide open to us. Through these open doors, we have watched dozens of people (many of them homosexuals) give their lives over to Christ through faith and repentance. In fact, by God's grace, we have yet to bury an AIDS sufferer connected with our program who did not first turn to Christ for salvation.

The Church (as a Church) and a Pastor (as a Pastor) Generally Ought to Stay out of Political Fights

Churches, pastors, and their staff members generally ought not to lead referendum drives on gay rights issues or thrust themselves into the center of the gay rights debates. American church experience with political involvement ought to give churches tremendous pause before they become embroiled in political fights about gay rights. Liberal churches in the 1960s and 1970s lost hundreds of thousands of members when many churchgoers concluded that they were not hearing the Bible being preached from the pulpit, but rather an echo of the liberal political establishment. Many conservative churches have failed to learn the lesson, and as a result, many cultural observers today see conservative Christianity and the Republican Party as virtually indistinguishable. A church that becomes known in its community as being a leader in the gay rights fight (no matter whether it's for or against it) will, in my opinion, sacrifice its principal calling, which is to promote the gospel of Jesus Christ.

Individual Christians (as Opposed to Churches) Ought to Be Encouraged to Be Politically Involved in the Moral and Political Issues That Shape Our Society

Pastors can serve an enormously important role as they privately counsel, encourage, and pray for those whose vocation is in the political realm. Rather than abdicate the realm of politics to the non-Christian world, I believe in serious political involvement by Christian individuals, as opposed to the church as a whole.

The Bible does speak clearly about moral issues such as homosexuality and idolatry. But it speaks with far less clarity about whether a practicing homosexual, adulterer, idolater, or greedy person ought to be allowed to teach children in a public school or rent an apartment without discrimination. Sincere Christians can agree on the rightness or wrongness of a particular practice, but honestly differ on how a pluralistic democratic society ought to treat that practice in different contexts. Taking different sides of a political debate is not the equivalent of denying the deity of Christ or rejecting the inspiration of the Bible (although some "Christian" political organizations make it sound like it is). Strongly discipled Christians who are gifted by God for a political calling ought to be allowed the freedom to wrestle with knotty political issues, supported by the care, counsel, and prayers of their pastors.

But what are the knotty issues raised by the gay rights movement? In the next chapter we'll look at the basic assumptions undergirding the entire gay rights agenda.

Questions for Reflection and Discussion

?

1.   What did you think about the various incidents of violence and discrimination related at the beginning of this chapter? Are you surprised by the place our society is in with regard to homosexuality, and if so, why?

2.   What is your position on gay rights? Do you think Christians have done a good job of representing Jesus Christ to the homosexual community? Explain your answer.

3.   Have you ever had to perform "eye surgery" on someone? What are some of the issues you would first want to consider before confronting someone about his or her sin?

4.   What would you say to a friend, coworker, relative—someone you know—who is caught up in homosexual sin? What would you *not* say, and why?

5.   Do you agree with the author's approach to Christian involvement in politics? If not, what is your position on the role of Christians in politics?

6.   Do you agree with the author's approach of "welcoming individuals without affirming the gay rights agenda"? If so, why? If not, why not? How, practically speaking, can a person do that—be compassionate toward individual homosexuals without endorsing the gay rights agenda?

9

Understanding the Homosexual

Eileen is a 40-something woman who has been living with AIDS for several years and raising her grandchildren. Eileen (not her real name) first became involved with our church's ministry to HIV/AIDS victims (Project Compassion) at our Easter party, held at the local children's hospital, when we gave her two Easter baskets for her grandchildren. You can imagine how difficult it was for Eileen to care for small children while living with AIDS, but she didn't want strangers from Children's Services raising her grandchildren. She saw the information cards about Project Compassion in the Easter baskets and decided to take a chance and call us.

Two volunteers from Project Compassion (we call them Faithful Friends) met regularly with her to support her through her illness and to encourage her in raising her grandchildren. These "faithful friends" overcame racial barriers and established trust over a period of time. Eileen had heard of Jesus, but had never given her life to him. Instead, she had become involved in drugs and in many sexual relationships with different men. After building relationships with the staff of Project Compassion and her two friends, Eileen decided to give her life to Christ and live only for him. She gave up using drugs and began pursuing a relationship with God with her whole heart. She now faithfully attends a church in her neighborhood and regularly shares her testimony. She is being used to lead others to Christ in her family and neighborhood and throughout the Project Compassion support group.

Perhaps you know someone with AIDS or someone who considers himself or herself to be a homosexual. How would you practice the welcome of the kingdom with this person? In order to help, it's important to know something about some of the assumptions that undergird the gay rights movement.

THREE ASSUMPTIONS OF THE GAY RIGHTS MOVEMENT

Thoughtful Christians (like other compassionate people) are horrified when they hear the details of Matt Shepard's brutal slaying as described in the last chapter. To a lesser degree, many other individual homosexuals have been victimized. One need not look very hard to find stories of shy, lonely teenage boys and girls who are called "queer" or "fags" or "sissies" by their taunting classmates.

As a pastor, I've had the opportunity to talk with many men and women who, at some point in their lives, labeled themselves "gay." They've told me stories of sexual abuse suffered at the hands of fathers, uncles, or older cousins—and, in one memorable case, abuse suffered at the hands of fellow Roman Catholic seminary students. They've also reported to me feelings of profound rejection by and alienation from their same-sex parent.

But I've also heard stories about rampant promiscuity, beatings at the hands of homosexual lovers, and sexual practices that were indescribably revolting. One of my dear friends, after describing a particularly bizarre sexual experience he had had in Greenwich Village, said to me, "Rich, you don't want to know what guys do with each other. It's just too horrible to talk about."

The gay rights movement regularly blurs the distinction between compassion for individual homosexuals (such as Matt Shepard and the many men and women my church and I have ministered to over the past two decades) and the political and social agenda of gay activists. They claim that a compassion for individual homosexuals must translate into a complete tolerance for homosexuality in all spheres of life. Anything less than viewing homosexuality as a completely equal and continually valid alternative to heterosexuality is seen as evidence of "homophobia." Opposition to homosexual practice on moral or religious grounds is stigmatized as a "hate crime." "Homophobia" (literally, the fear of homosexuals, or even the fear that one might be a homosexual) is viewed as the rough equivalent of racism and sexism.

The blurring of these two dimensions of life (individual homosexuals on the one hand and the gay rights political agenda on the other) is bolstered by three fundamental claims:

> 1. Science has determined as an irrefutable fact that homosexuality is biologically determined. Mountains of evidence exist, proving that homosexuality is as much an inherited trait as skin or hair color.
>
> 2. Psychology has determined that, because homosexuality is innate, it is irreversible. Efforts to "convert" homosexuals into heterosexuals are not only morally wrong, but are also doomed to failure. There is no such thing as an "ex-gay."
>
> 3. The Bible does not condemn same-sex partnerships or homosexual sexual practices per se. The biblical texts cited to show God's disapproval of homosexual practices have been historically misinterpreted. In short, homosexual practice is not at odds with biblical teaching.

Biological Arguments for Homosexuality

A decade ago, *Newsweek* featured a cover shot of a blue-eyed baby with the headline, "Is this child gay?" The article in *Newsweek's* "Lifestyle" section titled "Born or Bred?" stated in large, bold letters "SCIENCE AND PSYCHIATRY ARE STRUGGLING TO MAKE SENSE OF NEW RESEARCH THAT SUGGESTS THAT HOMOSEXUALITY MAY BE A MATTER OF GENETICS, NOT PARENTING." The article essentially argued that, while the causes of homosexuality are complex, science is converging on the conclusion that homosexuality is biologically determined. Today, a significant percentage of Americans believe that science has "proven" that homosexuality is as much an inherited trait as is "left-handedness" or "blue eyes." But has science really proven that homosexuality is biologically determined?

Twin Studies

Over the past ten years, many studies have attempted to scientifically establish the biological roots of homosexuality. One such study, by clinical psychologists J. Michael Bailey and Richard Pillard, discovered that among identical male twins where one twin was homosexually oriented, there was a 52 percent chance that his brother would also be so oriented. For fraternal twins, the concurrence was 22 percent. Among non-twin brothers, the rate was 9.2 percent and 11 percent for adoptive brothers. Similar rates of homosexuality were found among females.[1]

Initially, their findings were quite striking. After all, identical twins are genetically identical; therefore, if biology were a strong factor in determining homosexuality, you would expect the rates of concordance to be much higher for identical twins than for fraternal twins or for non-twin brothers.

But at least five issues mitigate against the widespread citation of the Bailey and Pillard study as "proof" of the biological basis of homosexuality. First, if biology (and not family structure or other environment causes) really determined a person's sexual orientation, then identical twins ought to have a 100 percent concordance rate, since they are genetically identical. The 52 percent concordance rate actually argues *against* the notion of biological determinism and suggests other factors have influenced sexual orientation.

Second, why is there a difference between the rates among fraternal twins (a 22 percent chance) as opposed to non-twin brothers (a 9.2 percent chance)? Fraternal twins have no more genetic similarity than do non-twin brothers. One obvious explanation is that fraternal twins are more likely to be raised similarly than siblings of different ages, pointing again to environment factors as the cause.

Third, unless twins are raised separately, one cannot determine the effect of environment and family structure on their eventual sexual orientation. Intuition would suggest that identical twins, raised in the same family, would experience essentially the same kind of upbringing. Fraternal twins, being different, would experience family life more dissimilarly than would identical twins. Finally, non-twin brothers would have the least amount of similarity in their experience of family life among sibling combinations. Therefore, we simply do not know how great a role family structure and other environmental causes play in determining sexual orientation.

Interestingly, as I was writing this section of this book, I met a young woman who just began attending our church. In our conversation, she mentioned that she had a twin sister, but because of her parent's divorce, she and her twin had lived apart for most of their lives. Her sister had lived with their dad on the west coast, and she had grown up with her mom in the east. I asked how her relationship was with her twin, remarking that her life situation sounded very much like the movie *The Parent Trap*, which had starred Haley Mills. She laughed and said, "Yes, I get that a lot. I guess my relationship with my sister is pretty good, except she's a lesbian and I don't agree with that."

"Your identical twin sister is a lesbian?" I asked.

"Yes," she responded, and then proceeded to tell me about the different circumstances in which her sister was raised compared to the way she was raised.

Even though situations like this are rare, they do form the best possible evidence to help us distinguish between biological and environment causes of homosexuality.

Fourth, these findings by Bailey and Pillard have not been replicated in studies by other researchers. A British study, for example, found only a 10 percent concordance for identical twins (as opposed to Bailey and Pillard's 52 percent rate). Among fraternal twins, the British researchers found an 8 percent concordance rate (as opposed to Bailey and Pillard's 22 percent rate).[2] This finding of a very similar rate of concordance between identical twins and fraternal twins suggests that biology may play no significant role in determining sexual orientation.

Finally, the British researchers, King and McDonald, in seeking to discover the nongenetic factors that might play into the relatively high concordance factor among twins, discovered "a high likelihood of sexual relations occurring with same-sex co-twins at some time, *particularly in [identical] pairs.*"[3] One out of five same-sex twins had sex with one another.

Brain Studies In Sexual Orientation

In a 1991 issue of *Science* magazine, Simon LeVay, a neuroscientist, published a study in which he compared the brains of heterosexual men and homosexual men. He focused on a microscopic cluster of neurons in the hypothalamus identified as INAH3 (which summarizes the daunting phrase "Interstitial Nuclei of the Anterior Hypothalamus—Group 3"). LeVay discovered in his autopsy of forty-one cadavers that this cluster of cells in "homosexual" men was less than half the size of that in "heterosexual" men. This finding was touted as the first direct evidence of what some gays have long contended—"that whether or not they choose to be different, they are born different."[4]

But like the twins studies, LeVay's conclusions are also subject to serious challenge. First of all, because LeVay's subjects were dead, he knew "regrettably little" (LeVay's own words) about their sexual histories beyond their declared or presumed orientation. "That is a distinct shortcoming of my study," [LeVay] concedes.[5] "Regrettably little" is actually a generous assessment of what LeVay knew. While LeVay claimed that nineteen of the males were homosexual (because they died of AIDS), he only "presumed" that the other sixteen males and six females were heterosexual. But six of the supposed heterosexuals also died of AIDS. Inasmuch as LeVay's entire study depends on reliably distinguishing between heterosexuals and homosexuals, the dependability of his findings is seriously undermined because he knew "regrettably little" about his subjects' sexual history.

Second, we do not know what effect, if any, the hypothalamus has on sexual orientation or sexual behavior. Some animal research attempts to connect the hypothalamus with sexual behavior, but there is absolutely no human research about it. So, even if LeVay could accurately distinguish between his homosexual subjects and heterosexual subjects, we don't know if the size of the hypothalamus means anything at all in terms of sexual behavior. And because the sample size is so small, we don't know if these findings would be consistent across the general population.

Third, we do not know the effect sexual behavior has on the brain. It is certainly plausible that one's brain affects sexual orientation and behavior. But it is also plausible that one's sexual behavior creates neurological changes in one's brain. For example, one study has demonstrated that sexual experiences in rats actually alters the size of the neurons in that animal's brain.[6]

The fact that behavior can alter the structure of the brain has been known by medical researchers for many years. For example, one study found that in people reading Braille after becoming blind, the area of the brain controlling the reading finger grew larger.[7]

Finger Length Ratios and Sexual Orientation

One other widely publicized study measured the finger length of 720 adults who were attending public street fairs in San Francisco. The participants were asked their gender, age, sexual orientation, handedness, and the number and gender of children their mother had carried before them.[8] The researchers discovered that heterosexual women had roughly the same size pointer finger as ring finger on their right hands. Heterosexual men had considerably shorter pointer fingers than ring fingers, as did homosexual men. But when the researchers factored in the presence of more than one older brother, the difference in size between the pointer finger and ring finger of homosexual men was more pronounced than the difference in size of these two fingers among heterosexual men. And the more older brothers a boy had, the more likely he was to develop homosexual orientations.

The researchers theorized that the presence of prenatal androgens (a male hormone) may influence adult sexual orientation. Prenatal androgen, according to the researchers, affects finger length differences and may be more present when one has more older brothers.

Like the other studies attempting to demonstrate a biological cause for homosexuality, this finger-length study also suffers from a number of defects. First, the differences between finger lengths for homosexuals versus heterosexuals are literally minute fractions of an inch. Because there is no standard way to measure a finger, any difference between the average heterosexual finger length and the average homosexual finger length may entirely disappear.

Second, this study, like many of the other studies, has not yet been replicated. Third, and perhaps the most serious flaw of this study, a plausible alternative explanation exists for the greater frequency of homosexuality in men who have older brothers than in men who do not. While it is possible that having older brothers results in higher levels of androgens in the womb for successive boys and that this higher level of androgens in the womb somehow affects homosexuality, a more plausible explanation is that boys who are raised with older brothers feel themselves to be at a competitive disadvantage. They are younger and smaller and as a result always feel somewhat inadequate as males. Life experience, therefore, and not finger length or androgen levels, forms, at the very least, a plausible explanation for homosexual orientation.

What can we conclude from the finger-length study, the hypothalamus study, the twins studies, and the other studies that claim a biological basis for homosexuality? William Byne, a neuroanatomist and psychiatrist at the Mount Sinai School of Medicine in New York, summarized the current state of our knowledge:

> The final perspective from which I wish to challenge the debate statement is to address the weakness of the biological database itself. Much of the commonly offered biological evidence has yet to be replicated or has to be discounted because it has failed replication. Even the replicable data are often uninterpretable because of confounded experimental designs.... Based upon our present knowledge of science, it

is absolutely unwarranted to say that science has "proven" that sexual orientation is determined by some biological cause. It seems wisest to say that biology may play some part. We presently do not know how large a part or how to segregate that part from other factors. We also know that human sexuality is so complex, that issues such as sexual attraction, sexual fantasies, and sexual behaviors are almost certainly linked to more than one single cause. Life experiences, family structure, traumas, choice, and perhaps, to some degree, biology are all inextricably intertwined.[9]

Despite the failure thus far of science to prove a biological base for homosexuality, it is important that we Christians not use Scripture to rule out the possibility of science ever finding a biological cause of or contributor to homosexuality. At this point, we should simply say that the present state of our scientific knowledge has not proven that sexual orientation is determined by biology. It is possible that at some future point such proof may occur. If that day ever comes, Christian opposition to homosexual practice would still not be undermined. Homosexuality is clearly not God's will, according to Scripture, but then neither are many chronic conditions such as asthma, multiple sclerosis, and birth defects. Yet, in this fallen and broken world, such things exist. Because God has clearly said "no" to homosexual behavior (and we believe that God's "no" in Scripture is designed not to hurt us, but rather because he loves us and desires to protect us), we must say "no" out of love for people and faithfulness to God. Science may someday affirm biological tendencies toward alcoholism, adultery, or even rage, but even if that were to happen, we would continue to assert that such tendencies ought to be resisted.

Psychological Arguments for Homosexuality

In the last chapter, I mentioned that attempts by counselors to change the sexual orientation of their clients have been severely attacked by the psychiatry, psychology, and social work professions. These professions are moving rapidly toward adopting a position that would discipline members of the various associations by removing counselors' licenses to practice for even attempting to change clients' sexual orientation. The fundamental assumptions of the psychiatry, psychology, and social work professional associations are that homosexuality is an innate, irreversible condition and that there is no such thing as an ex-gay.

A vocal minority of counselors, however, in the face of great opposition, assert that the origin of homosexual desire is not primarily biological. They suggest that homosexuality finds its origin in psychological issues and traumatic life circumstances.

Elizabeth Moberly, a Christian psychiatrist, is most often associated with the theory that homosexual men or women suffer from some deficit in their relationship with their parent of the same sex. Because of this deficit, there is a corresponding drive to make up this deficit through the medium of same-sex, or "homosexual," relationships.[10]

Moberly stresses that this deficit does not always imply willful maltreatment by the parent. Thus, parents of homosexuals should not necessarily blame themselves on account of this disruption in the attachment. Sometimes, however, there will be direct culpability. If a father makes little effort to find time for his son, or belittles him, or ill-treats him in some way, there is a risk of some form of psychological damage to the child—and the father may be considered at fault. But psychological damage does not stem from deliberate ill-treatment alone. A divorce may, in some cases, damage a child's relational capacity—without the parents wanting this to happen. Above all, early separation or parental absence at a crucial point in the child's development may, in some instances, have long-term negative effects. For example, a parent may be ill or hospitalized or may have to render military service or be separated because of an enforced employment absence. This theory of relational deficit, however, should not be read deterministically. Some children are very resilient and are not significantly affected by parental absence. Many children quickly recover from hurtful situations.[11]

Moberly's theory essentially boils down to this: "The homosexual impulse is essentially motivated by the need to make good earlier deficits in the parent/child relationship. The persisting need for love from the same sex stems from, and is correlated with, the earlier unmet need for love from the parent of the same sex or rather, the inability to receive such love, whether or not it was offered."[12] According to Moberly, the quest for homosexual expression is not merely a matter of "sexual activity." Its roots lie for males in a "male-gender deficit" and for females in a "female-gender deficit." In other words, there is a hole in the soul left by the disruption of attachment to the parent of the same sex.

Several years ago, I preached a series of messages titled "Restoring Your Sexual Sanity." In preparation, I interviewed eight men in our congregation who had come out of an exclusively homosexual lifestyle. The men I talked with fit Moberly's pattern exactly. All of them described very difficult relationships with their fathers. In fact, two things were common among the men with regard to their relationships with their dads. First, when asked, "How would you describe your father?" many of the men responded with a similar statement: "My dad is a mystery to me." Or ,"My father is a black box." I remember one man struggling and finally saying, "No. I don't know how to describe my father." This normally articulate man had no words with which to describe his father.

These men simply did not understand their dads and felt completely disconnected emotionally from their fathers. This disconnect extended to their present relationships with their fathers. Many of the men still felt like little boys whenever their fathers were around. They said things like, "There's something about being with my father that reduces me to child status." "Every time I'm around my dad, I revert to the same feelings of inadequacy and inner tension. I start acting like a little boy again and not like an adult." None of these men felt as though they could relate to their dads in an adult-to-adult way.

A second commonality among most (but not all) of the men I interviewed was an early experience of molestation by another man. Lesbians I interviewed had *all* been molested by men (often relatives) when they were young. Studies confirm a much higher degree of trauma through sexual abuse during the childhoods of adult homosexuals than in the childhoods of heterosexuals.[13] A less frequent kind of trauma suffered by homosexuals is an experience of rejection, physical abuse, verbal abuse, or sexual attack by the opposite-sex parent. This rejection sometimes shows itself later in an avoidance of opposite-sex relations.

My friend Andy Comiskey is the executive director of Desert Streams Ministries, one of the most effective Christian ministries that reaches out to the sexually and relationally broken. Comiskey believes that homosexual tendencies, whatever their origins, result in a profound sense of inadequacy in a person's own identity as a male or a female. "For some," he says, "that inadequacy is heightened by the threat of the opposite gender (often through childhood abuse). But for most with same-sex attraction, a tremendous yearning for same-sex attention and affection persists." According to Comiskey, gender inferiority is at the root of homosexuality.

But gender inferiority is not enough, Comiskey asserts. Three things contribute to lock a person into a homosexual identity and lifestyle. First, a person who struggles with a feeling of gender inferiority identifies himself or herself as a homosexual—he or she brands himself or herself with the label, "I am a homosexual." Second, having labeled himself or herself, he or she acts on his or her desires, thus intensifying and confirming the identity. Finally, the person identifies with the gay subculture or lifestyle, joining the community to "protect, celebrate, and advance the gay self."[14]

The Power of Addiction

In his book *Homosexuality and the Politics of Truth,* psychiatrist Jeffrey Satinover tells a little parable about the process of addiction. One day a white skylark flew over a Middle Eastern country when she heard a merchant cry out, "Worms! Worms! Worms for feathers! Delicious worms." Little did the skylark know that the merchant was the devil.

The merchant motioned the little skylark closer, saying, "See the lovely worms I have?" The skylark looked at the worms, which looked bigger and juicier than anything she had ever dug up for herself.

The merchant said, "The price isn't high. Two worms for a feather! Two worms for one!"

The skylark was unable to resist. After all, she had many feathers. So she plucked out one of her feathers, just a small one, and gave it to the merchant. Then she snatched up two of the plumpest and juiciest worms she had ever eaten and flew off.

The skylark returned day after day, trading one of her feathers for two worms. One day, however, when she leaped up in the air to fly away, she fell to the ground and had the stunning realization that she was unable to fly. All of the worms she had eaten made her body grow fatter and fatter. And all of the feathers she had plucked made her grow balder and balder.

Then the merchant came, picked up the little skylark, and put her in a cage. He slammed the little cage door shut, and with a loud SNAP! of his fingers, he vanished into the desert air.[15]

Satinover's point is that when we behave initially in a certain way, like the skylark who exchanges a feather for worms, we *choose* to do so. Along the way, we progressively lose the ability to choose not to do so. And finally we discover that we are completely trapped in compulsive addictive behaviors. Satinover calls this "the devil's bargain."

Of course, an addict often tries to manage his or her own problem. He or she will confess his or her sin to God and make a resolution to change—and set a new date for one last fling. Homosexual addicts, like all addicts, will attempt to deal with the depressing accompaniments of their lives (lies, depression, self-pity, isolation, the loss of intimacy) by going back to the same behavior that got them into bondage in the first place. In addition, the homosexual addict must make his or her way through a culture that suggests that self-denial is impossible and may even be injurious. But over time, every addict, whether they are addicted to a substance (alcohol, cocaine, barbiturates) or a behavior (pornography, work, gambling, homosexual sex), finds that his or her will has become significantly weakened and progressively enslaved.

Is There Any Evidence That
Homosexuals Can Change?

Exodus International is a coalition of Christian organizations that promotes the message of "freedom from homosexuality through the power of Jesus Christ." Since 1976, Exodus International North America has grown to include over one hundred local ministries in the United States and Canada. Many other independent ministries, not affiliated with Exodus International, also minister healing to homosexuals through the power of Jesus Christ. By simply clicking on Exodus International's Web site (www.exodusnorthamerica.org), one can find the testimonies of dozens of individuals who at one time in their lives considered themselves homosexual and who now believe themselves to be healed—changed through the power of Christ.

These are the kinds of stories that gay rights groups earnestly try to suppress, because they offer a stunning rebuke to the claim that homosexuality is an immutable trait, like race or eye color. Gay rights organizations go to great lengths in their attempts to silence those who would seek to promote the message that homosexuals can change. Newspapers across the country, under enormous pressure from gay rights organizations, often refuse to carry paid advertising by ex-gays who want to tell their stories. Most major media outlets self-censor reports of change from former homosexuals.

Jean Case, the wife of the founder of America Online, fell under enormous public criticism when she donated nearly $8.5 million dollars to Westminster Academy, a school run by Coral Ridge Presbyterian Church in Fort Lauderdale, Florida. Numerous pro-gay groups attempted to pressure the Cases to "reconsider their gift," because Coral Ridge has links to an Exodus member agency.

Doug's Story

Consider the story of Doug (not his real name), who has been, since 1995, a member of the church I pastor. Doug, the oldest of nine children, was raised in a strict Roman Catholic family. His father was absent a lot during the early years of his upbringing, spending an enormous amount of time assisting the church and taking part in various community events.

When Doug was fourteen, he went away to a Roman Catholic seminary. While there, he experienced sexual abuse from both faculty members and other students. Doug sought counseling from the seminary rector. What he didn't realize was that the rector was also involved in pedophilia (he was later convicted of child abuse in a very public trial). The rector even suggested to Doug's parents that Doug was delusional and that the alleged abuse never occurred. To Doug, what was most hurtful was that his parents believed his teachers, and for many years they thought Doug was crazy.

During college, Doug tried to repress what had happened to him, but the abuse left an enormous wound in his soul. When Doug moved to a new city, he plunged headlong into the gay lifestyle. He met men in bars and cruised the parks, looking for anonymous sexual encounters. During his late twenties, Doug got involved in a four-year relationship with another man. Doug didn't know that, almost from the outset, his lover cheated on him. He discovered the infidelity one day when he came home and found his lover in bed with another man.

Doug decided to return to church and to seek help for his ongoing struggle with homosexual desire and also with the sexual abuse that he had suffered in seminary. To Doug's chagrin, his new pastor didn't offer him counseling or refer him to a counselor. Instead, the pastor simply said, "I want you to leave this church and never show your face here again."

I asked Doug if he was acting out in church or creating a disturbance. Doug answered, "Absolutely not, Rich. I was the model church member and even sang in the choir. In fact, I tried to explain to the pastor that I wasn't expecting him to do anything for me, since I thought my problem may have been beyond his time or resources. Instead, I simply begged him to refer me to someone who could help me."

It is against this backdrop of abuse and rejection by church leaders that the miracle of Doug's life change occurred. Listen to Doug's story in his own words:

It was early in the summer of 1995, and my life seemed to be going pretty well. I had a good job and a nice apartment, and I was generally in good health. I was feeling a bit edgy about my upcoming trip home to attend my brother's wedding in Michigan. I knew it would be the usual barrage of questions: "Are you seeing anyone?" "When are you getting married?" I was ready to go and be the big brother at this wedding and would return to my wonderful life and my search for "Mr. Right."

Within a week of my return from my brother's wedding, I was faced with the only thing that could bring my plans for my life to an end. It was the one thing that I would not let myself believe could ever happen to me. I was diagnosed with HIV. I lost all perspective and hope and was certain of only one thing—my imminent death.

It was against this backdrop that a former college roommate and his wife asked me to be part of their search for a church here in Columbus. They proceeded to describe some of what they did and did not want in a church. I was only able to think of one place that even remotely sounded like the kind of church they were seeking. I remembered that, back in 1992, a friend had invited me to attend church with him at Vineyard for the last three weeks before he left for California. That church had stuck in my mind as "the warehouse with purple awnings." My friends insisted I go with them to show them where this place was. I eventually agreed so they'd stop bugging me about it.

We went to one of the Sunday morning services, and in the announcements, there was a ministry mentioned that helped people who had AIDS and who were HIV-positive. Although I didn't show it at the time, I was shocked that a church would have a ministry like this, but even more that they weren't afraid to announce it publicly. My previous experience with church was not only of blatant rejection of me for my gay life, but also for the fact that I would think of accusing church leaders of such horrible acts as sexual abuse. I was so blown away with the idea that a church was willing to look at the truth, regardless of its implications on their reputation, that I went home and cried uncontrollably for hours. At the Vineyard that day I recognized the loving heart of God that I had known as a child.

My friends and I returned the next week. We liked what we were seeing and had decided to give this church an honest try. It was only a few weeks before I gave Christ control of my life, and my former college roommate accepted Jesus, too. I began to understand God's gift to me. For the first time since the sexual abuse had occurred, I began to see hope restored to my life. I had abandoned God because of abuse from leaders in other churches. I discovered in a men's group four other guys who were willing to face their issues along with me. None of them was struggling with homosexuality. But I realized that every single man has issues that keep him from intimacy with God. I discovered healthy, normal relationships with other men. We were all going after God, and there was a safe place where we could go after him together.

Because of what God has done in my life through the church, I have entirely left the homosexual lifestyle. I still experience occasional temptation, but it is totally in check, and I no longer experience the consuming desire I used to. God has provided me with the complete suppression of HIV in my body through the use of new antiretroviral drugs.

I now help to colead Gideon's Call, a ministry at our church that assists men and women to leave the homosexual lifestyle. Because of what several of my friends have seen God do in my life over the past few years, three of my closest friends have come out of the gay lifestyle and have accepted Jesus.

I asked Doug what he would want to say to the church and also to men and women who were struggling with homosexual impulses. Doug responded, "We're all coming at life from some vantage point that is broken. I've really discovered that we are all sinners and that we need to stop judging each other for our particular variety of sin. The men's group I've been part of in the church helped me realize this. I saw that I had more similarities than differences with other men. That was incredibly healing to me.

"I'd also like to say to homosexual men and women that change is possible! The biggest lie of the enemy is that God wants to cut us off and that we must accept our 'gay identity.' But the only possible way you can be helped is by connecting with other loving people and with God. Homosexuality is the result of profound alienation from God, from others, and from our own beings. There are people who can help us reverse this alienation. God used people to restore his hope and life in me. I see myself now as a returned prodigal son of a loving Father."

A postscript to Doug's story: Dozens of former students testified in court about the sexual abuse they suffered at the hands of teachers at the seminary Doug attended. This made front-page news in the state where the seminary is located. Several of the teachers are now serving long prison sentences. Most wonderful of all, Doug's parents repented of believing the lie that Doug was crazy when he reported the molestation to them nearly two decades ago. They asked Doug's forgiveness for the pain they had caused him— forgiveness he was only too happy to grant.

Biblical Arguments for Homosexuality

These days, many church denominations that host general conventions or annual general assemblies of its leaders can expect to become the scene of dramatic protests by gay rights activists. Some churches, such as the United Church of Christ, have long supported the ordination of gays and lesbians. In fact, the United Church of Christ went so far as to set up a scholarship fund specifically designed to aid homosexuals who want to enter the ministry.

Episcopalians have officially declared that openly gay living is "incompatible with Scripture." But a number of dioceses have challenged this position. For example, Bishop Mary Adelia McLeod issued an "emancipation proclamation" in Vermont, where same-sex couples can now form legal civil unions. Bishop McLeod declared that "God's great gift of love and the expression of that love cannot and should not be denied to those among us who happen to be homosexual."

Delegates to the United Methodist general conference have continued to vote to retain the current language in the Methodist Book of Discipline, which states that "the practice of homosexuality is incompatible with Christian teaching." But Methodist pastors are openly defying Methodist church law. In 1999, sixty-eight Methodist clergy participated in the same-sex wedding ceremony for two Methodist lesbians.

When asked how denominations have gotten to this point, Episcopalian leader Todd Wetzel described three influences: First, liberal teachings in seminaries have resulted in church leaders who subscribe to moral relativism. In the soil of relativism, a second attitude has flourished: the elevation of experience above Scripture, tradition, or the Holy Spirit's guidance. Finally, the apathy and ignorance of many people in these denominations have enabled a theological shift to occur without protest.[16]

Some scholars have tried to argue that the Bible, as properly interpreted, does not condemn homosexual practice.[17] Still other scholars, most prominently John Boswell, have suggested that there was "widespread acceptance of homosexual desire and behavior among Christians until about the thirteenth century."[18] Both arguments do not stand up to critical appraisal. Dr. David Wright of Edinburgh University ends his article on homosexuality in the *Encyclopedia of Early Christianity* with these words: "The conclusion must be that, for all its interest and stimulus, Boswell's book provides at the end of the day not one firm piece of evidence that the teaching mind of the early church countenanced homosexual activity."[19]

It is beyond the scope of this book to thoroughly examine all of the arguments raised by gay rights advocates who attempt to reconstruct the meaning of Scripture or the practice of church history in a homosexual-friendly or, at least, a homosexual-neutral direction. Both John Stott and Stanley Grenz have done a great service to the church by considering and responding to these arguments at length.[20]

In brief, gay theology (yes, there is a burgeoning gay theology) suggests that the apostle Paul did not understand the difference between inversion and perversion. An *invert* is someone who is born gay. A *pervert* is someone who is naturally heterosexual, but who twists his or her nature by engaging in homosexual sex. Gay theology suggests that the biblical condemnations against homosexuality only apply to perverts and not to inverts.

The most serious problem with gay theology, however, is that its starting point is the biblical material directly applying to homosexuality rather than the plan of God for sexuality in general as found in Genesis 2. Foundational to biblical thinking about sexuality (whether heterosexual or homosexual) is God's creation of humanity as male and female and the blessing he placed on heterosexual marriage.

One author quoted the hymn "Just as I Am" and said, "The whole point of the Christian gospel is that God loves us and accepts us just as we are." Therefore, "it is the duty of heterosexual Christians to accept homosexual Christians [just as they are]." To this, John Stott responded in his customarily clear fashion:

> This is a very confused statement of the gospel.... God does, indeed, accept us just as we are, and we do not have to make ourselves good first; indeed, we cannot. But his "acceptance" means that he fully and freely forgives all who repent and believe, not that he condones our continuance in sin ... indeed, his offer of friendship to sinners like us is truly wonderful. But he welcomes us in order to redeem and transform us, not to leave us alone in our sins. No acceptance, either by God or by the church, is promised to us if we harden our hearts against God's Word and will. Only judgment.[21]

My friend Don Williams, a former Fuller Seminary professor and now Vineyard pastor, foresaw the debates that would take place over homosexuality and spoke in prescient terms:

> For the church at this point to surrender to gay advocacy and gay theology enough to give up her biblical faith would bring not only disaster upon herself, it would bring more havoc to the world as well. If the church simply blesses homosexuality, the hope for change in Christ will be destroyed. Millions of potential converts will have the only lasting hope for wholeness cut off from them. Untold numbers of children and adolescents who are struggling with their sexual identity will conclude that "gay is good," deny their heterosexual potential and God's heterosexual purpose for them, and slip into the brokenness of the gay world. Untold numbers of adults will follow suit.[22]

Don Williams wrote these words back in 1978. Tragically, his prediction of what would happen to the church that surrendered to gay advocacy and gay theology has proven to be true in all of its particulars.

MINISTRY TO THOSE STRUGGLING WITH HOMOSEXUALITY

Christians believe that Christ has come and that he will come again. In his first coming, Christ inaugurated the presence of his kingdom. By his second coming, Christ will bring about the fullness of his kingdom "on earth as it is in heaven." We now live between the times. This has been expressed as living "between the already and the not yet." We *already* may enjoy healing, but until Christ's second coming, that healing will *not yet* be total.

The "already" and "not yet" of the kingdom has profound implications for our ministry to those struggling with homosexual desires or those who engage in homosexual practices. On the one hand, Christ can and often does radically change and heal a person's desires. On the other hand, whether a person's desires completely change, a call to discipleship involves learning to act differently from one's desires.

But acting in ways inconsistent with one's desires is not a unique call to the homosexual. Discipleship requires this of all of us. To a man who *desires* to trade his wife in for a newer and younger woman, Christians would urge him to "crucify his desires" and to recommit himself to the faithful fulfillment of his marital vows. Likewise, to the compulsive shopper, the pornography addict, and the workaholic, the Bible calls each to learn to master his or her sinful desires. In similar fashion, alcoholics may experience a life-long desire to have a drink. Successful living with weakness and temptation is part of the "not yet" of God's kingdom.

My experience with homosexual strugglers is similar to my experience with heterosexual strugglers—healing is a process! The Fall has radically tainted all of our expressions of sexuality. "There is no one righteous, not even one."[23] Because of the extensiveness and compulsiveness of our sinful sexual behavior, healing generally does not take place instantaneously. Following Christ and picking up our crosses is not a one-time decision for anybody! Nor may we place conditions on Christ, such as "meeting and marrying a great opposite-sex partner" or "being freed from all homosexual temptation," before we choose to go the way of the cross.

A person typically needs to grow significantly in his or her intimacy and experience of Christ's love before healing from sinful sexual patterns can fully occur. Often a person needs to learn to identify and repent of false belief systems regarding sex and relationships.[24] For homosexuals, this may mean embracing a radically new self-identity, as well as new relational patterns with same-sex and opposite-sex persons. Forgiveness must, in a costly way, be applied—especially to past perpetrators of sexual, physical, or verbal abuse against the homosexual.

My friend Doug (whose story I told earlier in this chapter) told me that one of the most significant steps in his healing process occurred when he released his seminary teachers and other students, as well as the rejecting churches and former pastors, to God's justice and mercy.

Most important, the healing power of Christ almost always is experienced only within the context of loving Christian community.

It is essential that Christians and churches repent of all hatred toward and condemnation of homosexuals, especially the implication that homosexuals are uniquely deserving of God's judgment. It is also essential for a homosexual struggler to find some support group within the church or within a partnership of churches where he or she can work out a process for healing.

As we saw earlier in Doug's case, the power of Christ was released in a men's group. Interestingly, the men in Doug's group didn't have special "expertise" regarding "homosexual issues." None of the other men in the group had ever struggled with homosexuality. Nor had they ever gotten close to another man who did struggle with homosexual temptation. But they all were committed to radical honesty and vulnerability with regard to themselves and the stuff in their own lives.

This should give great hope to churches and individuals who want to help struggling homosexuals, but who feel that they are inadequate to do so. Of course, it is always profitable to learn and to grow in our ministry skills. If expert help is available, it's wise to make use of such help. But one doesn't need to be intimately acquainted with all the shapes that sin might take in another individual's life. There is enormous power when a group of men or women simply follow the apostle Paul's command: "Each of you must put off falsehood and speak truthfully to his neighbor, for we are all members of one body."[25]

Questions for Reflection and Discussion

?

1. What are the three claims the author suggests undergird the gay-rights position in the United States? Do you agree or disagree with each of these claims?

2. In your opinion, do the various studies cited by the author support or refute these three claims? Give specific reasons for your answer. How might

you use this information as a student in a college classroom, as a worker discussing the gay issue with colleagues, or as a friend or relative of a homosexual man or woman?

3. Do you think the psychological explanations for homosexuality cited by the author make sense? Why or why not?

4. Do you think homosexual behavior can be compared to other addictions such as alcoholism, gambling, or use of pornography? If so, in what ways are they similar? If not, why not?

5. Do you believe a person who practices homosexuality can change? If so, how? If not, why not?

6. How can you and your church minister to homosexuals more effectively?

RECOMMENDED READING

Grenz, Stanley J. *Welcoming But Not Affirming: An Evangelical Response to Homosexuality.* Louisville, Ky.: Westminster John Knox, 1998.

Plantinga Jr., Cornelius. *Not the Way It's Supposed to Be: A Breviary of Sin.* Grand Rapids: Eerdmans, 1995.

Satinover, Jeffrey. *Homosexuality and the Politics of Truth.* Grand Rapids: Baker, 1996.

Stott, John. *Same-Sex Partnerships? A Christian Perspective.* Grand Rapids: Revell, 1998.

Williams, Don. *The Bond That Breaks: Will Homosexuality Split the Church?* Los Angeles: BIM, 1978.

Part 4

Is the New Ager My Enemy?

10

A Closer Look at New Agers

A local realtor posted an ad in our daily paper that asked the following questions:

- Does your property have an unsettled feeling to it?
- Are you trying to purchase property, or a home you know that has potential, but something isn't quite right?
- Do you need peace restored with a House Blessing?

Let me be the realtor to help you find the land and home where your heart and soul is most at ease! I can help restore peace to your home!

This realtor, apparently an expert in feng shui, used her expertise to create calm, balance, and harmony in an individual's life. How? By creating a "perfect place to live by manipulating energy flows and by using color, aroma, and the light." Home buyers used to be content with four bedrooms, two-and-a-half baths, and a working fireplace. Now some real estate buyers want their realtors also to be experts in how the flow of energy affects their living space.

A major bookstore chain displayed children's coloring books on a stand that advertised "Gifts for the Holidays." One coloring book was titled, "I am God's Partner: A Spiritual Awareness Activity Book." Inside, the child is asked to draw her own pictures on a page with these words written across the top in large block letters, "I am creator—because together my God Partner and I create anything that is good." On another page the child is asked to draw his "God Partner," who is "a gentle spirit who welcomes you to this coloring book."

Our local convention center recently hosted the twelfth annual "Universal Light Expo," which was designed to honor "the living light." Touted as the Midwest's largest metaphysical event, it boasted "lectures on angels, sacred sites, crystals, art, music, ascension, Sufis and animals, healing auras, DNA, color, Native-American wisdom, Toltecs, spirituality, and much, much more!" Two-hundred-forty booths were displayed, and over one hundred lectures were given in this two-day event.

A local travel agency advertised, "A woman's journey to Ireland . . ." with the following enticement: "Join us for an unforgettable journey into the wild and beautiful, serene and sacred heart of Celtic Ireland. Discover what modern women can learn from the ancient tradition that honored the Goddess in Woman, the feminine in nature. Off the beaten path, join a dynamic traveling community of women exploring megalithic altars, healing wells, energy centers— a celebration of womanspirit." Traditional travel agents used to offer information about ticket prices and the availability of room service. Apparently, consumers now are demanding information about healing wells and energy centers as well.

What's going on?

THE GROWTH OF NEW AGE

What has been called "the New Age movement" has quickly moved from the fringe of American society in the early 1980s to the mainstream in the twenty-first century. In fact, New Age ideas have become so mainstream that the term "New Age" has fallen into disfavor in recent years. In current literature, marketers use such terms as "natural health," "spirituality," "alternative therapies," "global change," and "conscious living" when describing their product or services.

Interest in spirituality in America has increased over the past several decades, but it is often spirituality with a distinctively Eastern religious flavor. Most bookstores now have a burgeoning section of New Age and occult books, and "alternative" bookstores are springing up all over the country. Books such as *The Celestine Prophecy* and

Conversations with God (and its sequels) have remained at the top of best-seller lists for years. Whole Life Books in Austin, Texas, claims to carry 40,000 items, 25,000 of them books.[1] Alternative spirituality stores break down their specialty into hundreds of subcategories, such as voodoo, the fourth dimension, and birth awareness, that go well beyond just "New Age" or "Eastern spirituality." At Bodhi Tree in West Hollywood, California, bookstore manager Mark Labinger says he has "over 400 categories" of spirituality in his store.[2]

Yoga, another vehicle for New Age spirituality, is found in practically every health club, although most won't use the "Y" word. For example, one fitness center in our city offers a popular class called "Reebok Flexible Strength" that's based on hatha yoga positions (the more physical form of yoga and the one most familiar to Americans). "Most people go to yoga studios for physical reasons," says Catherine Arnold, editor-in-chief of the *Yoga Journal*, published in Berkeley, California, "a bad back or arthritis—once they start, they reach a point where they stumble on the spiritual component. It's a personal journey."[3] Yoga has become so popular that companies like J. Crew have come out with cool lines of yoga clothes.

Oprah Winfrey has been a major proponent of New Age spirituality through her popular talk show, her magazine *O*, and her book club recommendations. One recent show featured Iyanla Vanzant, who wrote two best-sellers, *Acts of Faith* and *One Day My Soul Just Opened Up*. Vanzant recently gathered a group of professional women to teach them how to meditate. "I want you to disconnect your brains," she told them, "so that you can be in complete contact with your own being. Take a cleansing breath ... repeat, it is God that works in me, may I be infused with the strength of God."[4]

The New Age and Alternative Health

Many alternative health therapies are rooted in the Eastern religious practice of balancing energy forces in the body. Alternative health therapies have become a multibillion dollar industry. Aroma therapy sales alone are estimated at over a half billion dollars and are growing at a rate of 30 percent a year. Even the Avon catalog features an aroma therapy calming gel that "helps to restore inner peace and harmony."

In 1992, Congress established the Office of Alternative Medicine as part of the National Institute of Health. It is now a multimillion-dollar budget expenditure in the new millennium. Many universities now offer classes for senior citizens in Eastern disciplines, such as Tai Chi, to assist heart patients and those who suffer inner-ear deterioration. Many alternative healing techniques have gained wide currency in nursing schools. Dolores Krieger, professor emerita of New York University, developed a healing technique known as "therapeutic touch," which is now taught in mainstream nursing schools. One of the practitioners of therapeutic touch at San Francisco State University's School of Nursing said that it is "a form of psychic healing, a channeling of super-conscious energy that is the source of an intelligence center of all of life." Many corporations offer wellness programs that include meditation, biofeedback, and yoga as part of the program.

The New Age and Tourism

New Age spirituality has also proven to be a boon for the tourism industry. Four million visitors a year travel to Sedona, Arizona—many drawn by a belief in the concept of a vortex, a place on the earth said to emit healing energies. "New Agers say that four such vortexes exist [in Sedona] and that they make it easier for humans to communicate with spirits, to get in touch with dead relatives, or to find their own past lives."[5] But many locals are not enamored with the reputation Sedona has earned, and they see other downsides to Sedona's popularity. "The only vortex I ever felt was all the money being sucked out of my wallet," says painter Rand Carlson, who lived in Sedona for two years before returning to Tucson. Spiritual living is costly because the rents paid by shop owners are so high the price of goods is high as well. Many residents, like Carlson, travel out of town to buy groceries.[6] Santa Cruz, California, is also a popular stop for New Age travelers, as is Eugene, Oregon; Boulder, Colorado; Santa Fe, New Mexico; and Madison;

Wisconsin. Those with the financial resources have made treks to Mexico, Peru, Cambodia, and more traditional New Age sites such as Glastonbury and Stonehenge in England.

The New Age and Business

Openness to all forms of spirituality has increased over the past decade. For example, 10 percent of Americans claim to have had an out-of-body experience (also known as astral projection), 14 percent claim to have seen a UFO, while thousands claim to have been abducted by aliens or to have seen them. Thousands of others have reported near-death experiences (NDEs), which have been popularized through television and various testimony books. And although the angel craze seems to have peaked, there are still plenty of angels-only boutiques, angel newsletters, angel seminars, and angel Web sites. Back in the mid-1990s, five of the ten best-selling books on religious topics were about angels. Blockbuster movies such as *The Sixth Sense*, starring Bruce Willis, have helped to popularize belief in various paranormal powers and visitation by spirits of the dead.

When a phenomenon spreads as ubiquitously as New Age spirituality, someone looking to make a quick buck is not going to be far behind. The so-called "New Age segment" of beverages is projected to grow into a $600-million-dollar wholesale industry by the year 2004. "New Age beverages" are often named for their supposed benefits. Stress Relief, Memory Mind, Energy Body, and Health Immune are actual names of bottled beverages.[7] Alternative health therapies for pets have appeared, along with a New Age line of makeup in glowing spring oranges and pinks. Even such megacorporations as Volkswagen, Nike, and Body Shop have jumped on the New Age bandwagon. In an article titled "Soul Branding: How to Do It," Jeffrey Durgee, a professor of marketing at Rensselaer Polytechnic Institute, pointed out many of the New Age connections in modern advertising.[8] Volkswagen, for example, draws on '60s' nostalgia for the traditional "Bug" by introducing the new Beetle with the slogan, "If you were really good in a past life, you come back as something better." Nike claims that its products come "straight from the soul of sports."

The Features of New Age Spirituality

New Age spirituality has spread so widely that it has already been co-opted by corporate America. But it is an often confusing, indeed self-contradictory spirituality. Are there some common features that make it identifiable to the average person? Features common to New Age spirituality include the following:

- Create your own religion.
- Create your own reality.
- Create your own God.
- Create your own afterlife.

Create Your Own Religion

George Gallup, America's premier pollster, said that the spiritual quest percolating among Americans today might best be described as "religion à la carte." In the twenty-first century, Gallup surveys suggest that Americans "are now picking and choosing what they want to believe, often mixing differing, or even contradictory, ideas from two or more different religions into a personal belief system."[9] So, for example, Gallup found that many evangelical Christians also believe in reincarnation.

Perhaps the most extreme example of creating a religion to satisfy one's own personal preference is found in the rising popularity of Wicca, sometimes known as "the Goddess Movement" or "the Craft." Thirty years ago almost no Wiccans could be found. Now, according to one scholar's estimate, there are more than 200,000 practitioners of Wicca and related neopagan faiths in the United States. Wicca may be the fastest growing religion in America.[10]

According to Wicca dogma, witchcraft is "perhaps the oldest religion extant in the West," beginning more than 35,000 years ago during the last ice age. At that time, people worshiped two deities, one of each sex—"the Mother Goddess, the birth giver, who brings into existence all life," and "the Horn God, a male hunter who dies and is resurrected each year." Throughout prehistoric Europe, people made images of the goddess. Each year these prehistoric worshipers celebrated the "season of cycles," which led to "Eight Feasts of the Wheel," the solstices, the equinoxes, and four festivals—Imbolc (February 2, now coinciding with the Christian feast of Candlemas), Beltane (May Day), Lammas (August 1), and Samhain (our Halloween).[11]

This "old religion" prevailed in Western Europe for thousands of years. It respected women and was egalitarian, nature-loving, and peaceful. (Is it surprising that Celtic society sounds very much like a twenty-first century vision of paradise?) Even during the rise of Christianity, the "old religion" was preserved through "Christian practices." But about four hundred years ago, many adherents to the "old religion" were slaughtered, because they were accused of being in league with the devil.

Wicca boasts a fascinating history, and one that apparently has convinced many Americans of its value and validity. There is just one problem. Virtually no truth exists in any single element of the story! Philip Davis, a professor of religion at the University of Prince Edward Island in Canada, published *Goddess Unmasked: The Rise of Neopagan Feminist Spirituality* in 1998. He argues that Wicca was the brainchild of an amateur anthropologist named Gerald B. Gardner in the 1950s. The religion sprang from Gardner's knowledge of Masonic practices, such as its blindfolding initiation, "degrees of priesthood," and commitment to secrecy, as well as various occult practices such as the use of wands, chalices, and five-pointed stars (which, when enclosed by a circle, is the Wiccan equivalent of the Christian cross). To Masonic rites and various occult practices, Gardner added ritual sex and nudity. But there is not a shred of historical evidence that the ancient Celts or any other pagan culture celebrated the "Eight Feasts of the Wheel."

A historian of pagan British religion who teaches at the University of Bristol, Ronald Hutton, wrote the book *The Triumph of the Moon*, in which he states, "The equinoxes seem to have no native pagan festivals behind them and became significant only to occultists in the nineteenth century. There is still no proven pagan feast that stood as an ancestor to Easter."[12] Neither is there any historical evidence that "hundreds of thousands of pagans" were persecuted or murdered during the seventeenth and eighteenth centuries, or that ancient people ever worshipped one goddess.

Further, a general consensus exists among archaeologists that pre-Christian culture in Western Europe was anything but women-respecting, peaceful, and egalitarian. Stone Age Europe, contrary to the portrayal by the creators of Wicca, is filled with evidence of fortifications and human bones bearing dagger marks.[13] Cynthia Eller, author of *The Myth of Matriarchal Prehistory*, suggests that no serious archaeologist believes that ancient Celtic culture was matriarchal or even women-focused.[14]

Why, in light of the absence of the least shred of historical credibility, is Wicca thriving? Allen Stairs, a philosophy professor at the University of Maryland who specializes in religion and magic, believes it is because "Wicca allows one to wear one's beliefs lightly, but also to have a rich and imaginative religious life."[15] In other words, Wicca has many of the advantages of Christianity in that it venerates a dying and rising God and a figure that is both virgin and mother, without having the burden of Christian ethics and especially the demand for self-denial.

In sharp contrast to New Age spiritualities, including Wicca, whose origins are almost entirely mythological and sheer hokum, Christianity claims to be backed up by history. For example, Luke, the physician and Gospel writer, begins his account of the story of Jesus this way:

> Many have undertaken to draw up an account of the things that have been fulfilled among us, just as they were handed down to us by those who from the first were eyewitnesses and servants of the word. Therefore, since I myself have carefully investigated everything from the beginning, it seemed good also to me to write an orderly account for you, most excellent Theophilus, so that you may know the certainty of the things you have been taught.[16]

Not empty philosophy or mythology, but history based on eye-witnesses, careful investigation, interviews, and evidence.

When talking with a New Ager, it is important to keep asking for clarification regarding almost every "spiritual" term that the person uses. I recently was invited to give a lecture at a Unitarian Universalist church, which I gladly accepted. My policy is to speak almost anywhere, as long as the inviting group puts no restrictions on what I can say. To me, this was a wonderful opportunity to share the story of God's love through Jesus Christ with 150 folks who would never darken the doorway of a Christian church.

After my half-hour message and an hour of questions and answers from the audience, I mingled with the crowd. A woman named Carol came up and told me that she was in agreement with a lot of what I said, because she also was a "spiritual" person.

I asked her to tell me a little bit about herself and her "spirituality." She told me that she prayed, believed in God, and believed in an afterlife, but did not believe in hell or that the only way to come to God was (as I had claimed) through the atoning blood of Jesus.

It would have been quite easy to focus on our points of disagreement. For example, by prayer she did not mean what I meant: communing with a personal, loving, holy Being who was other than a constituent part of every human soul. By prayer, Carol meant meditation that released her from illusory consciousness and assured her of God's (and her own and everyone else's) essential goodness. I spoke instead to Carol about the points of our so-called agreement. By asking questions and listening to her story, I was able to offer biblical content to a woman who had many of the right words, but almost none of the right definitions for those words.

Create Your Own Reality

The basic philosophical element underlying much of New Age religion or the "new spirituality" (as well as witchcraft and spiritism) is what philosophers call "monism"—the view that there are no distinctions among things or persons. All is one and all is God. Monism would teach that, in reality, there is no difference between

God, a worm, a baby, and a can of Diet Coke. Monism further teaches that there is no ultimate difference between good and evil or right and wrong.

The opening words of an old Zen poem put it this way:

> *The perfect way is without difficulty,*
> *Save that it avoids picking and choosing.*
> *Only when you stop liking and disliking*
> *Will all be clearly understood.*
> *A split hair's difference,*
> *And heaven and earth are set apart!*
> *If you want to get the plain truth,*
> *Be not concerned with right and wrong.*
> *The conflict between right and wrong*
> *Is the sickness of the mind.*[17]

In contrast, biblical religion begins with the story of God making distinctions where only undifferentiated chaos reigned. In the first chapter of Genesis, we are told that God separates light from darkness, the waters above from the waters below, the land from the sea, and the day from the night. Biblical religion further distinguishes good from evil and, most fundamentally, God from his creation.

Create Your Own God

If everything is one, including God, this naturally leads to the view that "all is God." The theological term for this is *pantheism,* the idea that everything—trees, bushes, animals, people—partakes of one divine essence. Since all is God, it is another very short step to the belief that all gods are the same. According to *Siri Guru Granth Sahib* (a collection of devotional hymns and poetry considered the Supreme Spiritual Authority and Head of the Sikh religion, rather than any living person), "everyone's God is the same and there is no other. Through Guru's grace, he manifests in a person's mind. God knows the innermost thoughts of all and resides in everyone. A person talks of bad and good only so long as he or she is lost in the duality. Through the (intercession of) Guru, one understands the One (God) and immerses oneself in him."

Since "all is God," each one of us is God in disguise. We, therefore, do not need to worship God, who is outside of ourselves. Pantheism inclines us to worship ourselves. Swami Muktananda, once a powerful Hindu spiritual leader, followed this pantheistic logic when he said, "Kneel to your own self. Honor and worship your own being. God dwells within you as You!"[18]

In sharp contrast, the apostle Paul reminds us that the obliteration of the distinction between the Creator and the creature is the essence of idolatry. To the Roman believers he wrote, "They exchanged the truth of God for a lie, and worshiped and served created things rather than the Creator—who is forever praised. Amen."[19]

The Christian philosopher Francis Schaeffer was fond of pointing out that in Michelangelo's famous Sistine Chapel painting of the creation of Adam, God's finger never touches Adam's finger. Adam was not simply the overflow of some cosmic ooze from the Creator. He was not made "from the stuff" of God. Adam, like all humanity, is separate from, different from, created by, but not made from the essence of God.

Christian theology has long taught the immanence of God, which is very different from what pantheism teaches. Christians believe that God is present to his creation and that he is active within the universe and within human history. In fact, our God is so immanent that, according to Paul's famous speech to the Athenians "[God] is not far from each one of us. . . . 'For in him we live and move and have our being.'"[20]

Yet, we must never forget that God is transcendent. Stanley Grenz and Roger Olson have pointed out that much of twentieth-century theology has so overemphasized God's immanence that it has lost this transcendence—the notion that God is wholly other, that he is apart from the world, above the world, and comes to the world from beyond.[21] As a result, the obliteration of distinction between God's thoughts and our thoughts, the Scriptures and our own ideologies, has gone unchecked.

Create Your Own Afterlife

Many New Agers believe in reincarnation, the idea that after death a person comes back as another being. Some even believe that this other being could be nonhuman; you could come back as a worm, a dog, or a tree. Most Western New Agers, such as Shirley MacLaine, would limit reincarnation to future existence in a human body.

Through "past-lives therapy," it is believed that one can uncover the mystery of previous reincarnations. Ronald Wong Jue, president of the Association for Transpersonal Psychology, places patients under hypnosis to evaluate past-life memories and dreams. As a licensed clinical psychologist, Dr. Jue believes that current fears and phobias stem from events that occurred in past lives. By healing one's past life, a person can experience peace and freedom in his or her present life.

Having a past life as a famous person has become big business. Nick Bunick, for example, is the subject of Julia Ingram's best-selling book *The Messengers*. In Ms. Ingram's book, Bunick reveals the extraordinary account of how angels intervened in his life and provided dozens of witnesses to encourage him to move ahead with the story of how his spirit and soul lived two thousand years ago as the apostle Paul! Bunick has since appeared on many national television and radio programs and has been featured in the *New York Times* and in *USA Today*. He recently released a book titled *In God's Truth*, which "clarifies and expands the original messages given to the world by Jesus and Paul" (as opposed to the distortions taught throughout church history).

Despite the popularity of reincarnation, many New Agers believe that individual existence continues after death but only as disembodied spirits. As a popular example of this perspective, recall the movie *The Sixth Sense*, which portrays a boy who sees the spirits of the dead.

In my city a man named Tana Hoy claims to be a psychic medium who can communicate with loved ones who have died and with guardian angels and spirit guides. Hoy, the subject of an article in a recent issue of *Entertainment Weekly* regarding his work as a medium for Hollywood movie stars, has convinced many people that he can get in touch with their loved ones who "do come and watch over us because it is natural for loved ones to stay near to those they love."[22]

Marguerite Marshall is a retired social worker from a local Catholic Social Services agency who gives frequent lectures on "dream encounters" with loved ones who have died. Mrs. Marshall believes that the spirits of dead loved ones frequently communicate to us through our dreams, just as we would communicate over the telephone or in person. She makes this claim:

> In the eighteen months since the death of my husband, he has visited me about thirty-eight times in my dreams.... From my [dead] husband I receive physical and emotional support, guidance in meeting a problem head-on, the use of humor, relaxation, no need to hurry, and cleaning up my eating concerns. Although he would always be there for me, he told me that he needed to take a different route for a while.[23]

What should we think of the New Age doctrine of reincarnation or the claims of contact with the departed spirits of the dead? These views do point to a deep need within every human being to believe in one's continued existence after death. But even more than acknowledging this need, Christians believe that faith in an afterlife springs from God, who "set eternity in the hearts of men."[24]

Christians sharply differ from New Agers, though, in describing the nature of our afterlife. Biblical religion knows nothing of reincarnation, but instead proclaims the message of the resurrection of our bodies. Individuals come back, not in the bodies of dogs, worms, or other human beings, but in their own bodies. The only difference is that the resurrected body has been cleansed from the stain of sin and is no longer mortal, but immortal.

Numerous studies have indicated that false memories can be induced by hypnosis.[25] This is the most likely explanation for the so-called "past-lives therapy" stories that claim to uncover previous incarnations (through hypnosis) in order to offer present help.

What about contact with the departed spirits of the dead through a psychic medium or through some kind of dream therapy? In numerous places, the Bible explicitly forbids contact with the dead. For example, consider this exhortation from the book of Deuteronomy:

> Let no one be found among you who ... engages in witchcraft, or cast spells, or *who is a medium or spiritist or who consults the dead.* Anyone who does these things is detestable to the LORD, and because of these detestable practices the LORD your God will drive out those nations before you. You must be blameless before the LORD your God.[26]

Some of the so-called contacts with the dead are pure fraud that play on people's gullibility or desperation. Communication from "departed loved ones" through dreams can best understood as being psychological in origin. But we ought never to discount the possibility of demonic impersonation. Satan does appear as "an angel of light" to deceive people.[27] We can receive revelation from "beyond," but that revelation is reserved exclusively to God speaking to a person through the Bible, through the biblical gifts of the Holy Spirit, and through *unsought* angelic communication.[28]

WHY IS NEW AGE SPIRITUALITY SO POPULAR?

New Age spirituality has become so popular that we now find it in areas as diverse as cancer therapy, organic gardening, dieting, hit movies, and even in many churches. For example, the parish wellness committee of a local mainline Protestant church recently held a workshop on feng shui, an ancient philosophy that explains how energy moves through our homes and offices. This workshop taught "the basic principles of feng shui and explained the nine aspects of a balanced and joyful life. Participants were encouraged to bring a floor-plan sketch of their home or office. Leadership for the workshop was provided by Paul Miller, *pastor and feng shui consultant.*"[29]

Failure of the Closed Universe Perspective

One reason for New Age spirituality's appeal is the failure of the "closed universe" perspective to resonate with most Westerners. A closed universe does not account for the spiritual dimension of life. Hardwired into every human being is the sense that we are more than just material beings—that we have a spiritual component. We are created in the image of God. We are not merely bodies. We have an intrinsic sense that existence does not end with death. We've all had experiences that cannot be explained by the mechanistic, materialistic universe offered to us by the modernist scientists and philosophers.

George Gallup agrees. He observes that "Americans are seeking something more meaningful, deeper, and healthier. It stems in part from what they perceive to be a failure of materialism in the twentieth century and the fact that there are so many problems that surround us without apparent solutions. That's why the seeking has intensified at this point in time. The surge in this desire for spiritual growth became, perhaps, one of the most dramatic movements of the late twentieth century."[30]

Failure of the Church

Another reason for New Age's appeal is the failure of the church. Individuals who thirst for spiritual meaning and spiritual experience often encounter in the church what I would call "Sadducean Christianity," a profoundly rationalistic and antisupernatural castration of real Christianity. In many churches, people are not taught how to discern the good side of the supernatural or how to walk in the power of the Holy Spirit or how to apply the biblical gifts of the Spirit. Even teaching on prayer or meditative Bible study has, in many cases, been replaced by discussions of politics, economics, and psychology.

Real spiritual fulfillment cannot be found in Sadducean Christianity. Moreover, according to George Gallup, churches by and large have done a poor job in equipping their own members in basic biblical beliefs. Too often, the Christian faith professed by the average church member is superficial. People simply do not know what they believe or why they believe it.

Fits Our Consumer Mind-set

A third reason for New Age spirituality's popularity is that it perfectly fits our consumer mind-set. If I can have two hundred choices of breakfast cereal and three hundred choices of athletic shoes, why can't I have choices in religion? Why can't I pick and choose those elements of religion I like and reject those elements I dislike? As mentioned earlier, Gallup's surveys have repeatedly found that Americans pick and choose what they want to believe, mixing differing and even contradictory ideas from religion or blending two or more different religions into a personal belief system.

If hell is an uncomfortable notion for me, New Age spirituality permits me to junk the notion of hell. If I prefer life without absolutes, played by my own rules, then New Age spirituality will accommodate that preference. In place of the "you shall's" and "you shall not's" of the Bible, New Age spirituality permits me to write my own list of "things I like and therefore choose to do" and "things I dislike and therefore choose not to do." New Age religion offers me the benefits of spirituality, such as rest and refreshment for my overstressed soul, without the interference of a meddling God who demands my obedience and my submission to his will.

The Power of Human Curiosity

A fourth, and frequently overlooked, reason for New Age's popularity is simply the power of human curiosity. Mary, a woman in our church, attended a party with some friends and observed a person reading tarot cards for guests of the party. Mary had been taught from her Protestant upbringing that fortune-telling, tarot cards, and other forms of divination were evil, but note what she said:

> I found my curiosity getting the best of me and decided to have this woman do a reading for me. The insight and the accuracy of the general reading really did apply to my life, and it astonished me! With my curiosity piqued, I decided I wanted to know more about divination and paganism. I asked an Internet friend about his religion—he was a

practicing pagan in the tradition of Isis. He recommended two books to give me a general understanding of neopaganism—*Goddess Spirituality* and *Wicca*. I came to believe that I had always experienced the goddess and the God through everyday activities of my life, through communing with nature, and through feeling a special connection to the gods and goddesses of ancient Rome and Greece. I felt this connection. I rationalized that all religions were essentially the same. They were merely different methods of worshiping God (and/or the goddess) based on a particular cultural setting. This made sense to me, since, even as a child, I had a difficult time believing that the God of Christianity could punish anyone.

For Mary, curiosity merged with both a thirst for spiritual connection and her consumer desire to have God be different from what he is.

Can Anything Positive Be Said about New Age Spirituality?

Despite all its inherent dangers, much of New Age spirituality can be affirmed by the biblical Christian. Recall from the first chapter of this book the discussion of the centered set. According to centered-set theory, the issue is not how far out an individual is at the moment, but whether this individual is moving toward or away from the center. In communicating with someone who is involved in New Age, it's easy to write that person off, convinced that he or she is just too far gone spiritually to be reached with the gospel message.

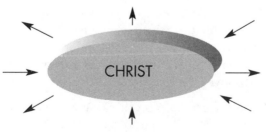

CHRIST

My friend Jeff recently e-mailed me a note about a woman named Julie, who had begun to attend Jeff's home group:

> I first met Julie a few months ago. She and her boyfriend were regulars at our Fruit of the Vine [Vineyard's ministry to the poor in the "short north" section of Columbus]. She was dressed entirely in black and was unable to make eye contact with anyone who spoke with her. It was quite obvious that this girl had been through a lot of trauma in her life. She openly spoke of her involvement in the occult. For years she had practiced magic, paganism, and "shadow realm" spirituality [witchcraft]. I'm ashamed to admit this, but I remember feeling really sorry for her and thinking to myself that she was almost too far-out to be reached for Christ.
>
> A few months later, a young woman in my home group struck up a friendship with Julie and brought her to the group. When she arrived at our home group for the first time, I was shocked to see her. She avoided most of the people in the group. Her hair dangled over her face, and her body shook during most of the teaching. After the meeting, one of the guys in our group started to talk to Julie. Soon they were sitting at a table, and he was explaining to Julie how to have a relationship with Jesus. You could tell that Julie was touched by his kindness. They prayed together, and she went home.
>
> Julie has been a frequent attender at our group over the last several months. I have watched her move closer and closer to Jesus. We have helped her see the difference between prayer and magic, and between Christianity and paganism. It's still too early to tell if she has really embraced Christ (she has prayed "the sinner's prayer" on several occasions), but I now understand at a deeper level how much Jesus loves the lost. No one is too far-out for Christ!

It's helpful to use centered-set thinking when conversing with a New Ager. Our church has run into dozens of people like Julie, who are about as far-out as anyone you could meet, but who with love and sensitivity have begun to move closer and closer to Christ.

I've also discovered things on the New Age radar screen that ought to be on the Christian's radar screen as well. The early church recognized that many of the most dangerous heresies arise when Christians are failing to vigorously proclaim the truth. What are some truths that New Agers may be pointing to more energetically than Christians?

Concern for God's Creation

Talk with the participants at Earth Day celebrations or pick up literature from any "green" organization, and you will immediately be struck by the association of recycling efforts, protests against deforestation, and New Age spirituality. Many people are drawn to New Age thinking because they are deeply concerned about creation's destruction. For example, one New Age group, called "the Rainbow Family of Living Light," says that their beliefs are based on Native-American traditions chosen because "we have a strong orientation to take care of the earth." Their literature quotes from an old Native-American prophecy that reads, "When the earth is ravaged and the animals are dying, a new tribe of people shall come unto the earth from many colors, classes, creeds, and who by their actions shall make the earth green again. They will be known as the warriors of the rainbow."[31]

Fortunately, in the last decade, Christians have become increasingly aware of the ways we have degraded creation. We are beginning to hear more Christian voices lifted in response to the biblical mandate to cherish and care for the creation. Sadly, many Christians still view the creation as simply "natural resources," and judge any vocal concern for creation as simply the ranting of New Age "tree huggers."

But a wonderful group of Christian believers has formed the Evangelical Environmental Network, whose objectives include fostering "substantial and visible progress on the care and restoration of God's creation, while building a national movement of Christians devoted to the cause of creation stewardship."[32] Evangelical work on behalf of the creation still woefully lags behind that of New Agers, however. Relatively few messages from evangelical pulpits address care for the environment. Even fewer churches would have an ongoing group or committee whose mission is to foster creation stewardship. One wonders how many evangelicals today would recognize that the author of "The Canticle of the Creatures," also known as "The Canticle of Brother Sun," was none other than the spiritual forefather Saint Francis of Assisi and not a New Age fanatic. Consider Francis's personification of nature:

> Most High, All-powerful, All-good, Lord!
> All praise is Yours,
> All glory, all honor
> And all blessing.

> To You alone, Most High, do they belong.
> No mortal lips are worthy
> To pronounce your name.

> All praise be Yours, my Lord, through all that You have made,
> And first my lord Brother Sun,
> Who brings the day; and light you give to us through him.
> How beautiful is he, how radiant in all his splendor!
> Of You, Most High, he bears the likeness.

> All praise be Yours, my Lord, through Sister Moon and Stars;
> In the heavens You have made them, bright
> And precious and fair.

> All praise be Yours, my Lord, through Brothers Wind and Air,
> And fair and stormy, all the weather's moods,
> By which You cherish all that You have made.

> All praise be Yours, my Lord, through Sister Water,
> So useful, lowly, precious, and pure.

> All praise be Yours, my Lord, through Brother Fire,
> Through whom you brighten up the night.
> How beautiful he is, how gay!
> Full of power and strength.

All praise be yours, my Lord, through Sister Earth, our mother,
Who feeds us in her sovereignty and produces
Various fruits and colored flowers and herbs.

If you are unfamiliar with Francis's poem, and feel that it sounds vaguely "New Age," compare it with Psalm 148, which reads as follows:

Praise him, sun and moon,
  praise him, all you shining stars.
Praise him, you highest heavens
  and you waters above the skies. . . .

Praise the LORD from the earth,
  you great sea creatures and all ocean depths,
lightning and hail, snow and clouds,
  stormy winds that do his bidding.
you mountains and all hills,
  fruit trees and all cedars,
wild animals and all cattle,
  small creatures and flying birds. . . .

Let them praise the name of the LORD,
  for his name alone is exalted;
  his splendor is above the earth and the heavens.[33]

A Rising Health Consciousness

Over the past several decades, Westerners have shown a heightened concern about diets. Study after study has suggested that Western diets not only are absurdly high in saturated fats and refined sugars, but many of the additives in our foods are demonstrably carcinogenic.

So one of the positive aspects of New Age spirituality is its emphasis on healthy living, and particularly on healthy diets. In my mind, it's unfortunate that a diet consisting of organically grown fruits and vegetables is so closely linked to New Age practices. New Age spirituality is the exclusive brand of spirituality promoted in health food stores and by popular magazines such as *Prevention*.

Where are the voices of biblical Christians concerning the importance of diet and health? One hopes they're not lined up at the local fast-food joint, asking a teenage vendor to "supersize it"! Where are the Christian newsletters advocating a more wholistic approach to wellness that goes beyond the "see your doctor once a year" kind of advice?

Millions of Americans, particularly aging seniors who are church-goers, would appreciate a Christian perspective regarding the ills that bedevil seniors, such as dementia, depression, and arthritis. But most alternatives outside of traditional medicine carry along with it New Age "baggage." One wonders why some enterprising Christian entrepreneur hasn't already published a Christian alternative to a magazine such as *Prevention*. We ought to be interested in the care of the body, since it is God's temple and will one day be resurrected from the dead. It would also be helpful for Christian physicians and other Christian professionals (dentists, physical and occupational therapists, midwives, and the like) to strategically place literature around their offices that explains the spiritual roots of alternative medical therapies. Many Christians simply do not know if it's OK to go to a reflexologist, to receive aroma therapy, to utilize iridology, or to be hypnotized.[34]

A Fuller Spirituality

I've read through dozens of New Age newsletters, and I'm struck by how often they quote Christians from the past. One newsletter quotes extensively from John of the Cross. A second quotes Julian of Norwich's *Revelations of Divine Love* (she is the best known of the English female spiritual writers). A third refers to Bernard of Clairvaux's *On Loving God*. The newsletters offer spiritual and silent retreats, lessons in meditation, and the opportunity to experience a community of like-minded friends.

However, the quotes from these spiritual forefathers are framed in such a way as to suggest that they support New Age ideas. Likewise, Christian meditation radically differs from Eastern meditation. Christian meditation is meant to engage all of our faculties, including our minds and spirits, while Eastern meditation attempts to shut off the operations of the mind. Nevertheless, New Age thinkers promote a spirituality that is fuller and richer than the typical Christian "daily quiet time," in which a person reads a chapter or two of Scripture and prays a list of items from a prayer list.

We see hopeful signs of a reinvigoration of Christian spiritual practices, evidenced by the popularity of spirituality books by Christian authors such as Dallas Willard and Richard Foster. If this trend toward interest in Christian spirituality continues unabated, evangelicals may be able to offer a satisfying answer for the spiritual thirst that is evident in so many New Age seekers.

Integration into Business and All of Life

Corporate training programs today may include sending an employee to a seminar that deals with some form of New Age spirituality under a repackaged title such as "Transformation" or "Reinvention."[35] John Naisbitt, the best-selling author of *Megatrends*, wove New Age themes into his book *Re-inventing the Corporation*. Naisbitt, who meditates, consults with psychics, and believes in reincarnation, states that "successful entrepreneurs score well above average on tests of intuitive ability such as precognition [psychically predicting the future] and remote viewing."[36]

The prevalence of books, seminars, and consultants that mingle New Age themes with business practices underlines the need for Christians to integrate a thoroughgoing Christian worldview with workplace concerns. Unfortunately, Christianity has been marked historically by a dualism that separates the sacred (concerns for prayer, Bible reading, and church attendance) from the secular (concern for commerce, cinema, the arts, and the like). It is once again a hopeful sign that the message of the kingdom of God is being embraced in our generation. The lordship of Jesus Christ over all of life—including political life, social life, and business life—is being rediscovered by many Christians. At present, however, it does appear that New Agers have done a better job than many Christians at integrating their belief system into all realms of life.

HOW CAN A NEW AGER BE REACHED?

It can be intimidating for Christians to encounter people with radically different worldviews—those who use spiritual terms (such as the name of Jesus) in distorted ways or who advertise their involvement in particularly weird rituals and practices. Some of this stuff is, frankly, very dark. Nonetheless, it's important to remember that no one is too far gone for Christ. Remember the story of Julie? How easy it is to write off as "unreachable" the person dressed in black and wearing a crystal or displaying a large pentagram tattoo. The truth is that many New Agers are spiritual seekers. Through love and genuine engagement, they can be pointed toward the only Fulfiller of spiritual seeking, namely, Jesus Christ.

At the same time, it is important to realize that, despite any claims to the contrary, many New Age practices profoundly wound their practitioners and others, and can result in great discouragement and despair. A member of my congregation wrote this about her involvement in a coven (a group of witches):

> We would meet on the evenings of the new and full moons, as well as on high holidays, to perform rituals, receive consecration, carry out magic, and have a feast. A feast was nothing more than a party with food, drinks, and, oftentimes, drugs. As the relationships between members of the coven developed, an emphasis was placed on staying out all night and using mind-enhancing drugs such as marijuana, mushrooms, and LSD. In addition to spiritual relationships, members of my coven began to have adulterous romantic and sexual relationships. This resulted in my own marriage being placed in jeopardy. Members of the coven forced my husband to make a decision between his role as high priest in the coven or his marriage with me.

When talking to a New Ager, you aren't talking to someone who is merely spiritually seeking and spiritually unfulfilled. You are often talking with someone who is deeply unhappy. As the book of Proverbs puts it so well, "The way of the unfaithful is hard."[37]

Furthermore, it's important to affirm what is positive about a New Ager's desires and concerns. Concern for the environment, for health, for integration, and for a more wholistic spirituality is commendable and even biblical, however muddled or confused the rest of the message may be.

Finally, every person, including every New Ager, has been made by God to give and receive love. Love is the universal language understood by everyone. My friend Jeff, who had first written me about Julie, e-mailed me again:

> Last week Julie came to our home group, and her hair was out of her face. She even smiled. She brought along an old King James Bible that had been in her family for years, and she followed along with the teaching. Following the teaching, she even asked if I could pray for her. She asked me to pray that her boyfriend, who was currently living with her, would get a job and stop bringing bad people into their apartment. She said she wanted to ask God for things and not rely on magic anymore. After we prayed, she asked if I could find her a ride to church so she could attend one of our Saturday morning classes.
>
> This week during prayer, several people gathered around Julie and communicated to her how precious she was to God. When we found out that Julie's boyfriend was being abusive to her, we prayed that God would give her the strength to get out of that destructive relationship. We are now helping her find a place to live.

Jeff believes that Julie is on the way to finding Christ!

Questions for Reflection and Discussion

?

1.   What products have you seen advertised that use New Age themes? What movies are based on New Age assumptions?

2. Regarding what issues do you find people (including those who profess to be Christians) creating their own religion?

3. What is the Christian view of the afterlife? How does it differ from reincarnation?

4. Are you aware of anyone who claims to have had an encounter with an angel? How would you evaluate such a claim?

5. How would you talk with someone who was into Wicca? What could you offer by way of Christian spirituality that would be more satisfying than Wiccan or New Age spirituality?

RECOMMENDED READING

Arnold, Clinton. *Power and Magic: The Concept of Power in Ephesians*. Grand Rapids: Zondervan, 1992.

_____. *Spiritual Warfare: What Does the Bible Really Teach?* Grand Rapids: Baker, 1997.

Groothuis, Douglas R. *Confronting the New Age*. Downers Grove, Ill.: InterVarsity Press, 1988.

_____. *Unmasking the New Age*. Downers Grove, Ill.: InterVarsity Press, 1986.

Hillstrom, Elizabeth. *Testing the Spirits*. Downers Grove, Ill.: InterVarsity Press, 1995.

Murphy, Ed. *The Handbook for Spiritual Warfare*. Nashville: Nelson, 1992.

Part 5

Is the Liberal My Enemy?

11

Practicing the Welcome of the Kingdom

The writer of the E-mail was outraged. She couldn't believe what I said to the congregation in the days prior to the last presidential election. She wrote these words:

> I couldn't believe my ears. You told people to become informed about the issues of our day such as abortion, race relations, ethics, and care for the poor. Then you told people to apply the Bible to these issues and to use an informed Christian conscience before voting. You also told people to not simply vote a party line. What is the matter with you? Why are you so weak? How can you call yourself a Christian pastor and not instruct your congregation in the correct way to vote? Don't you care about discipling people? Are you so afraid of people's opinions that you won't tell them the truth—that there is only one truly Christian way to vote in this election?

The rest of the E-mail, which was two pages of single-spaced criticism, explained how the author would disciple the congregation if she were the senior pastor.

Of course, my initial response was to fire back a curt reply. But in my nearly two decades as a pastor, I'm repeatedly learning the wisdom of putting into practice Proverbs 15:1: "A gentle answer turns away wrath, but a harsh word stirs up anger." I began my response by thanking the correspondent for her E-mail to me. I then proceeded to address the substance of her complaint by asking her several simple questions: What precisely was the one correct "Christian" way to vote? How exactly did one discern the correct way? Since there is no Bible verse that tells us whether to vote Republican or Democrat, was she claiming some secret spiritual knowledge to which I was not privy? I further described some of the complexity that exists in assigning to one particular political party the mantle of God's unique approval.

This chapter is, in a sense, my extended answer to the woman who wrote me that E-mail. It also is an attempt to weave together many of the themes raised in this book.

WHO IS MY ENEMY?

Cal Thomas and Ed Dobson, in their book *Blinded by Might: Can the Religious Right Save America?*, describe the fund-raising approach commonly used by the Religious Right (that they, in large measure, helped to create).

First, they identify an enemy—homosexuals, abortionists, Democrats, or "liberals" in general. Second, the enemies are accused of being "out to get us" or imposing their morality on the rest of us or destroying the country. Third, the letter assures the reader that something will be done: We will oppose these enemies and ensure that they do not take over America. Fourth, in order to help get the job done, the reader is politely asked to send money (and then the letter often suggests a specific amount).

Thomas cited one particularly disgraceful fund-raising letter in which the Moral Majority asked the question, "Who is the #1 enemy of the American family in our generation?" The letter identified America's worst enemy as Norman Lear, the founder of the liberal political group "People for the American Way." Thomas said he would have asked a different question, had he written a fund-raising letter—not *who* is the greatest enemy of the American family, but *what* is the greatest enemy of the American family? To this latter question, Thomas would have replied, "Divorce."[1]

The assumption of many Christians (as I've repeatedly pointed out in this book) is that readily identifiable enemies, such as feminists, New Agers, homosexuals, advocates of diversity, postmodernists, or liberals, can be blamed for the destruction of America's moral landscape. Among the many problems with this assumption, two stand out most prominently. First, *this approach is thoroughly unbiblical.*

Jesus never taught his disciples that the primary problem in first-century Jewish life was the rulership of Judea by the Romans. Rather, Jesus taught that the true enemy was the failure of God's people to act like the people of God should act.

It was because the salt of the earth (God's people) had lost its saltiness that it became good for nothing except to be thrown out.[2] The unfaithfulness of God's people—not the activity of those outside the community of faith (that is, the Romans)—was always the focus of Jesus' harshest criticisms. In contemporary culture, it would not be hard to imagine Jesus asking evangelical and Roman Catholic churches some pretty uncomfortable questions about the number of abortions or divorces within our own churches.

According to one abortion study conducted in the mid-1990s, one in five women who abort are "born-again" or evangelical Christians. In 1989, it was one in six, so the trend is worsening.[3] A CBS/*New York Times* poll asked the following question: "Do you favor or oppose using tax dollars to pay for a woman's abortion if she cannot afford it?" Fully 62 percent of Roman Catholics favored using tax dollars to pay for a woman's abortion; only 42 percent of other Americans favored the use of tax dollars. What's more, 45 percent of Roman Catholics believe that an abortion is a legitimate decision "for any reason during the first trimester," according to a *Time*/CNN poll. It is apparent that the churches that have been most outspoken regarding opposition to abortion, namely, evangelical and Roman Catholic churches, must focus more attention on persuading the members within our churches. As the comic strip character Pogo used to say, "We have met the enemy and he is us."

The second and most troubling aspect of the Religious Right's fundraising letters is that *they often appeal to the worst in us*—a self-righteous view that "sin" is located outside of us rather than a reality coursing through every human heart. The result is that someone who is on the wrong side of a particular "family values" issue is regarded as an enemy to be scorned rather than as a person to be won. Repentance is required of *them*, but not of *us*. Complex issues are reduced to simplistic either/or solutions. Since we are on the right side (God's side), we can always be assured of the ultimate victory of our particular viewpoint.

Abraham Lincoln was closer to the truth than both my e-mail correspondent or the Religious Right's fund-raising letters when he wrote, "In the presence of a war, it is quite possible that God's purpose is something different from the purpose of either party." He called the Civil War a "punishment inflicted upon us for our presumptuous sins to the needful end of our national reformation as a whole people."[4] Lincoln spoke of the sins of the whole nation rather than focusing on one particular sin (slavery) in one particular part of the country (the South). The North, as well as the South, in Lincoln's mind at least, was in need of the reformation and repentance. When asked by a reporter whether God was on the side of the North, Lincoln is said to have humbly responded, "My concern is not whether God is on our side, but whether we are on God's side!" Support for a particular political position does not in and of itself place an individual on the side of God.

CULTURE WARS

In the early 1990s, James Davison Hunter wrote a highly influential book in which he made the point that sectarian differences between Protestants and Roman Catholics had receded in importance and now were eclipsed by divisions that ran across denominational lines. The division, according to Hunter's analysis, was between those who had an "orthodox" view of the world and those who had a "progressive" view.[5] Or in the blunt words of James Dobson, the lines in the culture run between "those who say *God is*, and those who say *God is not*."

Theological Legalism

There is a very clear line that runs through America with regard to certain issues. On the religious front, theological liberalism may be viewed as an enemy of biblical Christianity, if by liberalism we mean a theology that attempts to thoroughly reconstruct Christian beliefs to bring them in line with modern cultural norms. Historic

Christian beliefs often are abandoned by theological liberals because they believe they rest on outdated or mistaken presuppositions. On other occasions, historic Christian beliefs are reinterpreted in a manner more conducive to the spirit of the age. For example, central doctrines relating to the person of Christ, including his divinity, are reinterpreted to suggest that by *divinity* we mean the modeling of qualities to which humanity as a whole can aspire.[6]

I had an unfortunate experience with a theological liberal some years ago. A pastor in our city had formed a group to assist in forming a Christian conciliation program. The purpose of the planned program was to assist Christians in settling their disputes out of court. The planning group included Christian professors of law (such as myself), Christian attorneys, several pastors, and a Christian professor of ethics at a local seminary. One of the Christian attorneys drafted a very simple statement of faith, which he suggested could be used as a basis for selecting future Christian conciliation board members. The brief statement of faith contained five items that could be commonly agreed to by all orthodox Christians. The statement of faith included belief in the triune God—Father, Son, and Holy Spirit; belief in Jesus Christ, who was fully man and fully God; belief in Christ's sacrificial death for our sins; belief in Christ's physical resurrection; and belief in Christ's return to judge the world.

It was, in my opinion, a statement of faith to which a Roman Catholic, a mainline Protestant, and an evangelical could all give hearty assent—but the professor of ethics didn't agree. He picked up the statement, and in a gesture of utter disdain, he threw it on the floor and said, "I don't believe any of this!" He then asked why we had to adopt a particular "metaphysical position" in order to do Christian conciliation: "Why can't we simply follow the ethics of 1 Corinthians 6, which instructs Christians to settle their disputes out of court without adopting a metaphysical position?"

I responded that "1 Corinthians 6 follows 1 Corinthians 5." I went on to say, "Horizontal reconciliation between Christians is rooted in the vertical reconciliation of a Christian to his or her Creator through the death of the Passover Lamb, Jesus Christ. It is because Christ has been sacrificed that we engage in Christian reconciliation." I then asked the professor what he expected me to do if I were to be one of the conciliators. I stated, "I'm approaching Christian conciliation with a whole set of metaphysical assumptions. For example, I would ask the participants to pray with me. Were we really praying to a God who was there, or were we merely engaged in a psychological exercise?"

The professor looked at me as though he had been accosted by a Neanderthal just unfrozen from a glacier somewhere in Greenland. He merely shook his head and said, "It is obvious that you and I have nothing in common." There is a very sharp line of demarcation that separates historic Christian orthodoxy and historic theological liberalism.[7]

Political Liberalism

A sharp line also separates biblical Christians from many political liberals on crucial cultural issues such as the sanctity of life and gay rights.[8] Concerning the sanctity of life, the biblical view is that all human life is sacred because human beings are created in the image of God. Human sin has not erased the divine image. Because we are image bearers, the lives of those still in the womb, those who have disabilities, and those who are elderly are entitled to the same legal and moral protections as are the lives of our most "productive" and healthy citizens. The "sanctity of life" view holds that from the moment of conception to the moment of one's natural death, every human being is afforded an inalienable God-given right to life.

On the other side of the cultural divide, many hold that personhood and any corresponding right to life are mere social constructions. Under this view, protection for human life exists only insofar as certain individuals (such as the mother of a fetus) or groups (such as the government) decide that that life is valuable. So, for example, Peter Singer, who was installed as Princeton University's first full-time professor of bioethics at its Center for Human Values, believes that the life of a human is no more sacred than that of a pig or a chimpanzee. Dismissing the notion of creation in the image of God as a relic of speciesism (the wrongful elevation of one species, namely, Homo sapiens, over another species, such as cows), Singer advocates a parent's right to kill severely disabled babies within twenty-eight days of birth. To the ethicist Singer, an infant is not a person, because it is not self-aware. On the other hand, slaughtering an animal (which *is* self-aware) would be wrong. *Self-awareness,* not creation in the image of God, becomes the new absolute for Singer.[9]

When human life is declared to be valuable only at a certain stage (upon birth or within twenty-eight days thereafter), or only if it is *wanted,* or only if it is *self-aware,* the door is opened to truly abominable practices such as partial-birth abortion. In September 1993, Brenda Pratt Shafer, a registered nurse with thirteen years of experience, was assigned by her nursing agency to an abortion clinic. Because Nurse Shafer considered herself "very pro-choice," she didn't think this assignment would be a problem. She was wrong. This is what Brenda Shafer saw:

> I stood at a doctor's side as he performed the partial-birth abortion procedure—and what I saw is branded forever on my mind. . . . The mother was six months pregnant (26–1/2 weeks). . . . On the ultrasound screen, I could see the heart beating. As the doctor watched the baby on the ultrasound screen, the baby's heartbeat was clearly visible on the ultrasound screen.
>
> The doctor went in with forceps and grabbed the baby's legs and pulled them down into the birth canal. Then he delivered the baby's body and arms—everything but the head. The doctor kept the baby's head just inside the uterus. The baby's little fingers were clasping and unclasping, and his feet were kicking. Then the doctor stuck the scissors through the back of the baby's head, and the baby's arms jerked out in a flinch, a startle reaction, like a baby does when he thinks that he might fall. The doctor opened up the scissors, stuck a high-powered

suction tube into the opening, and sucked the baby's brains out. Now the baby was completely limp. I was really completely unprepared for what I was seeing. . . .

I have been a nurse for a long time and I have seen a lot of death—people maimed in auto accidents, gunshot wounds, you name it. I have seen surgical procedures of every sort. But in all my professional years, I had never witnessed anything like this. . . .

That baby boy had the most perfect angelic face I have ever seen. . . . After I left that day, I never went back.[10]

While very clear lines of demarcation separate differing views of human life, as well as differing views of gay rights (see chapters 8 and 9 for an in-depth discussion of gay rights), other issues in the so-called culture war are fuzzier.

MOVING BEYOND THE CULTURE WARS

In the opening chapter I described various ways that items can be classified. One approach was fuzzy-set theory. As its name implies, the line separating one thing from another is not clear, but fuzzy. According to fuzzy-set theory, a person might ask the question, "When does a mountain begin?" or "When does an ocean begin?" The same could be asked regarding conservatism and liberalism. Contrary to the fund-raising appeals of "Religious Right" organizations, no clear biblical lines separate political conservatism from political liberalism.[11]

It is not surprising that the lines get very fuzzy when we attempt to apply the Bible to contemporary political agendas and issues. For one thing, the New Testament view of the state is not at all uniform. As D. A. Carson points out, "In the Apocalypse, the [Roman] Empire becomes the very embodiment of evil; Luke/Acts goes out of its way to persuade Roman leaders that the Christian movement is not politically dangerous; Paul can argue that the powers that be are ordained of God."[12] So when a person asks, "What is the biblical perspective of the Christian's relationship to the government," it is fair to answer, "There are biblical *perspectives*, but no singular perspective."

Second, not all liberal perspectives are necessarily antibiblical. For example, liberals would almost certainly be opposed to slavery. Likewise, liberals would be against child labor, cigarette smoking, and racism, just as they would be for equitable wages, safe working conditions, environmental protection, and women's rights. On these and a host of other issues, many biblical Christians would find themselves in substantial agreement with the perspectives of liberals. Indeed, we all ought to be grateful to liberals for calling attention to issues that are in line with biblical themes of justice, tolerance, human dignity, and compassion for the weak.

Third, not all conservative perspectives are necessarily Christian or biblical. For example, a conservative perspective may be fiercely nationalistic, adopting an "America first" mentality. But why would a Christian have primary loyalties to the United States or some other country, rather than to the world community of which the Christian is a part? A conservative perspective may be decidedly anti-immigration, a viewpoint that could be difficult to square with biblical injunctions regarding taking care of the alien and stranger.[13]

A conservative perspective may favor unrestricted gun ownership or unrestrained free enterprise. In the American South, a conservative perspective would have supported slavery and Jim Crow legislation. In South Africa, a conservative perspective supported apartheid. A strong case could be made that these conservative viewpoints are 180 degrees out of sync with the Bible.

Fourth, many politicians move back and forth across the lines, causing even more fuzziness. To cite one example, former president Bill Clinton (who was clearly a "lightning rod" of conservative attack) signed the first major welfare reform law in a generation and also signed the Defense of Marriage Act, authorizing federal agencies and state governments to give no validity to same-sex marriages. Clinton's strategy of triangulation, that is, his adoption of popular Republican agenda items such as "law and order," capital punishment, and balanced budgets, further demonstrates how fuzzy the lines of demarcation can be.

School Prayer and Culture Wars Rhetoric

Many issues do not resolve themselves into the neat biblical versus antibiblical distinctions suggested by political fund-raising letters. In fact, the complexity of applying Christianity and the Bible to contemporary political issues cannot be overstated. For example, it is often asserted that "the problem in our schools began when the Supreme Court kicked God and prayer out of the public school classroom. If we want our schools to stop being so violent, we simply need to restore prayer." Dismissing the question of whether a causal connection between a lack of public school prayer and school shootings could ever be established, it would be helpful for Christians to acknowledge that the issue of prayer in public schools is not at all straightforward or simple.

As a result of the increasing diversity of American and other Western societies, how shall we pray in the public schools? If prayer is the answer, which prayer should be offered—the prayer of the Muslims to Allah, or the prayer of Buddhists, Jews, Roman Catholics, agnostics, liberal Protestants, postliberals, Satanists? Some suggest that because we live in a democracy, the majority ought to rule. John Rawls, a professor of philosophy of law, once said, "A just rule is a rule that you would want applied if you didn't know whether or not you would be in charge." Majority rule makes sense to a Christian, *if the Christian is in the majority*.

But would you, as a Christian, want majority rule if you lived in a neighborhood in Dearborn, Michigan, that is 90 percent Muslim? Would you want your children subjected to prayers from the Qur'an? If we put it this way, it becomes easier to sympathize with Jewish students in Bible-Belt Texas towns whose parents object to the recitation of the Lord's Prayer from loudspeakers before high school football games.

An alternative to majority rule might be to have a government official (or committee) draft a bland, inoffensive, generic prayer to a higher power, whoever it, he, or she may be. The positive effect of a bland government-issued prayer can be seriously debated. I certainly don't want my children to be led in a government-sanctioned prayer. Moreover, I am amazed that Christian parents would want public school teachers, many of whom are agnostics or atheists, leading their children in any kind of prayer, even a Christian prayer.

My point is not that no solution could be worked out; a moment of silence may, in fact, be a reasonable solution. Rather, I object to the ease with which many members of the Christian Right seem to sweep aside the obvious difficulties of formulating a just solution to the problem of prayer in a public school setting. I also object to the demagoguery of suggesting that the elimination of prayer in an increasingly pluralistic public school setting can be traced to an anti-God, antibiblical, leftist conspiracy to take over the country. It is simply not that easy.

Is the Selection of a Candidate Obvious?

Fuzziness is not simply an issue in selecting between the competing merits of differing political proposals. Fuzziness is also an issue in selecting between political candidates who are running for office. How *does* one make a biblical choice of a political candidate? Should we pay attention to a politician's declaration of faith in Jesus Christ? Many Christians, even politically savvy Christians, have been taken in by politicians' declarations of faith.

Billy Graham's biographer wrote movingly about Graham's horror at the discovery that he had been deceived by Richard Nixon's regular use of evangelical terminology and biblical references in his notes to Graham. When Billy Graham heard tapes of Nixon's conversations, disclosed after the Watergate hearings, he heard Nixon using the foulest and most blasphemous language imaginable. Graham said that after listening to the Nixon tapes, he literally vomited and then wept for several days, like Samuel did over King Saul.[14]

This hits home because I have the personal experience of being taken in by politicians' professions of Christian faith. A local politician in my city stood before a predominantly Christian pro-life group and held up a Bible saying, "The problem with America is that we have moved away from this book. I believe that the words of this book are the words of God. If I am elected, I'm going to base my administration on this book." Christians in the crowd cheered wildly. A close friend of mine went backstage with the politician after the speech. My friend told me that this politician turned to one of his aides and said, "Can you believe how stupid those . . . Christians are. Maybe next time I'll hold up pictures of Jesus."

Obviously, not all professions of faith by Christian politicians are insincere. But stories such as the one my friend told me, or the banner headlines about a Christian prosecutor in South Florida who was arrested for soliciting prostitution after making the fighting of vice a central theme in his campaign, should make Christian voters wake up and take notice. We dare not be naive about the possibility that declarations of faith may either be false or be used in a manipulative way to garner votes.

If a candidate's declaration of faith is not a clear basis on which to decide whether or not to vote for that candidate, and if most issues do not resolve themselves neatly into a biblical versus antibiblical framework, then how should a Christian make decisions for or against a candidate or for or against a particular issue? It is here that centered-set theory continues to provide a solution.

SOME MODEST PROPOSALS FOR CHRISTIAN PUBLIC ENGAGEMENT

In contrast to those who want to reduce all issues to "us" versus "them," God versus anti-God, our views versus the views of our enemies, I don't believe that the bounded-set language (see chapter 1) of culture-wars rhetoric is particularly helpful when dealing with many of the complex issues in our culture. Throughout this book, I have suggested that centered-set language, in which we speak about moving toward or away from a Christian approach, would be far more useful.

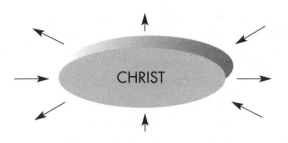

Centered-set language has great applicability to debates between political conservatives and political liberals. In the center of a Christian's approach to politics are, at a minimum, the following characteristics:

- A Christian approach is civil.
- A Christian approach uses persuasion, not force.
- A Christian approach is realistic.
- A Christian approach focuses on the main themes of the biblical story line.

A Christian Approach Is Civil

Some years ago I wrote a response paper to a critic of the charismatic movement. In this particular book, the critic claimed that "most charismatics fall back on the all too easy defense that virtually every critique of their movement is unfair and unkind. Noncharismatics, intimidated by that accusation, are effectively silenced."[15]

In my response, I pointed out that if the author wanted to understand why charismatics found it difficult to receive his message, all he would need to do is go through his book page by page and simply note the disparaging labels he used and the attacks he made on the motivations, intelligence, and orthodoxy of charismatics. Along the way, the author accused charismatics and Pentecostals of being immoral; "keen, but clueless"; anti-intellectual; not far removed from existentialism, humanism, and paganism; and being perilously close to neo-Baalism. He then expressed surprise that charismatics become defensive when he "speaks the truth in love" to them.[16] He also claimed that charismatic belief caused immoral behavior, resulted in sloppy exegesis, and tended to produce spiritual casualties.[17] He lumped charismatics with non-Christian leaders such as Sun Myung Moon, Joseph Smith, Edgar Cayce, and L. Ron Hubbard. Finally, he cited the most egregious examples of excesses from the charismatic and Pentecostal camps, instead of citing mainstream pronouncements from large Pentecostal or charismatic denominations.

In 1957, Carl Henry, then the editor of *Christianity Today,* wrote a critique of fundamentalism that applies not only to the way we Christians speak about each other, but also about persons with whom we differ culturally or politically:

> The real bankruptcy of fundamentalism has resulted not so much from a reactionary spirit—lamentable as this was—as from a harsh temperament, a spirit of lovelessness and strife contributed by much of its leadership in the recent past. . . .
>
> This character of fundamentalism as a temperament, and not primarily fundamentalism as a theology, has brought the movement into contemporary discredit. . . . Historically, fundamentalism was a theological position; only gradually did the movement come to signify a mood and disposition as well.
>
> If modernism stands discredited as a perversion of scriptural theology, certainly fundamentalism, in its contemporary expression, stands discredited as a perversion of the biblical spirit.[18]

It is this uncivil spirit, this temperament of lovelessness, that many contemporary critics of the Religious Right accurately (in my opinion) oppose. D. A. Carson points out that one of the reasons for Francis Schaeffer's influence was his ability to present his analysis of the culture with a tear in his eye.[19] Although a person may have disagreed with Schaeffer's analysis of culture, he or she could not disagree with Schaeffer's compassion. It is appropriate to ask whether the tone of much of contemporary Christian literature and preaching sounds as though it is written or spoken with tears in our eyes, or whether it sounds just plain angry.

A Christian Approach Uses Persuasion, Not Force

As we Christians engage our culture on a host of issues, our major weapon is persuasion. The Greek word *peithō* (often used in the sense of "to convince" or "to persuade") is used at least eight times in the book of Acts to refer to the proclamation of early Christians. Persuasion is mentioned a half dozen other times in the New Testament to refer to the way early Christians attempted to change people's minds through reasoning.

Many Christians today believe there is a shortcut to changing the moral landscape of our country through taking control of key political offices. "If we could only get a Christian president," many Christians feel, "then we could turn this country around." Cal Thomas offered this bleak assessment of Christians' attempt to change the moral landscape through legislation:

> Two decades after conservative Christians charged into the political arena, bringing new voters and millions of dollars with them in hopes of transforming the culture through political power, *it must now be acknowledged that we have failed.* We failed not because we were wrong about our critique of culture, or because we lacked conviction, or because there were not enough of us, or because too many were lethargic and uncommitted. We failed because we were unable to redirect a nation from the top down. Real change must come from the bottom up or, better yet, from the inside out.[20]

I have seen the effect of "bottom-up" persuasion. Our church has a very popular Sunday evening service for young adults in their twenties. Many of them have been influenced by popular messages about a woman's right to choose and a fetus being nothing other than a part of a woman's body. These young adults did not have their attitudes changed through the imposition of pro-life legislation. Instead, hundreds have reported that their perspectives changed as a result of the educational process of preaching, dialogue, group life, and testimonies from women who have had abortions.

Legislation is not wrong in its place. In a democratic society, the place of legislation is the same as the place of a cart with respect to a horse. The horse is the conversion of the hearts and minds of men and women to a biblical position through the power of persuasion; the cart is the passage of laws designed to reinforce the will of the people.

A Christian Approach Is Realistic

Theologians are fond of saying that we live "between the times," that is, between the first and second comings of Christ. A realistic approach to cultural engagement, therefore, will be neither overly optimistic or overly pessimistic. We are not overly pessimistic, because of God's common grace—"the grace of God by which he gives people innumerable blessings that are not part of salvation."[21] It is called *common,* because the grace is common to all people and is not restricted to believers.

Government and law are the result of common grace. We see the institution of government by God after the flood (Genesis 9:6), and we see it as a gift from God in Romans 13:4, where the apostle Paul says, "[The ruler] is God's servant to do you good," and he is "God's servant, an agent of wrath to bring punishment on the wrongdoer." Because of common grace, believers and nonbelievers can work together on issues of common concern, such as marriage, child rearing, education, and abortion.

On the other hand, common grace is not saving grace, and the political realm is not the kingdom of God. Sometimes when I listen to Christians speak, their rhetoric about what can be achieved through politics is wildly overinflated. While there is no absolute separation between the political and the personal, many of the church's concerns are primarily *pastoral and personal,* not political! In other words, the church must be realistic about the limits of politics in ministering to the broad range of human needs it faces.

Wilfred McClay, a Tulane University professor from 1987 until 1999, attended the funeral service of a young woman friend from his university who had died while giving birth to her second child. McClay wrote an outraged response to the minister's eulogy, which had shown gross insensitivity to the personal needs of the grieving audience:

> Where the rest of us had been stunned into reflective silence, awed and chastened by this reminder of the slender thread by which our lives hang, the minister had other things in mind.... He did not try to comfort her family and friends. Nor did he challenge us to remember the hard words of the Lord's Prayer, "Thy will be done." Instead, he smoothly launched into a well-oiled tirade against the misplaced priorities of our society, in which billions of dollars were being poured into "Star Wars" research while young woman such as this one were being allowed to die on the operating table. That was all the minister had to say. His eulogy was, in effect, a pitch for less federal spending on defense and more spending on the development of medical technology.... The only thing omitted was an injunction that we write our congressman, or Ralph Nader, about this outrage.
>
> I could hardly believe my ears. Leave aside the eulogy's unspeakable vulgarity, its unintentional cruelty to the woman's family, leave aside all the self-satisfied and self-righteous tone of easy moral outrage, leave aside the fashionable opinions; leave aside the flabby and clichéd quality of language and speech. I'm even willing to concede for the sake of argument that the minister may have been right in everything he said.... Nothing can alter the fact that he failed us, failed her, and failed his calling by squandering a precious moment

for the sake of a second-rate stump speech and by forcing us to hold our sorrow back in the privacy of our own hearts, at the very moment it needed common expression. That moment can never be recovered.

Nothing that religion does is more important than equipping us to endure life's passages by helping us to find meaning in pain and loss. With meaning, many things are bearable. But our eulogist did not know how to give it to us. All he had to offer were his political desiderata.[22]

Christian political involvement will also be realistic about the possibility of our being deceived by feigned confessions of faith. I referenced earlier the hypocritical use of faith by a local politician in our city. Realism reminds us to never fix our hope on a human political savior, however much he or she quotes the Bible. Realism also reminds us of our own susceptibility to being seduced by power. It is an incredibly heady experience to sit in the Oval Office with the world's most powerful political leader or to be invited to have lunch with the governor or a big-city mayor. Realism reminds us of the limitations imposed on us by our own needy egos and our desire to be accepted by those who hold earthly power.

A Christian Approach Follows the Biblical Story Line

When I say that a Christian approach to the great cultural issues of our day ought to be biblical, I do not mean that we should search for a Bible verse or a proof text to justify a particular political or moral decision. Often, even regarding the watershed issues of abortion and euthanasia, one has the uncomfortable feeling that the interpretation of individual Bible verses is being bent to support a pro-life position. Far stronger is an approach to politics (or the other issues raised in this book, such as homosexuality, feminism, postmodernism, or the New Age) that follows the biblical story line. The Bible can be described as a drama in three acts: Creation, the Fall, and Redemption.

Creation

Creation teaches us that every human being, wanted or unwanted, productive or unproductive, able-bodied or grossly deformed, is created in the image of God. From creation in the image of God, we derive our fundamental understandings of the sacredness of life and the equality of all human beings under the law. This leads to legal protection for the elderly, the dying, the weak, the alien, the pre-born, the disabled, racial minorities, and women.

The ordination of women in the church would find grounding in the biblical creation account: "So God created man in his own image, in the image of God he created him; male and female he created them."[23] Because creation involves sexually differentiated persons, and God placed his blessing on *heterosexual marriage,* we Christians find much in the gay rights agenda that is antithetical to the biblical story line.

The Fall

Act II of the biblical drama is *the Fall.* Because of sin, we Christians ought never to place naive confidence in the moral goodness of either individuals or collective groups such as a government, corporations, or unions. As Reinhold Niebuhr stated, "What is lacking among [liberal moralists], whether religious or rational, is an understanding of the brutal character of the behavior of all human collectives, and the power of self-interest and collective egoism in all inter-group relations."[24] Christians who have a profound biblical understanding of the Fall will recognize the need for limits on individuals and groups—whatever that individual's or group's religious profession may be. We are aware, as a result of the Fall, that power is poison, and so we are suspicious whenever too much unchecked power resides anywhere—whether among liberals or conservatives, Christians or non-Christians.

Because of the Fall, we Christians tend to be suspicious of root-cause explanations for bad behavior that do not contain a moral component. So, for example, regarding crime, Christians in general are suspicious about models that focus exclusively on education or economics. While education and economics undoubtedly play some role, a biblical perspective would be more at home with a moral poverty theory of crime. Princeton University professor and researcher John Dilulio has this to say about moral poverty:

> Moral poverty is the poverty of being without loving, capable, responsible adults who teach you right from wrong. It is the poverty of being without parents and other authorities who habituate you to feel joy at others' joy, pain at others' pain, happiness when you do right, remorse when you do wrong. It is the poverty of growing up in the virtual absence of people who teach morality by their own everyday example and who insist that you follow suit.[25]

A moral poverty theory can help explain why churchgoing, two-parent Black families in the Jim Crow South who lived in desperate economic straits and who had free access to guns never experienced anything like the gang violence and homicide rates that plague inner-city neighborhoods today. Moral poverty also explains why middle-class and upper-class white neighborhoods are experiencing epidemic levels of out-of-wedlock births, drug abuse, crime, and divorce.

Redemption

The answer that Christians look to is found in the third act of the biblical drama, namely, *redemption in Christ.* Christ alone is the focus of Christian hope. Nothing else and no one else can become an absolute, according to the biblical story line—not democracy, capitalism, or "family values." Democracy, for example, can be woefully wrong, as Abraham Lincoln argued in his famous debates with Stephen Douglas. Douglas advocated popular sovereignty (democracy) for determining whether slavery would spread to newly settled American territories. Lincoln, in contrast, rejected the spread of slavery not on democratic principles, but on the principle of higher law, namely, the law of Christ!

Likewise, family is a good, but it is not an absolute good. In fact, some of the contemporary conservative discussion about family values is much closer to the views of family held by the Pharisees than the views held by Jesus. One recent Jewish writer summarized the rabbinic view of family this way: "[Talmudic] literature is full of comments and statements on the value of family life. The sages . . . tried to invest family life with an aura of holiness. Family life is held in high value in most of the literature of the Second Commonwealth."[26]

Jesus regularly advocated behavior toward family that the Pharisees (and perhaps some contemporary family-values advocates) would find scandalous. For example, in first-century Judaism, the obligation to provide a proper burial for one's immediate family was so great as to override almost all other considerations.[27] But we read, "Another disciple said to [Jesus], 'Lord, first let me go and bury my father.' But Jesus told him, 'Follow me, and let the dead bury their own dead.'"[28] Similarly, we read this: "As Jesus was saying these things, a woman in the crowd called out, 'Blessed is the mother who gave you birth and nursed you.' He replied, 'Blessed rather are those who hear the word of God and obey it.'"[29]

We dare not miss Jesus' point that he alone is entitled to absolute loyalty, and that other relationships, such as one's relationship to family, work, or country, are only relative loyalties. We remember Jesus' words:

> "Do not suppose that I have come to bring peace to the earth. I did not come to bring peace, but a sword. For I have come to turn
>
> "'a man against his father
> a daughter against her mother,
> a daughter-in-law against her mother-in-law—
> a man's enemies will be the members of his own household.'
>
> "Anyone who loves his father or mother more than me is not worthy of me; anyone who loves his son or

daughter more than me is not worthy of me; and anyone
who does not take his cross and follow me is not worthy
of me."[30]

Following Jesus takes precedence over every other loyalty. It's not
enough to merely *assume* that Christians understand this. Sometimes
in the discussion of "traditional values," "family values," or "orthodox
values," the primacy of Jesus' claims is all but lost.

Redemption has an agent. That agent is not the government or
the political realm, but it is *the church*. Government can exert great
pressure for moral good around the world. But redemption can only
be effected by the church. I am personally encouraged by the focus
on faith-based (or, rather, church-based) initiatives as a solution for
social problems such as substance abuse, homelessness, child care,
and vocational training. How did we ever arrive at a place of
believing that without faith and without the church, we could
ultimately solve moral problems?

Finally, the ethos of redemption is *love*. Throughout this book, I
have repeatedly referred to ways that a bridge of welcome has been
built to those typically considered to be enemies by many conservative
Christians. Bridge building almost always involves the practice of love.

Two Stories of Welcome

How many times have you passed by a homeless person and
decided to keep a safe distance from where they were sleeping on
the street or on a park bench? A man in our church named Willy
had a church background, but wasn't much interested in Christ. To
him, Christianity was a giant list of do's and don'ts—mostly don'ts.
Here is Willy's story in his own words:

> I've spent most of my life as rootless drifter. I was
> estranged from my family and every other kind of
> healthy relationship. I eventually found myself com-
> pletely homeless, living just south of downtown by the
> river. I spent three years down there and was completely
> without hope.

A church group from Vineyard came down to the river on a regular basis to pass out food and blankets, as well as other supplies. I began to develop a relationship with some of the people who came down. I was almost always drunk, yet they kept offering me friendship. The Christianity I saw in their lives was not just a bunch of rules. Instead, they were offering relationship.

One year ago, a small group of people from the church came to the camp where I was sleeping. They gave me food and a blanket. But most important of all, they laid hands on me and prayed for me. That morning, I had cried out for God. I had just consumed a forty-ounce bottle of malt liquor, and I felt sicker than ever. I felt like I was going to die.

After I received prayer, God began to change me. I spent the next week going through detox. A pastor at the church helped to arrange a place for me to stay at a halfway house. I was able to get a job as well. I began having difficulty at the halfway house and felt like going back to the river. That same day, the phone rang at the halfway house, and it was the pastor of the church's ministry to the homeless. He told me to hang on and that he would call back in a little while. In an hour, he called me back. He had found an apartment for me to live in. I soon moved out of the halfway house and into an apartment near one of the families from the church. They gave me work as an independent contractor for a business they ran. I've been sober for over a year. I recently reconciled with my father, and I'm currently attempting to reconcile with my son, who is twenty-seven years old.

Each Saturday I take groups from the church over to the river to minister to my old friends and to introduce them to my Jesus. They see how much God has done to help me. Several of my old friends have followed me off the streets.

This week you may encounter a "Willy" hanging out near your university, in front of a downtown office building, by a McDonald's, or at the boardwalk. What difference would it make to you if you said to yourself, "This man or woman is not my enemy." How could you or your church begin to practice the welcome of the kingdom with men and women like Willy?

A member of our church, whom I'll call Jim, is another example of someone you might regard to be an enemy of Christianity. Jim had been an atheist for as long as he could remember. When he was a student at our state university, he had joined an atheist club called "the Society of Humanists." The basic agenda for this club was to actively discourage students from pursuing Christianity. Here is how Jim described his involvement in this organization:

> After I had been a member of the club for a while, we decided to pursue becoming an officially sanctioned student organization in order to receive funding from the school. As part of the application process, we had to elect an officer to preside over our organization. I agreed to become the officer and was able to choose my own title. I decided on the title "chaplain," because it was yet another way to mock Christianity.
>
> Shortly after graduating, I found a job in the mental health field. I worked very closely with a woman named Lisa. Lisa would often tell me that Jesus loved me. Even though I was very steadfast in my atheism, Lisa continued to show me unwavering kindness. She would often invite me to church, and each time I would decline her invitations. I said I might take her up on the offer in two years.
>
> One day Lisa told me that she really loved me (in a nonromantic way) and that she often prayed for me. I told her that I appreciated the sentiment, but I didn't believe in God. Undaunted by my statement, Lisa told me that Jesus loved me even more than she did. That really impacted me. I now had a reference point for the

love she was talking about. She was consistently loving toward all of her coworkers, and her words had real authority.

Shortly after our conversation, a friend of mine, Bill, who was also a longtime atheist, invited me out to lunch. I had heard that he recently had become "born again," and I expected that he would try to convert me. I was not surprised when he pulled out the Bible at lunch and started sharing the gospel with me. In a way, Lisa's kindness toward me primed me to hear my friend's gospel presentation. When he was finished, Bill invited me to receive Christ, but I turned down the offer. Even though I was intrigued by what he had shared, I did not respond. Bill shared that the reason he called to invite me to lunch was that he had had a dream about me. In his dream, I was dying. I thought, "That's weird. I'm not planning on dying anytime soon."

One week later I was in the hospital with spinal meningitis, completely bedridden, and I had a debilitating headache. As I lay there, I thought about my conversations with Lisa and Bill. One night I had a very vivid dream. I was driving my car and was overcome by the stench of filth in my trunk. I stopped the car, opened the trunk, and attempted to shovel the filth out, but it kept slipping off the shovel. I was powerless to clean out the filth in the trunk of my car. I awoke from the dream and knew what it meant. I could not deal with my sin on my own. I knew I needed God to change me.

While I still resisted giving my life to Jesus, I now believed in God. I just wasn't sure that Jesus was the way to God. After some investigation, I discovered that no other religion addressed the issue in my dream. No one but Christ claimed to be able to wash away my sin. So I prayed to receive Christ into my life. As I was praying, I felt that God was holding me, saying, "I love you, my son."

I recovered from spinal meningitis and started to pursue my newfound faith by reading the Bible. After getting back to work, I told Lisa and Bill what I had done. Lisa invited me to go to church, but I declined. I thought I could walk as a Christian alone. However, Lisa opened her calendar and showed me where, exactly two years before, I had promised that I would go to church with her. My two years were up!

We attended a church outreach event in the summer of 1995. The band that was playing impressed me, and I was surprised to hear Jimmy Hendrix licks on the guitar. During the teaching, I was challenged that I had to acknowledge Jesus before other people by making a public confession. So I went forward at the invitation and publicly proclaimed my faith in Jesus Christ.

Since Jim's conversion, he has led several small groups, been involved with the drama and children's ministry, led worship, and graduated from the church's training school for future pastors and leaders. It would have been easy to write off Jim as unreachable, especially because of his vocal and very public anti-Christian positions. The most natural thing in the world would have been to respond in kind to Jim.

But consider the fact that the two people at the center of two of the most unpopular United States Supreme Court decisions (at least with Christians) have since become outspoken believers in Christ: Norma McCorvey (a.k.a. Jane Roe) and William J. Murray (son of noted atheist Madalyn Murray O'Hair). Norma McCorvey was the plaintiff in the Supreme Court case (*Roe* v. *Wade*) that legalized abortion in all fifty states. William Murray was one of the plaintiffs in the Supreme Court case that prohibited prayer in schools. Consider further that the "poster child" of the culture left, Jane Fonda, a woman who has been vilified over the years by many Christian newsletters and magazines, has also declared her faith in Christ. What would the "Christian press" have said about Saul, the persecutor of the church, before Damascus Road?

The truth is, it is impossible to know what is going on in the hearts of the "Jims" or the "Janes" or the "Normas" or the "Williams." It is also impossible to know what effect a loving witness will have on such people—no matter what their initial positions or protestations may be. Nothing on earth (or in heaven) compares to the joy felt "over one sinner who repents."[31] Share the joy! Be an agent of one of God's greatest miracles. Let God use you to proclaim the welcome of the kingdom to persons certain other Christians have tended to treat as enemies!

Questions for Reflection and Discussion

?

1. Have you noticed a tendency to designate one political party to be "the only acceptable Christian choice"? If you have noticed this tendency, do you agree or disagree with it?

2. What issues in the contemporary "culture wars" debate do you think can be clearly determined by an appeal to the Bible? What issues cannot be clearly determined by appealing to Scripture?

3. Do you agree or disagree with the author's assigning of prayer in public schools as a fuzzy-set issue?

4. Where have you witnessed the absence of civility by Christians in either a contemporary theological or political debate?

5. Apply the author's "biblical story line" approach (Creation, the Fall, Redemption) to the following: big government, sex education in public schools, and gun control.

RECOMMENDED READING

Bork, Robert H. *The Tempting of America: The Political Seduction of the Law.* New York: Touchstone, 1990.

Guinness, Os. *The American Hour: A Time of Reckoning and the Once and Future Role of Faith.* New York: Macmillan, 1993.

Hunter, James Davison. *Culture Wars: The Struggle to Define America.* New York: Basic Books, 1994.

Medved, Michael. *Hollywood vs. America: Popular Culture and the War on Traditional Values.* New York: HarperCollins, 1992.

Olasky, Marvin. *The Tragedy of American Compassion.* Washington, D.C.: Regnery, 1992.

Thomas, Cal, and Ed Dobson. *Blinded by Might: Can the Religious Right Save America?* Grand Rapids: Zondervan, 1999.

Appendix: Listing of Web Links

WEB LINKS ON POSTMODERNISM

1. www.regenerator.com/
   Home page of The Regeneration Forum
   According to the Web site, its mission is as follows: "Rooted in orthodox Christianity, The Regeneration Forum gathers emerging Christian leaders across deep differences, advancing conversations and relationships that will impact the future of the church and the culture." Provides excellent discussions for Christians who want to make an impact in our postmodern world.

2. www.joshuahouse.org/
   Joshua House is the young adult ministry of Vineyard Columbus (Ohio) that strives to be "a growing community gathered around Jesus, and to express a missional heart by sharing the love of Jesus with those around us."

WEB LINKS ON FEMINISM

1. www.cbeinternational.org/
   Home page of Christians for Biblical Equality
   According to the Web site, "Christians for Biblical Equality is a church and individual membership-organization of men and women from over 100 denominations, who believe that the Bible, properly interpreted, teaches the fundamental equality of believers of all racial and ethnic groups, all economic classes, and all age groups, based on the teachings of Scripture as reflected in Galatians 3:28: *There is neither Jew nor Greek, there is neither slave nor free, there is neither male nor female; for you are all one in Christ Jesus.*"

2. www.feministsforlife.org/
   Feminists for Life of America provides an exploration of the feminist roots of the pro-life movement. According to the Web site, "Feminists for Life is a nonsectarian, grassroots organization that

seeks true equality for all human beings, particularly women. We oppose all forms of violence, including abortion, euthanasia, and capital punishment, as they are inconsistent with the core feminine principles of justice, nonviolence, and nondiscrimination."

WEB LINKS ON HOMOSEXUALITY

1. www.exodusnorthamerica.org/ ; also www.exodusintl.org/

Exodus is a nonprofit, interdenominational Christian organization promoting the message of "freedom from homosexuality through the power of Jesus Christ."

2. www.desertstream.org/

According to the Web site, "Desert Stream is a local, national, and international ministry proclaiming the transforming power of Jesus Christ. All of our efforts are fueled by the confidence that Jesus Christ is the only hope for a world struggling under the weight of sexual and relational brokenness and the resulting destruction." Its mission statement reads as follows: "Based on the biblical foundation of compassion, integrity, and dependence on God, Desert Stream Ministries proclaims to the world the transforming power of Jesus Christ. We equip the body of Christ to minister healing to the sexually and relationally broken, and to those with life-defining illnesses, through healing groups and leadership training for the local church."

3. www.projectcompassion.com/

The ministry of Vineyard Columbus (Ohio) to those afflicted with the AIDS virus. According to the Web site, its mission statement is as follows: "Project Compassion reaches out to the men, women, and children in our community and beyond who have HIV/AIDS. We provide physical, emotional, and spiritual support. We also educate the public on the facts and issues surrounding AIDS."

WEB LINKS ON THE NEW AGE MOVEMENT

1. cesc.montreat.edu/ceo/CEA/

Home page of the Christian Environmental Association

For Christians interested in finding ways to become involved in environmental stewardship.

According to the Web site, "The Christian Environmental Association is a nationwide organization joined together to promote Biblical environmental stewardship within the Christian community." Its mission is defined as "Serving the Earth, Serving the Poor." Its Target Earth program (www.targetearth.org/) "is active in 15 countries— buying up endangered lands, protecting people, saving the jaguar, sharing the love of Jesus, feeding the hungry, and reforesting ravaged terrain. We are a movement that is marked by a spirited desire to live a life of value. And a belief that Christians have a unique role in today's world that is so pressed by poverty, destruction, and violence."

2. www.theatlantic.com/issues/2001/01/allen.htm

"The Scholars and the Goddess: Historically speaking, the 'ancient' rituals of the Goddess movement are almost certainly bunk."

This insightful article by Charlotte Allen, senior editor of *Crisis* magazine, critiques the historicity of Goddess worship.

WEB LINKS ON LIBERALISM

1. www.esa-online.org/

Home page of Evangelicals for Social Action

According to the Web site, this organization is made up of "Evangelicals working together to challenge and equip the church to be agents of God's redemption and transformation in the world." They do this through

- reflection on church and society.
- training in holistic ministry.
- linking people together for mutual learning and action.

Notes

CHAPTER 1: WHO IS MY ENEMY?

1. Michael Cromartie, "Up to Our Steeples in Politics," in *No God but God: Breaking with the Idols of Our Age*, eds. Os Guinness and John Seel (Chicago: Moody Press, 1992), 58.
2. *The Best of G. A. Studdert-Kennedy* (New York: Harper and Brothers, 1924).
3. Acts 17:24.
4. John 1:10.
5. John 3:16.
6. David Wells, *God in the Wasteland* (Grand Rapids: Eerdmans, 1994), 40. When I use the term *culture* in this book, I'm using it as a combination of the second and third senses of the term *world*. According to H. Richard Niebuhr, "culture is the artificial, secondary environment which man superimposes upon the natural. It comprises language, habits, ideas, beliefs, customs, social organization, inherited artifacts, technical processes, and values. . . . Culture is human achievement. We distinguish it from nature by noting the evidence of human purpose and effort" (H. Richard Niebuhr, *Christ and Culture* [New York: Harper & Row, 1951], 32–33).
7. James Hefley and Marti Hefley, *By Their Blood* (Milford, Mich.: Mott Media, 1979), 27.
8. Hefley and Hefley, *By Their Blood*, 25.
9. Paul Marshall, "Keeping the Faith: Religion, Freedom, and International Affairs," *Imprimis* 28, no. 3 (March 1999): 2.
10. Marshall, "Keeping the Faith," 4.
11. Eugene H. Peterson, *The Contemplative Pastor* (Grand Rapids: Eerdmans, 1993), 10.
12. Marshall, "Keeping the Faith," 1.
13. Patrick Glynn, *God: the Evidence: The Reconciliation of Faith and Reason in a Postsecular World* (Rocklin, Calif.: Prima, 1997), 3–4.
14. Karl Barth, *The Word of God and the Word of Man* (New York: Harper & Row, 1956), 104.
15. Jeremiah 8:11.
16. Paul G. Hiebert, "Sets and Structures: A Study of Church Patterns," in *New Horizons in World Missions*, ed. David J. Hesselgrave (Grand Rapids: Baker, 1979), 217–27.
17. See Ephesians 2:13.
18. 1 John 3:14.
19. N. T. Wright, *Jesus and the Victory of God* (Minneapolis: Fortress, 1996), chapter 10.

20. This is why we read of so many challenges by the Pharisees concerning Jesus' practice of the Sabbath (see, for example, Mark 2:23–3:7; Luke 13:10–17; John 9:13–16). Jesus was challenging the fundamental identity of Israel by suggesting that keeping the Sabbath in a certain fashion did not make one a *true Israelite*.
21. John 13:35; 6:40.
22. See Matthew 8:13.
23. See Mark 8:34–38.
24. Matthew 16:4.
25. See Luke 16:14–15.
26. Matthew 13:24–30, 47–50.
27. 1 Corinthians 5:12–13.
28. See Matthew 5:13–16.
29. Wright, *Jesus and the Victory of God*, 308–9.
30. Wright, *Jesus and the Victory of God*, 449.
31. Luke 19:42, emphasis added.
32. Acts 2:5–11.
33. "Bible Salesman Inspired to Found Translators," *Arizona Republic*, 12 July 1998, A–14.
34. The Edict of Milan, agreed to by the Roman emperors Constantine and Licinius, proclaimed absolute freedom of the conscience and placed Christianity on a full legal equality with any religion of the Roman world.
35. Matthew 9:36.
36. John 7:49.

CHAPTER 2: THE HODGEPODGE ON THE HIGHWAY

1. Lisa Miller, "The Age of Divine Disunity: Faith Now Springs from a Hodgepodge of Beliefs," *Wall Street Journal*, 10 February 1999, B–1.
2. Miller, "The Age of Divine Disunity," B–1.
3. Richard J. Mouw, "Babel Undone," *First Things* 83 (May 1998): 9.
4. See David S. Dockery, ed. *The Challenge of Postmodernism: An Evangelical Engagement* (Grand Rapids: Baker, 1995), 254.
5. Thomas Oden, "The Death of Modernity and Postmodern Evangelical Spirituality," in *The Challenge of Postmodernism*, 26.
6. Stanley J. Grenz, *A Primer on Postmodernism* (Grand Rapids: Eerdmans, 1996), 60.
7. Oden, "The Death of Modernity and Postmodern Evangelical Spirituality," 23.
8. Marie-Jean-Antoine-Nicolas de Caritat, *Sketch for a Historical Picture of the Progress of the Human Mind*, trans. June Barraclough (New York: Hyperion, 1955), 124.
9. Cited in J. Richard Middleton and Brian J. Walsh, *Truth Is Stranger Than It Used to Be: Biblical Faith in a Postmodern Age* (Downers Grove, Ill.: InterVarsity Press, 1995), 14.

10. C. S. Lewis, *Surprised by Joy* (New York: Harcourt Brace Jovanovich, 1955), 207–8.
11. Anselm (Christian Classics Ethereal Library), on the Internet at http://ccel.org/a/anselm/basic_works/htm/iv.I.htm.
12. Stanley F. Grenz, "Star Trek and the Next Generation: Postmodernism and the Future of Evangelical Theology," in *The Challenge of Postmodernism*, 91.
13. Philosophers use the term *verisimilitude*, which means, according to Karl Popper (one of the twentieth-century's greatest philosophers of science), that, given a pair of rival theories, we ought to adopt the one that is nearer the truth than the other. "While there is some truth in Newton and some falsehood, and while Einstein's theory is no doubt false and certainly not known to be true, it is at least more approximately true" (W. H. Newton-Smith, *The Rationality of Science* [Boston: Routledge & Kegan Paul, 1981], 54–55).
14. John 14:6.
15. Mark E. Dever, "Communicating Sin in a Postmodern World," in *Telling the Truth: Evangelizing Postmoderns*, ed. D. A. Carson (Grand Rapids: Zondervan, 2000), 143–44.
16. Bertrand Russell, *Why I Am Not a Christian* (New York: Touchstone, 1957), 22–23.
17. John Lennon, "Imagine" (Bag productions, Inc., 1971).
18. James W. Sire, *The Universe Next Door* (Downers Grove, Ill.: InterVarsity Press, 1988), 63.
19. C. S. Lewis, *God in the Dock* (Grand Rapids: Eerdmans, 1970), 72.
20. Oden, "The Death of Modernity and Postmodern Evangelical Spirituality," 25.

Cʜᴀᴘᴛᴇʀ 3: Uɴᴅᴇʀꜱᴛᴀɴᴅɪɴɢ ᴛʜᴇ Pᴏꜱᴛᴍᴏᴅᴇʀɴɪꜱᴛ

1. Discussed in D. A. Carson, *The Gagging of God: Christianity Confronts Pluralism* (Grand Rapids: Zondervan, 1996), 100.
2. Cited in Thomas C. Oden, *Two Worlds: The Death of Modernity in America and Russia* (Downers Grove, Ill.: InterVarsity Press, 1992), 23.
3. Cited in Stanley J. Grenz, *A Primer on Postmodernism* (Grand Rapids: Eerdmans, 1996), 25.
4. Cited in David Steward and H. Gene Blocker, *Fundamentals of Philosophy*, 3d ed. (New York: Macmillan, 1992), 245.
5. Stanley Fish, *Is There a Text in this Class?* (Cambridge, Mass.: Harvard Univ. Press, 1980), 180.
6. Gertrude Himmelfarb, *On Looking into the Abyss* (New York: Vintage, 1994), 9.
7. William J. Clinton, Grand jury testimony, August 17, 1998.
8. J. Hillis Miller, "On Edge: The Crossways of Contemporary Criticism," in *Romanticism and Contemporary Criticism*, eds. Morris Eaves and Michael Fischer (Ithaca, N.Y.: Cornell Univ. Press, 1986), 102–11.

9. Allan Bloom, *The Closing of the American Mind* (New York: Simon & Schuster, 1987), 25–26.

10. Dennis Prager, radio broadcast.

11. Cited in Daniel Taylor, "Deconstructing the Gospel of Tolerance," *Christianity Today,* 11 January 1999, 44.

12. Alan Sokal and Jean Bricmont, *Fashionable Nonsense: Postmodern Intellectuals' Abuse of Science* (New York: Picador USA, 1998), 109.

13. Charles Colson, "The Ugly Side of Tolerance," *Christianity Today,* 6 March 2000, 44.

14. See Jon Hinkson and Greg Ganssle, "Epistemology at the Core of Post-modernism: Rorty, Foucault, and the Gospel" in ed. D. A. Carson, *Telling the Truth,* 82–83, 86–87.

15. Hinkson and Ganssle, "Epistemology at the Core of Postmodernism," 86.

16. The process of "unmasking" truth claims is not merely a postmodernist preoccupation, but is an essential part of twentieth-century philosophical hermeneutics. Marxists would see power claims below the surface, Freudians would find unconscious urges, feminists would discover patriarchy, and so forth. What I am urging is the turning of the weapon of "unmasking" against the postmodernists themselves.

17. Cited in Francis Schaeffer, *The God Who Is There* (Downers Grove, Ill.: InterVarsity Press, 1968), 129–30.

18. Ephesians 2:1.

CHAPTER 4: TODAY'S DIVERSITY

1. See Jerelyn Eddings, "Counting a 'New' Type of American," *U.S. News and World Report,* 14 July 1997, 22.

2. "Number of American mosques grows by 25 percent," Shia News report on the Internet at www.shianews.com, 27 April 2001. The news report summarizes the findings of the Council on American-Islamic Relations (CAIR) in their major study titled "The Mosque in America: A National Portrait."

3. See Marcia Mogelonsky, "Watching in Tongues," *American Demographics,* April 1998, 48.

4. Reported in Jeremy Paxman, *The English* (New York: Penguin Group, 1998), 72–75.

5. Cited in George Fredrickson, "America's Diversity in Comparative Perspective," *Journal of American History,* December 1998, 859–75.

6. Genesis 1:20.

7. See C. Lavett Smith, *World Book Encyclopedia,* 1998 ed., s.v. "Fish."

8. See Ward B. Watt, *World Book Encyclopedia,* 1998 ed., s.v. "Insects."

9. Matthew 28:18–20, emphasis added.

10. Cited in Ralph Winter, "Unreached Peoples: Recent Developments in the Concept," *Mission Frontiers,* August/September 1989, 12. The strategy group sprang from the Lausanne Congress on World Evangelization held in 1974. It was convened by an international group of 142 evangelical leaders under the honorary chairmanship of Billy Graham.

In part, the congress attempted to identify those who were still unreached with the gospel.

11. Reported in Winter, "Unreached Peoples," 12.
12. Revelation 7:9, emphasis added.
13. Revelation 5:9, emphasis added.
14. Revelation 15:4, emphasis added.
15. See John Piper, *Let the Nations Be Glad: The Supremacy of God in Missions* (Grand Rapids: Baker, 1993), 216.
16. See Piper, *Let the Nations Be Glad,* 216.
17. See David Barrett's statistics on the Global Evangelization Movement's Web site at http://www.gem-werc.org/
18. Richard J. Foster, *Streams of Living Water* (New York: HarperCollins, 1998), 120.
19. Foster, *Streams of Living Water,* 119.
20. Acts 10:1–5.
21. Lesslie Newbigin, *The Gospel in a Pluralist Society* (Grand Rapids: Eerdmans, 1989), 9–10.
22. Acts 10:5.
23. Acts 11:13–14, emphasis added.
24. Acts 10:43, emphasis added.
25. Acts 4:12, emphasis added.
26. John R.W. Stott, *The Contemporary Christian* (Leicester, U.K.: Inter-Varsity Press, 1992), 306.
27. 1 Timothy 2:5.
28. John 3:18.
29. Acts 4:12, emphasis added.
30. Acts 10:43, emphasis added.
31. Romans 10:13, emphasis added.
32. Philippians 2:9–11.
33. Matthew 1:21.
34. Thomas J. Hopkins, *The Hindu Religious Tradition* (Encino, Calif.: Dickenson, 1971), 44.
35. Hopkins, *The Hindu Religious Tradition,* 55.
36. Cited in Edward T. Oakes, "Pascal: The First Modern Christian," *First Things* 95 (August/September 1999): 45.
37. Matthew 7:13–14.
38. Acts 4:12.
39. See Romans 10:9–10.
40. Ephesians 1:20b–21.
41. Colossians 2:2b–3.

Chapter 5: Was Jesus a Feminist?

1. Jung Chang, *Wild Swans* (New York: Anchor Books, 1991), 24.
2. Chang, *Wild Swans,* 24.
3. "The Taliban's War on Women," Editorial, *New York Times,* 5 November 1997, A-26.

4. John F. Burns, "Sex and the Afghan Woman: Islam Straitjacket," *New York Times*, 29 August 1997, A-4.
5. Burns, "Sex and the Afghan Woman," A-4.
6. H. McKeating, "Jesus ben Sira's Attitude toward Women," *Expository Times* 85 (1970): 85–87.
7. Ecclesiasticus 42:13–14.
8. See Ecclesiasticus 25:24.
9. Ecclesiasticus 42:9–11.
10. *The Testament of Reuben* 5:1–2.
11. *The Testament of Reuben* 5:3–4.
12. *The Testament of Reuben* 5:5–6.
13. *The Testament of Reuben* 5:3.
14. Menahot 43b, emphasis added.
15. Many Jewish communities, such as Reformed and Conservative, have, of course, done away with the prayers in modern times. C. G. Montefiore comments, "No amount of modern Jewish apologetics, endlessly poured forth, can alter the fact that the rabbinic attitude toward women was very different from our own. No amount of apologetics can get over the implication of the daily blessing, which orthodox Judaism has still lacked the courage to remove from its official prayer book. 'Blessed art Thou, O Lord, our God, who has not made me a woman'" (C. G. Montefiore, *A Rabbinic Anthology* [Philadelphia: Macmillan, 1938], 507).
16. The Talmud was composed by the spiritual descendants of that part of Judaism known in Jesus' day as the Pharisees. The Sadducees lost their spiritual and political position in Judaism following the destruction of the Jewish temple in A.D. 70. Talmudic Judaism is the Judaism of the Pharisees.
17. Montefiore, *A Rabbinic Anthology,* xviii.
18. Abraham Cohen, *Every Man's Talmud* (New York: Schocken, 1949), 160–61.
19. Cohen, *Every Man's Talmud,* 161.
20. Cohen, *Every Man's Talmud,* 161.
21. Exodus 22:18.
22. See Cohen, *Every Man's Talmud,* 161.
23. Cohen, *Every Man's Talmud,* 162.
24. Cohen, *Every Man's Talmud,* 163.
25. Cohen, *Every Man's Talmud,* 167.
26. Discussed in Cohen, *Every Man's Talmud,* 168–69.
27. Genesis 24:1.
28. Cited in Cohen, *Every Man's Talmud,* 171.
29. Numbers 6:24.
30. Cited in Cohen, *Every Man's Talmud,* 172.
31. Discussed in Cohen, *Every Man's Talmud,* 175–76.
32. Cited in Cohen, *Every Man's Talmud,* 179.

33. Discussed in *Women in the Classical World*, eds. Elaine Fantham, Helene Peet Foley, Natalie Boymel Kampen, Sarah B. Pomeroy, H. Alan Shapiro (Oxford: Oxford Univ. Press, 1994), 212.
34. Cited in *Women in the Classical World*, 39–41.
35. Cited in Mary R. Lefkowitz and Maureen B. Fant, *Women's Life in Greece and Rome* (Baltimore, Md.: John Hopkins Univ. Press, 1982), 16.
36. Discussed in *Women in the Classical World*, 118–21.
37. Cited in *Women in the Classical World*, 123.
38. See Mark 10:12.
39. Matthew 19:9.
40. There was recently a major controversy in Israel regarding a woman's right to pray aloud from the Torah at the Western Wall (generally considered the holiest site in modern Judaism). Orthodox rabbis were enraged, claiming that for women to do so would be a violation of Jewish law and the division of roles that God assigned men and women.
41. See Luke 10:38–42.
42. See Luke 8:1–2.
43. See Luke 1:32–35.
44. See John 2:1–11.
45. See John 4:7–42.
46. See John 4:26.
47. See Matthew 15:21–28.
48. See John 11:23–27.
49. See Matthew 28:9.
50. See John 20:18.
51. Dorothy L. Sayers, *Are Women Human?* (Grand Rapids: Eerdmans, 1971), 47.
52. Cited in Richard Foster, *Streams of Living Water* (New York: Harper-Collins, 1998), 120.
53. Cited in Foster, *Streams of Living Water*, 66.
54. Noted in Sheila Rowbotham, *A Century of Women: The History of Women in Britain and the United States* (London: Viking, 1997), 22.
55. Noted in S. Jay Kleinberg, "American Women in the Twentieth Century," in *America's Century: Perspectives on U.S. History Since 1900*, eds. Iwan W. Morgan and Neil A. Wynn (New York: Holmes and Meier, 1993), 226.
56. *America in the Twentieth Century: 1910–1919, vol. 2*, ed. Janet McDonnell (New York: Marshall Cavendish, 1995), 160.
57. Constance Jones, *1001 Things Everyone Should Know About Women's History* (New York: Doubleday, 1998), 131.
58. David Traxwell, *1898: Birth of an American Century* (New York: Random House, 1998), 73.
59. Traxwell, *1898: Birth of an American Century*, 74.
60. Traxwell, *1898: Birth of an American Century*, 76.

61. *Encyclopedia Britannica, vol. 12* (Chicago: Encyclopedia Britannica, 1998), 733.

62. Noted in Sheila Tobian, *Faces of Feminism* (Boulder, Colo.: Westview, 1997), 12.

CHAPTER 6: WHAT SHOULD WE THINK OF FEMINISTS?

1. Germaine Greer, *The Female Eunuch* (New York: Bantam, 1972), 62, 65, 66, 74, 108, 148, 208, 303, 336.

2. Betty Friedan, *The Feminine Mystique* (New York: Dell, 1982), 351.

3. Friedan, *The Feminine Mystique*, 77.

4. Kate Millett, *Sexual Politics* (New York: Ballantine, 1978), 86.

5. "Sex, Society, and the Female Dilemma: A Dialogue Between Simone de Beauvoir and Betty Friedan," *Saturday Review*, 14 June 1975.

6. Millet, *Sexual Politics*, 178–79, 186.

7. Cited by Marlene Nathan in an unpublished sermon, 1994.

8. Interestingly, the attempt to turn child rearing over to the experts in order to free women from the "stifling" duties of domesticity was tried and initially celebrated on Israeli kibbutzim (collective farms) during the 1950s. By 1980, the situation had drastically changed. Not only had kibbutzim reverted back to traditional roles involving a disproportionate amount of women's time spent tending to home and family, but it was women who led the way back to these traditional roles. They were unhappy with the unisex model of life on a kibbutz. Women wanted more time with their children and more time to work in their homes, and they wanted men to stay out of their "female" responsibilities.

9. Titus 2:4–5.

10. Cited in Mary Thorn, "Hearts & Minds," *Ms.*, April/May 1999, 73, 76.

11. Thorn, "Hearts & Minds," 74.

12. See, for example, Daphne Hampson, *Theology and Feminism* (Oxford: Blackwell, 1990), 121–24, and Rosemary Radford Ruether, *Sexism and God-Talk* (Boston: Beacon, 1983), 184–89.

13. Hampson, *Theology and Feminism*, preface.

14. Ruether, *Sexism and God-Talk*, 233.

15. Cited in Gayle White, "Is God a She?" *Atlanta Journal-Constitution*, 22 May 1994, D-2.

16. Cited in Stanley Grenz and Roger Olson, *20th-Century Theology* (Downers Grove, Ill.: InterVarsity Press, 1992), 236.

17. Cited in Grenz and Olson, *20th-Century Theology*, 235.

18. *People Magazine* article cited in Barbara Dafoe Whitehead, "Dan Quayle Was Right," *Atlantic Monthly*, April 1993, 9–10.

19. Judith S. Wallerstein and Sandra Blakeslee, *Second Chances* (New York: Ticknor & Fields, 1989), xii.

20. Cited in Whitehead, "Dan Quayle Was Right," 32.

21. David Popenoe, "The Vanishing Father," *Wilson Quarterly Review*, Spring 1996, 15.

22. Noted in Popenoe, "The Vanishing Father," 18, 21, 23–25.

23. Charles Ballard, "Prodigal Dad: How We Bring Fathers Home to Their Children," *Policy Review,* Winter 1995.

24. Millet, *Sexual Politics,* 93–94.

25. Noted by Gregg Johnson, "The Biological Basis for Gender-Specific Behavior," in *Recovering Biblical Manhood and Womanhood,* eds. John Piper and Wayne Grudem (Wheaton, Ill.: Crossway, 1991).

26. Deborah Tannen, *You Just Don't Understand* (New York: Ballantine, 1991), 77.

27. Found on the Rape Abuse and Incest National Network (RAINN) Web site at www.RAINN.com.

28. See Alister E. McGrath, *Intellectuals Don't Need God and Other Modern Myths* (Grand Rapids: Zondervan, 1993), 66–73. McGrath has a wonderful section in his book on the things that keep people from becoming Christians or even from giving Christianity a fair hearing. One of the major obstacles McGrath lists is the problem of the historical association of Christianity with oppression.

CHAPTER 7: WHAT ROLES ARE OPEN TO WOMEN IN THE CHURCH?

1. The first challenge, discerning the meaning of the text to its original readers, is the task of *exegesis.* But even if scholars agreed about the meaning of 1 Timothy 2 for Paul's original hearers (which they don't), the more difficult task of *hermeneutics*—applying the text to an entirely different cultural situation—would remain. Much of the recent and most exciting work in New Testament studies has been in the area of hermeneutics—how one applies agreed-to biblical meanings to the modern world.

2. Among the many books on the egalitarian perspective on the role of women, a few of the best are Stanley J. Grenz and Denise Muir Kjesbo, *Women in the Church* (Downers Grove, Ill.: InterVarsity Press, 1995); Ruth Tucker, *Women in the Maze* (Downers Grove, Ill.: InterVarsity Press, 1992); Craig S. Keener, *Paul, Women and Wives* (Peabody, Mass.: Hendrickson, 1992); Don Williams, *The Apostle Paul and Women in the Church* (Glendale, Calif.: Regal, 1977).

  From the complementarian, or hierarchicalist, perspective, these include Wayne Grudem and John Piper, eds., *Recovering Biblical Manhood and Womanhood* (Grand Rapids: Zondervan, 1991); James B. Hurley, *Man and Woman in Biblical Perspective* (Grand Rapids: Zondervan, 1981); Ben Witherington III, *Women in the Earliest Churches* (Cambridge: Cambridge Univ. Press, 1988).

  For a comprehensive overview of the two primary views, see James R. Beck and Craig L. Blomberg, eds., *Two Views on Women in Ministry* (Grand Rapids: Zondervan, 2001).

3. Revised Standard Version, alternate reading.

4. It is important not to merge texts regarding male headship in the home with the issue of the appropriate roles for women in the church. While there are many texts concerning male headship in the home, nowhere does any text ever use the word *head* to signify a male's role in the church. These two realms—home and church—can be treated separately. While some tricky issues can arise (for example, a wife who is a senior pastor leading her husband in the church, but not at home), these are not necessarily any trickier than the issue of a woman such as Margaret Thatcher leading a whole nation (which many Christians would support), but also taking a submissive role at home. The issue of exactly what is meant by headship in the home is also widely debated.

5. See Acts 2:17–18.

6. See Romans 16:3.

7. Some scholars and Bible translators have changed Junia's name into the masculine Junias. This is likely an untenable rewriting of the text. We have no evidence before the thirteenth century of any commentary or text translating this name as masculine. And in the Eastern part of the church (the Greek-speaking part), the feminine form of the name was always used until the nineteenth century. For a convincing discussion of the Junia versus Junias controversy, see C. E. B. Cranfield, *Romans,* vol. 2 (Edinburgh: T.&T. Clark, 1975, 1979). James D. G. Dunn suggests in his commentary on Romans that there are over 250 examples of Junia before the modern period and none of Junias (James D. G. Dunn, *Romans 9–16,* Word Biblical Commentary [Dallas: Word, 1988], 894).

8. See Romans 16:1–2, 3, 6, 7, 12.

9. See Philippians 4:2–3.

10. Keener, *Paul, Women and Wives,* 246–47.

11. See 1 Corinthians 11:2–16.

12. 1 Corinthians 11:16.

13. See Romans 16:16; 1 Corinthians 16:20; 2 Corinthians 13:12; 1 Thessalonians 5:26; 1 Peter 5:14.

14. Some would prohibit senior leadership or primary leadership (for example, becoming a senior pastor), but would permit women to be staff pastors or small group leaders over men. Such distinctions, while culturally comfortable for some, could not possibly have been understood by Paul's original hearers or intended by Paul himself. Either Paul's restriction of women's power to lead men was meant to be universal in scope, or it was designed to address a local situation. Nothing in the text, however, permits us to make the fine distinctions between some kinds of church teaching and other kinds, or some kinds of church leadership and other kinds—the kinds of distinctions that many Christians make today.

15. Gleaned from Earl O. Roe, *Dream Big: The Henrietta Mears Story* (Ventura, Calif.: Regal, 1990).

16. See Gordon Fee and Douglas Stuart, *How to Read the Bible for All Its Worth*, rev. ed. (Grand Rapids: Zondervan, 1993), 72–76.

17. 2 Timothy 3:6–9.

18. Keener, *Paul, Women and Wives*, 116.

19. See Judges 4:4–24.

20. See 2 Kings 22:14; 2 Chronicles 34:14–33.

21. See Acts 18:18–26; Romans 16:3; 1 Corinthians 16:19.

22. See Romans 16:16; 1 Corinthians 16:20; 2 Corinthians 13:12; 1 Thessalonians 5:26; 1 Peter 5:14.

23. See 1 Corinthians 11:5–16.

24. Titus 2:5.

25. Titus 2:10.

26. 1 Corinthians 8:4–13.

27. 1 Corinthians 6:1–8.

28. See, for example, Romans 16:7 (apostle); Colossians 4:15 (hosted a house church); 1 Timothy 3:11 (women deacons).

29. See 1 Corinthians 9:7–15; 2 Corinthians 11:7–12.

30. Dorothy L. Sayers, *Are Women Human?* (Grand Rapids: Eerdmans, 1971), 47.

CHAPTER 8: JUDGMENT, TOLERANCE, AND THE SPREAD OF GAY RIGHTS

1. Gleaned from James Brooke, "Gay Man Beaten and Left for Dead: Two Are Charged," *New York Times*, 10 October 1998; Becky Orr, "Guilty," *Washington Tribune-Eagle*, 24 October 2000.

2. James Brooke, "Gay Man Dies from Attack," *New York Times*, 13 October 1998.

3. Ephesians 4:19.

4. Information gleaned from "TransTeen's School Dress Allowed," PlanetOut News & Politics at www.planetout.com/, 13 October 2000.

5. Ronald Bayer, *Homosexuality in American Psychiatry: The Politics of Diagnosis* (New York: Basic Books, 1981), 3–4.

6. Doug Haldeman, president of the APA Society for the Psychological Study of Lesbian, Gay and Bisexual Issues, helped to write a resolution that would have branded therapists engaged in reparative therapy as "unethical." This was defeated by the American Psychological Association in 1995; however, in 1997, a resolution passed just short of this. The APA resolution asked that the therapist obtain "informed consent from the client." This would include: (1) a full disclosure of the client's potential for happiness as a homosexual; (2) communication to the client that there is no sound scientific evidence that the therapy works; (3) raising the possibility that therapy may exacerbate the client's problems; and (4) an analysis of the client's true motive for wanting to change. Haldeman said, "In the past ten years, Christian fundamentalists have enlisted a coalition of old-style psychologists, psychiatrists, and social workers who have become very visible in this country and inter-

nationally and who have as a mission to 'help' homosexuals get rid of their sexual orientation.... Our aim is not to try to stop them per se or interfere with anyone's right to practice [therapy], but we want to expose the social context that creates this market."

7. "Policy Statement: Lesbian, Gay, and Bisexual Issues" (approved by Delegate Assembly, August 1996), *Social Work Speaks: NASW Policy Statements* (Washington, D.C.: NASW Press, 1997).

8. "Position Statement: Psychiatric Treatment and Sexual Orientation," American Psychiatric Association (approved at December 1998 meeting of its Board of Trustees).

9. Action taken by the American Counseling Association governing council, April 1999.

10. Cited in Jeffrey Satinover, *Homosexuality and the Politics of Truth* (Grand Rapids: Baker, 1996), 43.

11. See Council on Scientific Affairs, American Medical Association, "Health Care Needs of Gay Men and Lesbians in the United States," *Journal of the American Medical Association 275,* no. 17 (1 May 1996): 1354–59.

12. Cindy Beal, "Context Matters: An Investigation into the Allegations Contained in the Article 'Kids Get Graphic Instruction in Homosexual Sex'" at www.bridges-across.org.

13. Gleaned from Mac Daniel, "2 Lose Jobs over Workshop on Sex," *Boston Globe,* 20 May 2000.

14. Many school curriculum changes, government funding for outreach to gay students, and gay pride celebrations have been based on supposed evidence from a government study showing that gay teens are more likely to commit suicide because of public rejection. The claim has been made that 30 percent of teen suicides are homosexuals and that homosexual young people are two to three times more likely to attempt suicide than heterosexual young people. This was built on a report written by a homosexual social worker named Paul Gibson. Gibson never claimed that his report was a research study. Representatives of the National Institute of Mental Health, the Centers for Disease Control, the American Psychological Association, and the American Association of Suicidology have said there is no scientifically valid evidence that a sexual-orientation suicide link exists in teens. However, the national media continue to cite a suicide link in teens with homosexuality so often that it is now part of conventional wisdom. See Delia M. Rios, "Statistics on gay suicides are baseless, researchers say," *Seattle Times,* 22 May 1997.

15. "Vermont Gives Marital Protections to Lesbian and Gay Couples," LAMBDA Press Release, 25 April 2000.

16. There are numerous other laws affecting gay rights, not the least of which are "hate crimes laws." Hate crimes are those crimes motivated by prejudice based on, among other things, a person's sexual orientation. In

addition to being convicted of assault or murder, a person who is motivated by prejudice against another's sexual orientation might be additionally convicted of committing a hate crime, for which there are additional penalties. A bill to combat hate crimes was introduced in the United States Senate in 1999 (S.1406), mentioning in its opening declaration that hate crimes "are committed to send a message of hate to targeted communities, usually defined on the basis of immutable traits." Since sexual orientation would have been covered by this proposed federal hate crimes bill, homosexuality would as a result have been declared by federal law to be an immutable (unchangeable) characteristic, just as a person's race is.

17. *Boy Scouts of America and Monmouth Council* v. *James Dale* (June 28, 2000).

18. Cited in Randy Bishop, "Politics of Sexuality," *Christianity Today*, 17 May 2000.

19. Matthew 7:1–5.

20. Matthew 7:6.

21. Matthew 7:15–16.

22. Mark 8:15.

23. One of the most successful and biblically sound healing ministries, Desert Stream Ministries, was founded by Andy Comiskey, who himself was a former practicing homosexual. Through his Living Waters program, Comiskey trains leaders to establish and run similar ministries around the country. Among the many other healing programs that God has used to bring change to homosexuals is Leanne Payne's Pastoral Care Ministries, centered in Wheaton, Illinois.

CHAPTER 9: UNDERSTANDING THE HOMOSEXUAL

1. J. Michael Bailey and Richard Pillard, "A Genetic Study of Male Sexual Orientation," *Archives of General Psychiatry* 48 (December 1991): 1089–96.

2. M. King and E. McDonald, "Homosexuals Who Are Twins: A Study of Forty-six Probands," *British Journal of Psychiatry* 160 (1992): 407–9. J. Michael Bailey, one of the authors of the original study, along with two other researchers, Michael Dunne and Nicholas Martin, discovered in a much more recent study of Australian twins that the concordance rate for homosexual orientation was much lower than in his prior study. Bailey has been unable to replicate his own original findings. See J. Michael Bailey, Michael P. Dunne, and Nicholas G. Martin, "Genetic and Environmental Influences on Sexual Orientation and Its Correlates in an Australian Twin Sample," *Journal of Personality and Social Psychology* 78 (March 2000): 524–36.

3. King and McDonald, "Homosexuals Who Are Twins," 407–9, emphasis added.

4. Cited in David Gelman, et al., "Born or Bred?" *Newsweek*, 24 February 1992, 46. See Simon LeVay, "A difference in hypothalamic structure between heterosexual and homosexual men," *Science* 258 (1991): 1034–37.

5. Cited in Gelman, "Born or Bred?" 50.

6. See S. Marc Breedlove, "Sex on the Brain," *Nature* 389 (October 1997): 801.

7. See Jeffrey Satinover, *Homosexuality and the Politics of Truth* (Grand Rapids: Baker, 1996), 79.

8. Reported in S. Marc Breedlove, et al., "Finger Length Ratios and Sexual Orientation," *Nature* 404 (30 March 2000): 455.

9. William Byne and Bruce Parsons, "Human Sexual Orientation: The Biologic Theories Reappraised," *Archives of General Psychiatry* 50 (1993): 228–39.

10. Elizabeth R. Moberly, *Homosexuality: A New Christian Ethic* (Cambridge: James Clarke & Co., 1983), 2.

11. Gleaned from Moberly, *Homosexuality: A New Christian Ethic*, 3.

12. Moberly, *Homosexuality: A New Christian Ethic*, 3.

13. Noted in Satinover, *Homosexuality and the Politics of Truth*, 106.

14. Gleaned from Andrew Comiskey, *The Kingdom of God and the Homosexual* (Anaheim, Calif.: Desert Streams Ministries, 2000), 9–10.

15. Satinover, *Homosexuality and the Politics of Truth*, 130–32.

16. Noted in Rob Reynolds, "Divisions Challenge Mainstream Churches," *Moody*, November/December 1997, 46–47.

17. See, for example, D. Sherwin Bailey, *Homosexuality and the Western Christian Tradition* (London: Longmans, Green & Co., 1955; reprint, North Haven, Conn.: Shoe String Press, 1975).

18. See John Boswell, *Christianity and Social Tolerance* (Chicago: Chicago Univ. Press, 1980), and *Same-Sex Unions in Premodern Europe* (New York: Villard, 1994).

19. Everett Ferguson, ed., *The Encyclopedia of Early Christianity* (New York: Garland, 1990), s.v. "homosexuality."

20. See John Stott, *Same-Sex Partnerships? A Christian Perspective* (Grand Rapids: Revell, 1998), and Stanley J. Grenz, *Welcoming, But Not Affirming: An Evangelical Response to Homosexuality* (Louisville, Ky.: Westminster John Knox, 1998). "Some people say that God made them gay and God would not create people homosexual and then deny them the right of sexual expression. Such folks may argue that the apostle Paul's claim that homosexuality is 'against nature' in Romans 1 applies to hetero-sexual people who act against their 'nature.' But a homosexual person acts consistently with his or her own nature when he or she engages in homosexual practices.... By 'nature' and 'unnatural,' the apostle Paul was not talking about the individual's subjective inclination or inner nature. Rather, by nature, he was talking about that which is against God's created order. Charles Cranfield, in his commentary on the book of Romans, writes that by 'natural' and by 'unnatural' Paul clearly

means *in accordance with the intention of the Creator and contrary to the intention of the Creator respectively.* For Paul, homosexual practice is contrary to the biblical doctrine of creation" (Stott, *Same-Sex Partnerships,* 46).

21. Stott, *Same-Sex Partnerships,* 58–59.
22. Don Williams, *The Bond That Breaks: Will Homosexuality Split the Church?* (Los Angeles: BIM, 1978), 128.
23. Romans 3:10.
24. Observed in Patrick Carnes, *Out of the Shadows* (Minneapolis: CompCare, 1983), 82–85.
25. Ephesians 4:25.

CHAPTER 10: A CLOSER LOOK AT NEW AGERS

1. Margaret Langstaff, "Mind + Body + Spirit = New Age," *Publishers Weekly,* 15 May 2000, 65–69.
2. Langstaff, "Mind + Body + Spirit = New Age," 65–69.
3. Cited in Elizabeth Large, "Yoga Is Stretching into the Mainstream," *Ft. Worth Star-Telegram,* 7 February 2000, 6.
4. Cited in Hamil R. Harris, "Meditating Their Way to a Happy New Year: Believers Crowd Self-Help Gurus Day of Workshops," *Washington Post,* 1 January 1999, B3.
5. Cited in Leo W. Banks, "Of Spirits and Wider Reality in Arizona," *Boston Globe,* 7 February 1999, A8.
6. Gleaned from Banks, "Of Spirits and Wider Reality in Arizona," A8.
7. Noted in Kate MacArthur, "New Age Still the Rage in Beverage," *Advertising Age,* 15 May 2000, 32.
8. Noted in Andrew Brownstein, "Products' Souls Linked to Bottom-Line Sales," *Patriot Ledger,* 26 February 2000, 28.
9. Cited in Cecil S. Holmes, "Seeking Spirituality: Americans Are Picking and Choosing Their Religion," *Salt Lake City Tribune,* 12 February 2000, C3.
10. Noted in Charlotte Allen, "The Scholars and the Goddess," *Atlantic Monthly,* January 2001, 18.
11. Gleaned from Allen, "The Scholars and the Goddess", 18.
12. Cited in Allen, "The Scholars and the Goddess," 19.
13. Noted in Allen, "The Scholars and the Goddess," 22.
14. Noted in Allen, "The Scholars and the Goddess," 22. For more, see Cynthia Eller, *The Myth of Matriarchal Prehistory: Why an Invented Past Won't Give Women a Future* (Boston: Beacon Press, 2000).
15. Cited in Allen, "The Scholars and the Goddess," 22.
16. Luke 1:1–4.
17. Cited in Allen Watts, *The Way of Zen* (New York: Vintage, 1989), 115.
18. Cited in Douglas R. Groothuis, *Unmasking the New Age* (Downers Grove, Ill.: InterVarsity Press, 1986), 21.
19. Romans 1:25.
20. Acts 17:27–28.

21. See Stanley J. Grenz and Roger E. Olson, *20th-Century Theology: God and the World in a Transitional Age* (Downers Grove, Ill.: InterVarsity Press, 1992).
22. Cited in Rosemary Goodburn, "Hoy Says He Sees Future Through Spirit World," *Westerville Suburban News,* 20 December 2000, 30.
23. Marguerite Marshall, "There Is No Separation in Love," *Pattern Pieces,* July/September 2000, 13.
24. Ecclesiastes 3:11.
25. See the Web site at http://www.bennet.com/research/falsemem.htm.
26. Deuteronomy 18:10–13, emphasis added.
27. 2 Corinthians 11:14.
28. At this time of rampant interest in guardian angels and angelic communication, it's important to note that, in the Bible, communication from an angel to a human being occurs solely at the initiative of Almighty God. Nowhere in the Bible do we have an example of an individual who sought communication from an angel. Believers' prayers are to be directed exclusively to God. If God chooses to use an angel or some other intermediary to communicate with us, that is his divine prerogative. Seeking angelic guidance is, in my mind, an extremely dangerous practice that potentially can leave a person open to spiritual counterfeits.
29. "Feng Shui Workshop Offered," *Eastside Messenger,* 15 March 1999, 4, emphasis added.
30. Cited in Holmes, "Seeking Spirituality," C3.
31. Cited from the Rainbow Family Web page at www.welcomehome.org.
32. Information about the Evangelical Environmental Network and its resources can be found on the Web at www.creationcare.org.
33. Psalm 148:3–4, 7–10, 13; see also Job 38 and 39.
34. *Reflexology* is a form of compression massage applied to the feet and sometimes to the hands. It is based on the idea that the whole body is represented by various zones on the feet. Practitioners claim that massaging the correct spot on the foot will restore to normal the energy flow in the corresponding part of the body. This abnormality in energy flow is said to be the cause of the disease of the affected part. (While it undoubtedly feels nice to have your feet massaged, there is simply no evidence that the body is represented by the feet. Moreover, "the laying on of hands" by a reflexologist may communicate to a person a demonic spirit.) *Aroma therapy* involves rubbing essential oils (distilled plant essences) into one's skin. These oils are said to release "essential cosmic energy" to heal imbalances within the body. (Much of aroma therapy is linked with Eastern religious practices. Some practitioners use pendulums to decide which oils to use.) *Iridology* is a method of diagnosing disease by carefully examining the iris (the

colored portion) of the eyes. Iridologists believe that the discoloration or flecks in the iris indicate the body's energy and health state. Iridology often involves psychic diagnoses. *Hypnosis* modifies one's will by allowing the conscious mind to be distracted. (Hypnosis can induce mental passivity and allow a person to become controlled by another person; this openness to another person can also lead to openness to spiritual counterfeits.) For a comprehensive Christian perspective on alternative medicine, see Donal O'Mathuna and Walt Larimore, *Alternative Medicine: The Christian Handbook* (Grand Rapids: Zondervan, 2001).

35. Observed in Douglas Groothuis, *Confronting the New Age* (Downers Grove, Ill.: InterVarsity Press, 1988), 156.
36. Cited in Groothuis, *Confronting the New Age,* 158.
37. Proverbs 13:15.

CHAPTER 11: PRACTICING THE WELCOME OF THE KINGDOM

1. Noted in Cal Thomas and Ed Dobson, *Blinded by Might: Can the Religious Right Save America?* (Grand Rapids: Zondervan, 1999), 54.
2. See Matthew 5:13.
3. Noted in the *Chicago Tribune,* 12 August 1996.
4. Cited in Donald McCullough, *The Trivialization of God* (Colorado Springs: NavPress, 1995), 27.
5. See James Davison Hunter, *Culture Wars: The Struggle to Define America* (Oxford: Oxford Univ. Press, 1994).
6. Observed in Alister E. McGrath, *Christian Theology: An Introduction* (Oxford: Blackwell, 1994), 92–94.
7. It is becoming increasingly difficult to label contemporary theological positions. These have multiplied well beyond traditional "liberal versus conservative" perspectives. A few of the many theological labels in current use are postliberalism (or the Yale School), neoorthodox, evangelical, feminist, charismatic, nonfoundationalist, Black, historic liberalism, and Roman Catholic. Some observers have proposed doing away with labels altogether, since the boundary lines have become increasingly ill defined.
8. There is no simple definition for liberalism, since it not only differs in its English, German, and American expressions, but it also varies in America from one decade to another. Currently, liberalism has come to be associated with left-wing ideologies that believe an individual ought to be free to do what he or she wants (especially in matters pertaining to sex), completely free of government interference. This is often coupled with a demand for government intervention in the marketplace to ensure social betterment and equality.
9. Noted in John Leo, "Singer's Final Solution," *U.S. News and World Report,* 4 October 1999, 17.

10. Statement of Brenda Pratt Shafer, R.N., "Hearing on the Partial-Birth Abortion Ban Act (HR 1833), March 21, 1996," cited on the Web at www.priestsforlife.org/testimony/brendatestimony.html.

11. Many observers have made similar points regarding the fuzziness of the divide in the culture wars. See, for example, Jeremy Rabkin, "The Culture War That Isn't," *Policy Review,* August/September 1999, 3–19.

12. D. A. Carson, *The Gagging of God* (Grand Rapids: Zondervan, 1996), 406.

13. In the Bible, especially in the book of Deuteronomy, *aliens* (a.k.a. immigrants) are classed along with widows and the fatherless as objects of God's special concern and protection (see, for example, Deuteronomy 10:18–19; 24:17–22; 26:12–14; 27:19).

14. Noted in William Martin, *A Prophet with Honor: The Billy Graham Story* (New York: Morrow, 1991), 428–31.

15. John F. MacArthur, *Charismatic Chaos* (Grand Rapids: Zondervan, 1992), 17.

16. See MacArthur, *Charismatic Chaos,* 21, 40–41, 43. In Martin Marty's *Fundamentalism Observed* (Chicago: Univ. of Chicago Press, 1991), *fighting* is described as "a key feature that separates fundamentalism from traditional Christian expression. Fundamentalists fight when they perceive a challenge or threat to their core identity. They fight for their particular worldview. They fight against others, especially those who are perceived more moderate than themselves, and they fight under the supposed banner of God."

17. See MacArthur, *Charismatic Chaos,* 21, 159.

18. Carl F. H. Henry, "Dare We Renew the Controversy?" *Christianity Today,* 24 June 1957, 26.

19. Noted in Carson, *The Gagging of God,* 439.

20. Thomas and Dobson, *Blinded by Might,* 23, emphasis added.

21. Wayne Grudem, *Systematic Theology: An Introduction to Biblical Doctrine* (Grand Rapids: Zondervan, 1995), 657.

22. Wilfred M. McClay, "Religion in Politics; Politics in Religion," *Commentary,* October 1988, 48–49.

23. Genesis 1:27.

24. Reinhold Niebuhr, *Moral Man and Immoral Society* (New York: Charles Scribner's Sons, 1932), xx.

25. John J. Dilulio Jr., "The Coming of the Super-Predators," *Weekly Standard,* 27 November 1999, 25.

26. Samuel Safrai, "Home and Family," quoted in N. T. Wright, *Jesus and the Victory of God* (Minneapolis: Fortress, 1996), 401.

27. Noted in Wright, *Jesus and the Victory of God,* 401.

28. Matthew 8:21–22.

29. Luke 11:27.

30. Matthew 10:34–39.

31. Luke 15:7, 10.

index